New Approaches in Applied Musicology

This book presents four extended essays that are rooted in the growing interdisciplinary field of applied musicology, in which music theory – in particular, the zygonic conjecture – is used to inform thinking in the domains of music psychology, music education and music therapy research. It is essential reading for academics and postgraduate students working in these fields. The topics covered include a new study on the emergence of musical abilities in the early years, using the *Sounds of Intent* framework of musical development; an exploration of how the *Sounds of Intent* model can be extended to map how people with learning difficulties engage in creative multisensory activities; an investigation of the expectations generated on hearing a piece of music more than once evolve in cognition, using evidence from a musical savant; and a report on the effect on listeners of repeated exposure to a novel melody. Data are drawn from the findings of postgraduate and postdoctoral projects. It is hoped that this exciting new work will act as a catalyst in the emerging field of applied musicological research, and bring recognition to a group of new young academics.

Adam Ockelford is Professor of Music at Roehampton University, where he directs the Applied Music Research Centre. He is widely published in music psychology, education, theory and aesthetics. He has particular interests in special educational needs and the development of exceptional abilities; learning, memory and creativity; the cognition of musical structure and the construction of musical meaning.

Graham Welch holds the Institute of Education, University of London Established Chair of Music Education. He is elected Chair of the internationally based Society for Education, Music and Psychology Research (SEMPRE), immediate past President of the International Society for Music Education (ISME) and past Co-Chair of the Research Commission of ISME. His publications number over 300 and embrace musical development and music education, teacher education, the psychology of music, singing and voice science, and music in special education and disability.

Angela Voyajolu holds a Masters in Music from the University of York, UK and a Masters in Music Therapy from Montclair State University, USA. She is currently completing a PhD at the University of Roehampton in London. Her research focuses on the musical development of children in the early years.

Ruth Grundy studied Music at Lady Margaret Hall, Oxford, before completing the MSc in Music, Mind and Brain at Goldsmiths, University of London, where she undertook the research project reported in this volume with Adam Ockelford. She has an interest in the relationship between music and medicine, and is currently working as a junior doctor in Shropshire, UK.

Hayley Trower gained her MSc and PhD at the University of Roehampton. Her research focused on the memory processes that support the development of melodic expectations in the context of familiar music in children and adults with 'typical' brain development, and in children with autism spectrum condition. She is currently working as a research psychologist in the Lifespan Health & Wellbeing Group at the University of Warwick, UK, exploring risk factors, adaptation and positive life outcomes associated with premature birth.

SEMPRE Studies in The Psychology of Music
Series Editors
Graham Welch, UCL Institute of Education, University College London
Adam Ockelford, University of Roehampton, UK
Ian Cross, University of Cambridge, UK

The theme for the series is the psychology of music, broadly defined. Topics include (i) musical development at different ages, (ii) exceptional musical development in the context of special educational needs, (iii) musical cognition and context, (iv) culture, mind and music, (v) micro to macro perspectives on the impact of music on the individual (from neurological studies through to social psychology), (vi) the development of advanced performance skills and (vii) affective perspectives on musical learning. The series presents the implications of research findings for a wide readership, including user-groups (music teachers, policy makers, parents) as well as the international academic and research communities. This expansive embrace, in terms of both subject matter and intended audience (drawing on basic and applied research from across the globe), is the distinguishing feature of the series, and it serves SEMPRE's distinctive mission, which is to promote and ensure coherent and symbiotic links between education, music and psychology research.

Musical Creativity Revisited
Educational Foundations, Practice and Research
Oscar Odena

Aural Education
Reconceptualising Ear Training in Higher Music Learning
Monica Andrianopoulou

Expertise in Jazz Guitar Improvisation
A Cognitive Approach
Stein Helge Solstad

New Approaches in Applied Musicology
A Common Framework for Music Education and Psychology Research
Adam Ockelford and Graham Welch

For more information about this series, please visit: www.routledge.com/music/series/SEMPRE

New Approaches in Applied Musicology
A Common Framework for Music Education and Psychology Research

Adam Ockelford and Graham Welch

LONDON AND NEW YORK

First published 2020
by Routledge
2 Park Square, Milton Park, Abingdon, Oxon OX14 4RN

and by Routledge
52 Vanderbilt Avenue, New York, NY 10017

Routledge is an imprint of the Taylor & Francis Group, an informa business

© 2020 Adam Ockelford and Graham Welch

The right of Adam Ockelford and Graham Welch to be identified as authors of this work has been asserted by them in accordance with sections 77 and 78 of the Copyright, Designs and Patents Act 1988.

All rights reserved. No part of this book may be reprinted or reproduced or utilised in any form or by any electronic, mechanical, or other means, now known or hereafter invented, including photocopying and recording, or in any information storage or retrieval system, without permission in writing from the publishers.

Trademark notice: Product or corporate names may be trademarks or registered trademarks, and are used only for identification and explanation without intent to infringe.

British Library Cataloguing-in-Publication Data
A catalogue record for this book is available from the British Library

Library of Congress Cataloging-in-Publication Data
A catalog record has been requested for this book

ISBN: 978-1-4724-7358-5 (hbk)
ISBN: 978-1-315-59786-7 (ebk)

Typeset in Times New Roman
by codeMantra

Affectionately dedicated to Dr Desmond Sergeant, founding member of the Society for Education, Music and Psychology Research (SEMPRE) and founding editor of *Psychology of Music* – an inspiration to us all.

Contents

Series' editor's preface: SEMPRE Studies in The Psychology of Music	x
Acknowledgements	xiii

1 Introduction 1
GRAHAM WELCH AND ADAM OCKELFORD

2 The development of music-structural cognition in the early years: a perspective from the *Sounds of Intent* model 13
ADAM OCKELFORD AND ANGELA VOYAJOLU

3 Extending the *Sounds of Intent* model of musical development to explore how people with learning difficulties engage in creative multisensory activities 64
ADAM OCKELFORD

4 Expectations generated on hearing a piece of music on more than one occasion: evidence from a musical savant 108
ADAM OCKELFORD AND RUTH GRUNDY

5 Exploring the effect of repeated listening to a novel melody: a zygonic approach 141
ADAM OCKELFORD AND HAYLEY TROWER

6 Conclusion 247
GRAHAM WELCH AND ADAM OCKELFORD

References	259
Index	271

Series' editor's preface
SEMPRE Studies in The Psychology of Music

Series Editors: Graham Welch, UCL Institute of Education, London, UK; Adam Ockelford, Roehampton University, UK; and Ian Cross, University of Cambridge, UK

The enormous growth of research that has been evidenced over the past three decades continues into the many different phenomena that are embraced under the psychology of music 'umbrella'. Growth is evidenced in new journals, books, media interest, an expansion of professional associations (regionally and nationally, such as in Southern Europe, Africa, Latin America, Asia), and accompanied by increasing and diverse opportunities for formal study, including within non-English-speaking countries. Such growth of interest is not only from psychologists and musicians, but also from colleagues working in the clinical sciences, neurosciences, therapies, in the lifelong health and well-being communities, philosophy, musicology, social psychology, ethnomusicology and education across the lifespan. There is also evidence in several countries of a wider political and policy engagement with the arts in general and music in particular, such as in arts-based social prescribing for mental and physical health.

As part of this global community, the Society for Education, Music and Psychology Research (SEMPRE) – looking forward to celebrating its 50th Anniversary in 2022 – continues to be one of the world's leading and longstanding professional associations in the field. SEMPRE is the only international society that embraces formally an interest in the psychology of music, research and education, seeking to promote knowledge at the interface between the twin social sciences of psychology and education with one of the world's most pervasive art forms, music. SEMPRE was founded in 1972 and has published the journals *Psychology of Music* since 1973 and *Research Studies in Music Education* since 2008, both now produced in partnership with SAGE (see www.sempre.org.uk/journals) and we continue to seek new ways to reach out globally, both in print and online. This includes the recent launch of *Music and Science* in 2018 – an additional peer-reviewed, open-access academic journal. We recognise that there is an ongoing need to promote the latest research findings to the widest possible audience. Through more extended publication formats, especially books, we believe

Series' editor's preface   xi

that we are more likely to fulfil a key component of our distinctive mission, which is to have a positive impact on individual and collective understanding, as well as on policy and practice internationally, both within and across our disciplinary boundaries. Hence, we welcome the strong collaborative partnership between SEMPRE and Routledge (formerly Ashgate Press).

The Routledge Ashgate 'SEMPRE Studies in The Psychology of Music' has been designed to address this international need since its inception in 2007 (see www.sempre.org.uk/about/5-routledge-sempre-book-series). The theme for the series is the psychology of music, broadly defined. Topics include (amongst others) musical development and learning at different ages; musical cognition and context; culture, mind and music; creativity, composition, and collaboration; micro to macro perspectives on the impact of music on the individual – from neurological studies through to social psychology; the development of advanced performance skills; musical behaviour and development in the context of special educational needs; music education; therapeutic applications of music and affective perspectives on musical learning. The series seeks to present the implications of research findings for a wide readership, including user-groups (music teachers, policy makers, leaders and managers, parents and carers, music professionals working in a range of formal, non-formal and informal settings), as well as the international academic teaching and research communities and their students. A key distinguishing feature of the series is its broad focus that draws on basic and applied research from across the globe under the umbrella of SEMPRE's distinctive mission, which is to promote and ensure coherent and symbiotic links between education, music and psychology research.

Series editor's preface to *New Approaches in Applied Musicology*

In this volume in the SEMPRE series, the authors explore the application of music theory – the nature of how music is organised – to aspects of musical behaviour and development. The driving force for *New Approaches in Applied Musicology: A Common Framework for Music Education and Psychology Research* is Adam Ockelford's extensive research since the early 1990s into the fundamental underlying structuring of sounds as something that is experienced as 'music'. Zygonic theory seeks to elaborate how music is made up of patterns of sounds, particularly based on imitation, and that these patterns shape our perception and cognition by creating expectations as such sounds unfold over time. At the core of the book are four chapters by Ockelford, singly and with colleagues – Angela Voyajolu, Ruth Grundy, Hayley Trower. Three of these chapters use zygonic theory to explore and explain how young children (Chapter 2) and children and young people with special educational needs and disabilities (Chapters 3 and 4) make sense of music. These illustrative examples from Chapters 2 to 4 are unpacked further in Chapter 5, which examines in more detail how the underlying principles of this approach to musical analysis can be combined with theories

xii *Series' editor's preface*

from cognitive psychology to demonstrate why music might be engaging for the listener. In terms of my own contribution, I have had the honour and pleasure of working with Adam on child-focused research in music education for nearly three decades. Consequently, I was delighted to have an opportunity to be involved as a co-author in the creation of this innovative text and to help in bringing this perspective from applied musicology to a wider audience.

Professor Graham Welch,
UCL Institute of Education, London,
20 September 2019

Acknowledgements

The authors are grateful to the children and staff of Eastwood Nursery School Centre for Children and Families in South West London who participated in the research reported in Chapter 2. They also extend their thanks to David Hargreaves for his comments on an earlier version of Chapter 2, and to the publications team at Routledge.

1 Introduction

Graham Welch and Adam Ockelford

Introduction

The current volume presents four chapters rooted in the growing interdisciplinary field of applied musicology, in which music theory – in particular, the zygonic conjecture – is used to inform thinking in the domains of music-psychological, educational and therapeutic research (Ockelford, 2012a). The zygonic conjecture holds that the cognition of musical structure occurs through one sound or group of sounds being heard as deriving from another or others through imitation. The power of this proposition lies in its very simplicity: it enables both qualitative and quantitative analyses to be undertaken in a range of contexts and to a number of different ends. These include tracing the path of musical development in children with learning difficulties (set out in the *Sounds of Intent* framework; see Welch *et al.*, 2009), tracking how pieces are learnt through repeated exposure (Ockelford and Pring, 2005; Mazzeschi, 2015), defining patterns of influence in group improvisation (Shibazaki, Ockelford and Marshall, 2013) and articulating the melodic expectations that are engendered in listeners as they attend to serial (atonal) music (Ockelford and Sergeant, 2012).

In the current volume, three topics are chosen that have been the subject of postgraduate research projects at the Applied Music Research Centre of the University of Roehampton, in collaboration with the International Music Education Research Centre at the Institute of Education, University College London, and Goldsmiths, University of London. Data from the projects are subject to fresh analysis with a view to interrogating the deeper cognitive processes involved in perceiving, understanding and remembering music (see Chapters 2, 4 and 5). In Chapter 3, it is theory that drives empirical research, as initial attempts are made to gauge the potential relevance of the zygonic conjecture to other areas of artistic and creative endeavour.

Zygonic theory

Zygonic theory made its first appearance in the academic literature around three decades ago (Ockelford, 1991). It seeks to explain how music makes sense: how it is that human beings, with no formal music education and limited (if any) understanding of musical concepts, come to have an intuitive grasp of what is effectively a form of natural language. The theory holds that the essence of music is that one sound or group of sounds, or a feature or features thereof, should be heard as deriving from another or others through imitation.

In order to describe zygonic theory in more detail, we will consider first the issue of how language-based art forms work, which, as a reflection of an external 'reality' or potential, have a more evident source of meaning construction. According to T.S. Eliot (1933, 1960), literature has three principal sources of meaning (couched in terms of aesthetic response):

- an *objective correlative* – a set of objects, a situation, a chain of events, which shall be the 'formula of a particular emotion';
- the *manner of representation* (including, for example, the use of metaphor);
- the *sound qualities* and *structure* of the language itself.

This thinking is shown in Figure 1.1. In semiotic terms, the model captures the stages corresponding to the transition from:

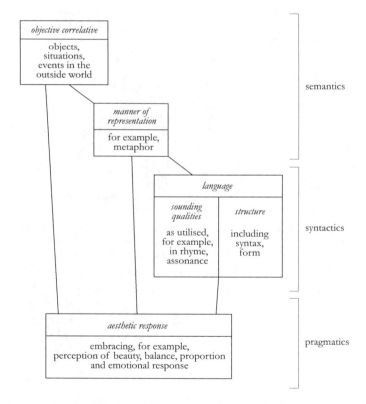

Figure 1.1 Representation of T.S. Eliot's model of aesthetic response to literary works, and its correspondence to semiotic thinking.

- *semantics* (the relationships between the signs and the things to which they refer); through
- *syntactics* (the relationships between the signs themselves); to
- *pragmatics* (the relationships between the signs and the effects that they have on readers or listeners).

However, absolute music (and the abstract component of music with referential meaning, which overtly refers to extra-musical ideas) has no objective correlative – no semantic component (see Figure 1.2). In these circumstances, how is meaning constructed and conveyed?

In the absence of semantics, it follows that the meaning of music must derive solely from its syntax – the logical arrangement of its constituent sounds – which has two elements: the qualities of the sounds themselves (in zygonic theory referred to as 'content') and their organisation (termed 'structure').

First, we consider 'content'. Zygonic theory asserts that *all* sounds and the relationships we perceive between them can potentially cause or enable an emotional response (*cf.* Johnson-Laird and Oatley, 1992; Sparshott,

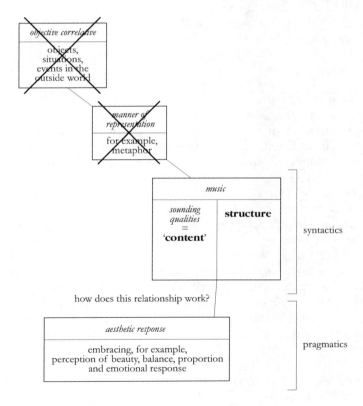

Figure 1.2 Absolute music has no objective correlative – so how is meaning conveyed?

4   *Graham Welch and Adam Ockelford*

1994, p. 28; Reybrouck and Podlipniak, 2019). There appear to be two main sources of such responses: 'expressive non-verbal vocalisations' and 'music-specific' qualities of sound.

'Expressive non-verbal vocalisations' comprise the cues used to express emotions vocally in non-verbal communication and speech (Juslin, Friberg and Bresin, 2001). They are present cross-culturally (Scherer, Banse and Wallbott, 2001), suggesting a common phylogenetic derivation from 'non-verbal affect vocalisations' (Scherer, 1991) and apparently embedded ontogenetically in early maternal/infant interaction (Malloch, 1999; Trehub and Nakata, 2001/2002). It seems that these cues can be transferred in a general way to music, and music-psychological work from the last 80 years or so has shown that features such as register, tempo and dynamic level do relate with some consistency to particular emotional states (Gabrielsson and Lindström, 2000). For example, passages in a high register can feel exciting (Watson, 1942) or exhibit potency (Scherer and Oshinsky, 1977), whereas series of low notes are more likely to promote solemnity or to be perceived as serious (Watson, *op. cit.*). A fast tempo will tend to induce feelings of excitement (Thompson and Robitaille, 1992), in contrast to slow tempi that may connote tranquillity (Gundlach, 1935) or even peace (Balkwill and Thompson, 1999). Loud dynamic levels are held to be exciting (Watson, *op. cit.*), to be triumphant (Gundlach, *op. cit.*) or to represent gaiety (Nielzén and Cesarec, 1982), while quiet sounds have been found to express fear, tenderness or grief (Juslin, 1997). Conversely, as the musicologist Leonard Meyer observed (2001, p. 342), 'one cannot imagine sadness being portrayed by a fast forte tune played in a high register, or a playful child being depicted by a solemnity of trombones'.

'Music-specific' qualities of sound, like those identified above in relation to early vocalisation, have the capacity to induce consistent emotional responses, *within* and sometimes *between* cultures, especially for core emotional states such as joy or sadness (Gabrielsson, 2011). For example, in the West and elsewhere, music typically utilises a framework of relative pitches with close connections to the harmonic series. These are used idiosyncratically, with context-dependent frequency of occurrence and transition patterns, together yielding the sensation of 'tonality' (Krumhansl, 1997; Peretz, 1998). Such frameworks of relative pitch can accommodate different 'modalities', each potentially bearing distinct emotional connotations. In Indian music, for example, the concept of the 'raga' is based on the idea that particular patterns of notes are able to evoke heightened states of emotion (Jairazbhoy and Khan, 1971), while in the Western tradition of the last four centuries or so, the 'major mode' is typically associated with happiness and the 'minor mode' with sadness (Hevner, 1936; Crowder, 1985), differences which have been shown to have neurological correlates (Suzuki *et al.*, 2008; Nemoto, Fujimaki and Wang, 2010).

On their own, however, separate emotional responses to a series of individual sounds or clusters would not add up to a coherent musical message – a unified aesthetic response that evolves over time. So what is it that binds these discrete, abstract experiences together to form a cogent musical narrative? It is our contention that the organising force is 'structure', as defined in zygonic theory.

To understand how this works, consider verbal language once more. Eliot's 'objective correlative' is likely to be a series of events, actions, feelings or thoughts that are in some way *logically related*, each contingent on another or others through concepts such as causation. Relationships like these will be conveyed and given additional layers of meaning through language-specific relationships such as metaphor (in the domain of 'manner of representation'), rhyme and meter (in the domain of 'sounding qualities') and syntax (in the domain of 'structure') – see Figure 1.3.

But how does a comparable sense of coherence and unity – a sense of structure – come about in music, when it cannot borrow a sense of contingency from the external world? In the absence of an objective correlative, musical events can refer only to *themselves* (Selincourt, 1920). Self-evidently, one sound does not *cause* another one to happen (it is performers who do that), but one can *imply* another (Meyer, 1989, pp. 84ff) through a sense of derivation. That is, one musical event can be felt to stem from another, and it is our contention that this occurs through imitation: if one fragment or feature of music echoes another, then it owes the nature of its existence to its antecedent. And just as certain perceptual qualities of sound are felt to derive from one another, so too, it is hypothesised, are the emotional responses

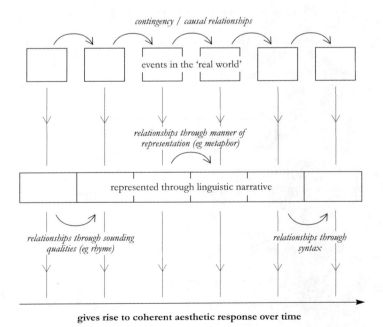

Figure 1.3 The forms of logical relationship underpinning meaning in language.

to each. Hence over time a metaphorical (musical) narrative can be built up through abstract patterns of sound (Figure 1.4).

The agency through which musical implication occurs is held to be a particular kind of perceived relationship that acknowledges the qualities of separate sounds that are the same or similar. Such relationships – purely mental constructs – are termed 'zygonic', after the Greek term 'zygon', meaning a 'yoke' or connection between similar things (Ockelford, 1991). The musical effect of a zygonic relationship is that a second event seems to *derive from* one that precedes, or, conversely, that a given event appears to *generate* one that follows (see Figure 1.5).

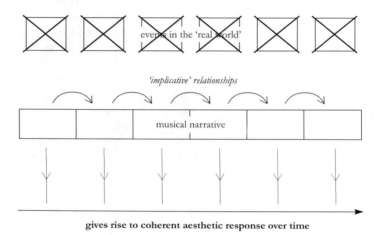

Figure 1.4 Relationships underpinning logic in music.

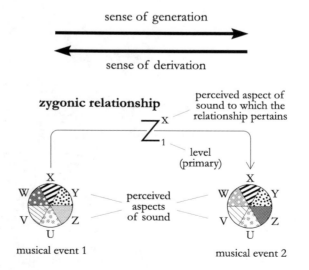

Figure 1.5 Representation of a primary zygonic relationship.

Introduction 7

The underlying imitation can be exact ('perfect') or approximate ('imperfect'), and refer to part or the whole of a musical event. Relationships can be of different levels: 'primary', between percepts themselves; 'secondary', between perceptual differences (which are gauged through 'primary interperspective relationships') and 'tertiary', between the relationships between differences (which are determined through 'secondary interperspective relationships'). Examples in relation to pitch, onset and duration are shown in Figure 1.6.

As well as pertaining to events, zygonic theory holds that a sense of derivation through imitation can also pertain at higher hierarchical levels in the domains of pitch and perceived time: to 'groups' of notes and 'frameworks' (Ockelford, 2006, 2011). The way in which zygonic relationships of pitch can function between events, groups and frameworks to create perceived coherence at different structural levels, and the cognitive demands that each is hypothesised to pose on listeners can be illustrated in relation to the opening bars of Beethoven's fifth symphony (see Figure 1.7).

Recognising imitation between *events* is postulated to take the least mental processing power, requiring (at least) two items of musical information (which comprise notes in the current example) to be held in working memory and compared. The temporal envelope within which such structures occur and are perceived is generally constrained, sometimes extending to little more than the perceived present. Zygonic connections between *groups* necessarily involve four events or more (Ockelford, 2006, p. 109), which may be separated over longer periods of time, possibly implicating long-term memory. Here there may also be a greater degree of abstraction from the perceptual 'surface', when, as in the example shown in Figure 1.7 between the two opening motifs, it is the relationships between the events within each group that are being imitated. The nature of the relationship between them is explained in more detail in Figure 1.8.

Imitative links between *frameworks* appear to be the most cognitively demanding of all. They depend on the existence of long-term 'schematic' memories (Bharucha, 1987) – in the case of a listener stylistically attuned to the Beethoven symphony, for example, built up from substantial exposure to other pieces in the minor mode. Here, it is assumed that the details of the perceptual surface and individual connections perceived between musical events are not encoded in long-term memory discretely or independently, but are combined with many thousands of other similar data to create probabilistic networks of relationships between notional representations of pitch and perceived time. That is, large amounts of perceptual information are merged to enable the requisitely parsimonious deep level of cognitive abstraction to occur.

In summary, then, it is hypothesised that the cognitive correlates of musical structure grow in complexity as one moves from events to groups and frameworks, reflecting an increasing amount of perceptual input, experienced over longer periods of time, and processed and stored using progressively more abstract forms of mental representation. Moreover, the logic

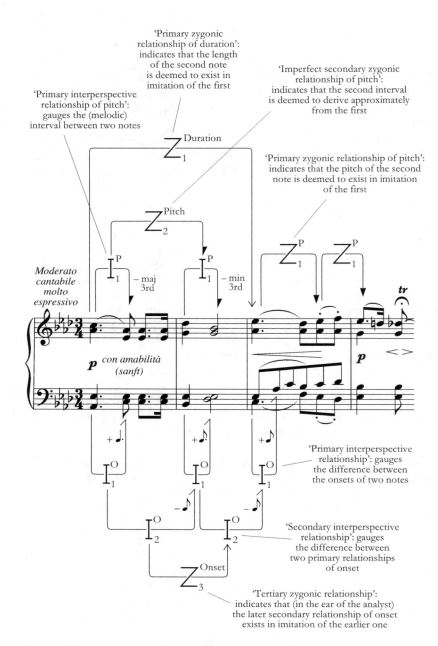

Figure 1.6 Examples of the zygonic relationships that are believed to underpin the cognition of musical structure in action in the opening bars of Beethoven's piano sonata, op. 110.

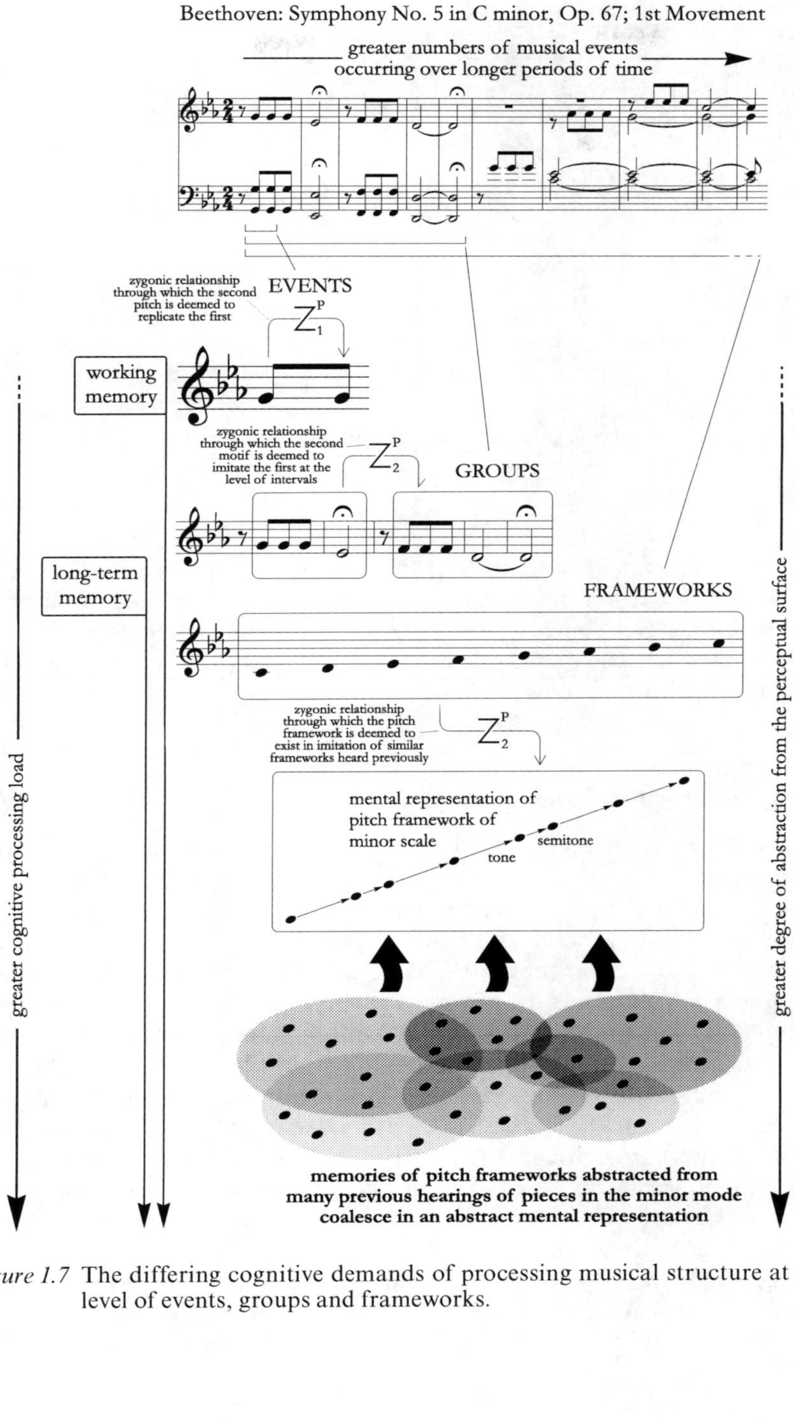

Beethoven: Symphony No. 5 in C minor, Op. 67; 1st Movement

Figure 1.7 The differing cognitive demands of processing musical structure at the level of events, groups and frameworks.

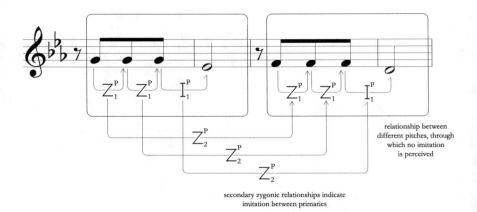

Figure 1.8 Relationships between groups ultimately comprise associations between events.

of the zygonic model suggests that the cognitive operations pertaining to higher levels of structure must build on and incorporate those required to process lower levels, since connections between groups comprise series of relationships between events (see Figure 1.8), and links between frameworks are established by acknowledging the correspondences that exist between groups.

The structure of the book

If this theory is correct, and musical structure is indeed hierarchical – functioning in distinct ways at the level of events, groups and frameworks, which make successively greater demands on cognitive processing power and memory – then it is reasonable to assume that these interlocking forms of structure should be reflected developmentally in children's evolving capacity to understand music. This hypothesis, which underpins the *Sounds of Intent* model of musical development (Welch *et al.*, 2009), is tested in the research reported in Chapter 2. This takes snapshots of young children's engagement in music and other organised sound, and uses the results of these assessments to sketch out a provisional music-developmental trajectory in the early years. Although the findings are preliminary in nature, there appear to be a number of factors that bear on infants' musical development, including, principally, the provision of a nurturing environment.

Chapter 3 is a response to the requests of a number of teachers working in special schools to ascertain whether the thinking underpinning the *Sounds of Intent* framework could be used to model development in other

Introduction 11

areas of creative activity, including art, drama and dance. This is particularly important because, for children and young people with complex needs, the distinction between activities in different sensory modes can be somewhat artificial: life typically passes by as a series of irreducible multisensory experiences.

The approach adopted is a theoretical one, identifying forms of supramodal cognition that underpin the six *Sounds of Intent* levels in the auditory domain, and ascertaining whether these may have a function in processing data arising from other types of sensory input. The new frameworks that are constructed suggest that this may indeed be the case as they have credible descriptive and explanatory power in relation to the (often limited) developmental literature that exists in relation to art forms other than music.

Chapter 4 reports on research that forms part of the 'REMUS' ('Researching Exceptional MUsical Skills') project – an extended exploration of how musical savants learn, remember and reproduce the music that they hear. The study presented is one in which a musical savant, Derek Paravicini, was asked to 'play along with' (or 'shadow') an original piece, the *Romantic Rollercoaster*, on ten occasions over a two-month period. The zygonic model of implication and expectation in music (Ockelford, 2006) was used to assign an expectancy rating to each note of the stimulus. It was hypothesised that notes with higher expectancy ratings would be predicted more consistently by Derek during his attempts to play along with *Romantic Rollercoaster*. This proved to be the case, and the analysis of the data sheds new light on our understanding of the relationship between expectation and memory in music.

Implication and expectation in music in the context of repeated hearings are also the subject of Chapter 5. In the course of eight trials, a slow-paced melody (previously used by Thorpe, Ockelford and Aksentijevic, 2012) was presented to (neurotypical) listeners, who registered the perceived strength of expectation that each note engendered in them by moving an index finger, left or right, along a touch-sensitive ribbon. So, in contrast to the research reported in Chapter 4, in which Derek anticipated what he believed would occur next, here participants' responses were retrospective. Different forms of musical structure that exist in the melody are categorised as events, groups or frameworks, and by identifying the extent to which these influence each response, sophisticated analyses are undertaken that provide insights into the evolving aesthetic response as the melody is heard – both on the first and subsequent occasions.

Conclusion

As noted above, one of the striking features of this collection of extended chapters is its theoretical parsimony. A single underlying principle – that of music-structural creation or recognition through imitation – is sufficient to offer concise and elegant explanations of apparently diverse cognitive phenomena that pertain to music. It appears to be a case that the simpler a theory is, the greater its potential power and the more general its applicability. Moreover, the zygonic conjecture, which draws on ideas from the fields of music theory, psychology and education, promotes the type of interdisciplinary thinking that is both epistemologically challenging and enriching, and must surely point the way to future empirical research in the domain of music science that is both theoretically rigorous and of practical pedagogical value.

2 The development of music-structural cognition in the early years

A perspective from the *Sounds of Intent* model

Adam Ockelford and Angela Voyajolu

Introduction

This chapter reports on new research that explores how musical structures at the level of events, groups and frameworks that are identified by zygonic theory in a psychomusicological context may arise developmentally. The findings build on evidence derived from earlier empirical work, including the *Sounds of Intent* project (for example, Vogiatzoglou *et al.*, 2011). This investigated the course of music development in young people with learning difficulties, and, incidentally, from the observations of 'neurotypical' children's engagement with music in the early years, reported in music-psychological literature in the last three decades of the twentieth century and into the early years of the twenty-first century, ranging from the pioneering work of Helmut Moog (1968/1976) to Esther Mang's notion of vocal play as creativity (2005). The new data are taken from the first of the *Sounds of Intent in the Early Years* studies (Ockelford, 2015, 2019), and support the notion of three levels of music-structural understanding. The data analysis suggests that their emergence in cognition, while broadly sequential (events, groups and then frameworks), is complex, 'fuzzy' and context-dependent.

Evidence for the existence of the postulated cognitive correlates of musical structure from the musical engagement of children in previous research (i): the *Sounds of Intent* project

We begin with the premise of zygonic theory that the human cognition of musical structure occurs at three levels in the domains of pitch and perceived time that pertain to 'events', 'groups' and 'frameworks' (see Chapter 1 and Ockelford, 2006, 2011). The existence of the cognitive correlates of musical structure was first corroborated empirically in the *Sounds of Intent* studies, which were designed to explore the musical development of children with learning difficulties (for example, Ockelford *et al.*, 2005; Cheng, Ockelford and Welch, 2009; Welch *et al.*, 2009; Ockelford *et al.*, 2011; Vogiatzoglou *et al.*, 2011; Himonides, Ockelford and Voyajolu, 2017). Here, the evidence of music-structural processing pertaining to events, groups and frameworks comes from hundreds of observations of young people engaging with music in a range of everyday contexts.

14 *Adam Ockelford and Angela Voyajolu*

For example, an appreciation of imitation at the level of *events* is implied by Zeeshan's laughing and rocking 'when he hears his teacher imitating Tom's vocal sounds', an understanding that is translated into action by Xavier, who 'distinctly tries to copy high notes and low notes in vocal interaction sessions' (Ockelford, 2013, pp. 130 and 133).[1] Lottie seems to be able to recognise *group* structures, since she 'cries whenever she hears the "goodbye" song. It only takes the first two or three notes to be played on the keyboard, and she experiences a strong emotional reaction'. This capacity is realised in sound by Lottie, who 'hums distinct patterns of notes and repeats them. Her favourite sounds rather like a playground chant, and she repeats it from one day to the next' (Ockelford, *op. cit.*, pp. 129 and 130). Quincy, who 'knows that when his music teacher plays the last verse of *Molly Malone* in the minor key it signifies sadness', shows some non-conceptual understanding of how pitch *frameworks* work in the Western musical vernacular, while Janet, with severe learning difficulties, has taken Quincy's intuitive grasp of mode a stage further, having 'developed the confidence to introduce new material on her saxophone in the school's jazz quartet'.

Although much of the data gathered in the course of the *Sounds of Intent* project comprised 'snapshots' of children's musical engagement at a single point in time, rather than offering longitudinal accounts (notable exceptions being Cheng, Ockelford and Welch, 2009, and Wu, 2017), two developmental features of music-structural cognition did become apparent. First, as one would expect, it appeared that the successively more extensive cognitive abilities required to process musical structure at the level of events, groups and frameworks arise sequentially in development. The evidence for this stemmed from the observation that there were no instances of children showing music-structural engagement at the level of frameworks who were not able to recognise or create imitative patterns involving groups, nor of children who could process or produce group structures who could not operate cognitively at the level of events. Second, it became evident that the cognitive capacities pertaining to each structural level do not emerge fully functioning, but themselves evolve incrementally: that is to say, as well as music-structural processing developing *between* levels, there appeared to be development *within* each of them.

In addition, the *Sounds of Intent* data suggested precursors to the three phases of music-structural cognition whose postulated existence they substantiated. To frame these developmental antecedents theoretically, consider that imitation, which lies at the heart of zygonic theory, can only have significance in the context of potential *variety*. This is because for one sound (or aspect of sound) to be heard as deriving from another – for the concept of agency in repetition to exist – requires a (hypothetical) range of options to be available. That is to say, before children can appreciate or make imitatively generated patterns in sound, they need to be able to process or create a range of sonic alternatives. This in turn implies that they will have had many, diverse listening experiences and sound-making opportunities. Examples of children functioning at this level who were observed in the

A perspective from the Sounds of Intent *model*   15

course of the *Sounds of Intent* project include Rick, whose 'eye movements intensify when he hears the big band play', and Oliver, who 'scratches the tambourine, making a range of sounds ... whenever he plays near the rim and the bells jingle, he smiles' (Ockelford, *et al.*, 2011, pp. 179 and 180).

A few of the children who were involved in the *Sounds of Intent* research appeared to be at a stage before this one of developing auditory perception, when the processing of sound had yet to get underway at all. Examples included Anna, who

> sits motionless in her chair. Her teacher approaches and plays a cymbal with a soft beater, gently at first, and then more loudly, in front of her and then near to each ear. She does not appear to react.

and Yerik, who

> usually makes a rasping sound as he breathes. He seems to be unaware of what he is doing, and the rasping persists, irrespective of external stimulation. His class teacher has tried to see whether Yerik can be made aware of his sounds by making them louder (using a microphone, amplifier and speakers), but so far this approach has met with no response.
>
> (Ockelford, 2013, p. 129)

It seemed that nothing distinctive could precede this pre-perceptual phase, so it was termed (*Sounds of Intent*) Level 1. The pre-structural phase, referred to above, of which Rick and Oliver provided examples, was called Level 2. The three phases of structural cognition, pertaining to events, groups and frameworks, were designated respectively Levels 3–5. Collectively, these five levels, while covering a vast range of musical development, did not seem to present a complete picture, however, as there were examples of children engaging with music who were more or less consciously manipulating the parameters of sound – pitch, timing, loudness and timbre – to achieve particular expressive ends. For instance, Ciara,

> who is a good vocalist despite having severe learning difficulties, is learning how to convey a range of different emotions in her singing through using techniques such as vibrato, rubato, consciously using a wider range of dynamics, and producing darker and lighter sounds.

And Ruth,

> who sings well, and is used to performing in public, although she has severe learning difficulties and autism. She can learn new songs just by listening to her teacher (who is not a trained singer) run through them, and as she gets to know a piece, she intuitively adds expression as she feels appropriate. ... Later, when she listens to other people singing

16 *Adam Ockelford and Angela Voyajolu*

the songs she knows, she clearly prefers some performances to others. Her teacher believes this shows that she has a mature engagement with pieces in mid-to-late twentieth-century popular style.

(Ockelford, 2013, p. 129)

This phase of musical development, in which young people appeared to be aware of the culturally determined rules of expressive performance, was labelled Level 6.

The six *Sounds of Intent* levels, and the core cognitive abilities associated with each, can be summarised as follows (Ockelford, 2013, p. 148). See Table 2.1, in which the levels pertaining to musical structure (3, 4 and 5) are highlighted.

The *Sounds of Intent* research further divided the universe of potential musical engagement into three domains: 'reactive' ('R'), which entailed listening and responding to sounds; 'proactive' ('P'), which involved causing, creating or controlling sounds and 'interactive' ('I'), which meant participating in sound-making activity in the context of others. Conceptually, the three domains and six levels were orthogonal, implying that they could be represented as a matrix with 18 cells. This was represented visually as a series of concentric circles divided into segments, ranging from the centre (Level 1), with its focus on self, to the outermost ring (Level 6), with its reference to wider communities of others. The convention of denoting each segment by its domain (R, P or I) followed by its level (1, 2, 3, 4, 5 or 6) was used. Hence 'R.1' refers to 'Reactive Level 1', 'P.3' to 'Proactive Level 3' and 'I.6' to 'Interactive Level 6'. Brief descriptors were developed for the segments, which sought to summarise the nature of the musical engagement that each involved. See Figure 2.1.

Table 2.1 The six levels underpinning the *Sounds of Intent* framework (acronym 'CIRCLE')

Level	Description	Acronym	Core cognitive abilities
1	Confusion and Chaos	C	No awareness of sound
2	Awareness and Intentionality	I	An emerging awareness of sound and the variety that is possible within the domain of sound
3	**Relationships, repetition Regularity**	**R**	**A growing awareness of the possibility and significance of relationships between sonic *events***
4	**Sounds forming Clusters**	**C**	**An evolving perception of *groups* of sounds and the relationships that may exist between them**
5	**Deeper structural Links**	**L**	**A growing recognition of whole pieces, and of the *frameworks* of pitch and perceived time that lie behind them**
6	Mature artistic Expression	E	A developing awareness of the culturally determined 'emotional syntax' of performance that articulates the 'narrative metaphor' of pieces

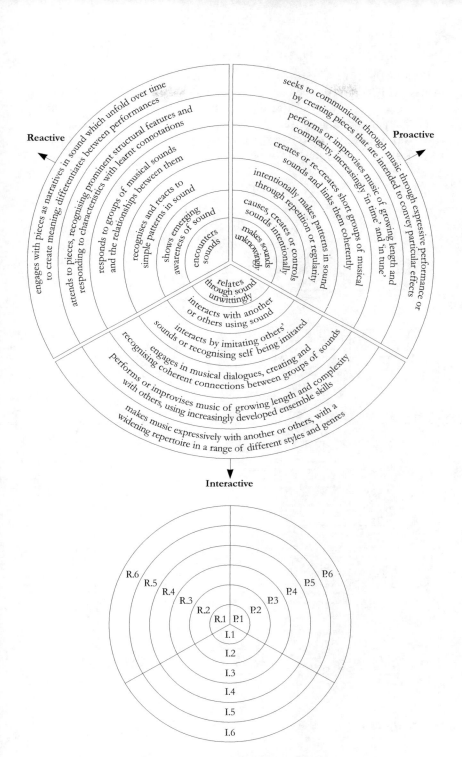

Figure 2.1 Visual representation of the *Sounds of Intent* framework.

18 *Adam Ockelford and Angela Voyajolu*

Finally, the 18 descriptors were broken down into four more detailed 'elements', which the *Sounds of Intent* research team believed offered a fair reflection of each segment (Ockelford, 2013, pp. 166–168); see Figures 2.2a–2.2c. Some elements related purely to engagement with sound and music, other to sound and music in relation to other sensory input and the remainder to technical matters pertaining to performance, which it was felt became

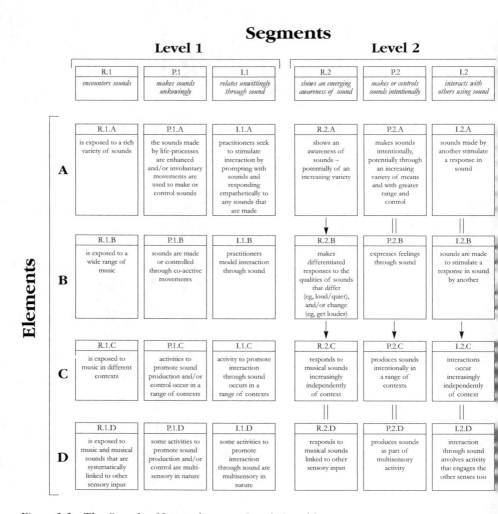

Figure 2.2a The *Sounds of Intent* elements, Levels 1 and 2.

A perspective from the Sounds of Intent model 19

important at Levels 5 and 6. The elements that pertain particularly to the cognition and creation of musical structure at Levels 3–5 are shaded in Figures 2.2b and 2.2c. Where a developmental *sequence* between these can be identified, it is marked with an arrow; developmental *equivalence* is shown with parallel lines.

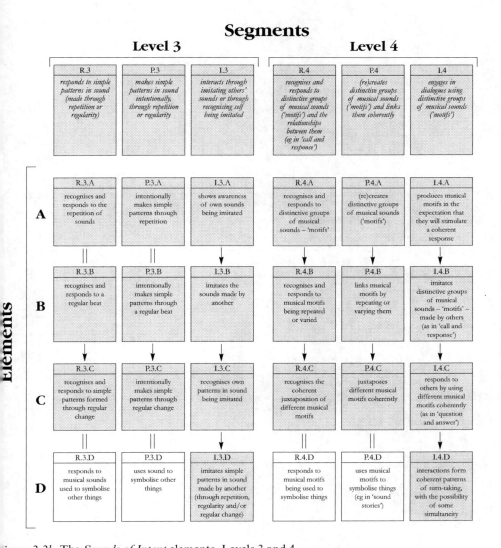

Figure 2.2b The *Sounds of Intent* elements, Levels 3 and 4.

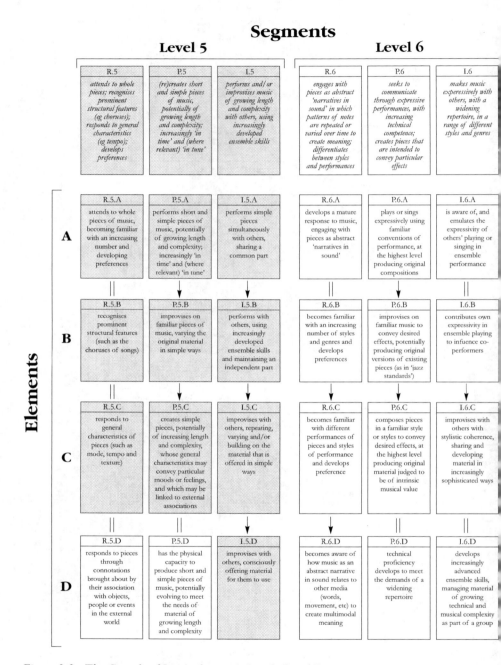

Figure 2.2c The *Sounds of Intent* elements, Levels 5 and 6.

Evidence for the existence of the postulated cognitive correlates of musical structure from the musical engagement of children in previous research (ii): work in the early years

Further corroboration of the existence of three levels in our music-structural processing capacity (pertaining to events, groups and frameworks) is to be found incidentally in the literature pertaining to 'neurotypical' music development in the early years. For example, as we noted above, it seems that young children's built-in propensity to imitate others (Meltzoff and Prinz, 2002) soon comes to play a part in early sound-making at the level of musical *events*. Auditory and acoustic analyses of preverbal communication at two, three, five and seven months demonstrate that 34%–53% of infant vocal sounds are part of reciprocal matching sequences, framed by mothers' modelling or matching utterances or both (Papoušek, 1996, p. 97). Moreover, it appears that infants below five months of age can imitate individual pitches (Kessen, Levine and Wendrich, 1979), pitch contours (Kuhl and Meltzoff, 1982) and vowel-like harmonic resonances (Legerstee, 1990).

Later, from seven to eleven months, the notion of repeating and varying *groups* of sounds as the basic units of proto-musical structure appears, when 'canonical babbling involves production of short musical patterns or phrases that soon become the core units for a new level of vocal practising and play' (Papoušek, *op. cit.*, p. 106). Gradually, groups of sounds may be linked through repetition or transposition to form chains, and the first self-sufficient improvised pieces emerge. 'Between the ages of one to two years ... a typically spontaneous infant song consists of repetitions of one brief melodic phrase at different pitch centres' (Welch, 2006, p. 318). These are unlike adult songs, however, because 'they lack a framework of stable pitches (a scale) and use a very limited set of contours in one song' (Dowling, 1982, pp. 416 and 417). From the age of two and a half, 'pot pourri' songs may appear (Moog, 1968/1976, p. 115), which borrow (and may transform) features and fragments from others – standard songs that are assimilated into the child's own spontaneous song schemes (Hargreaves, 1986, p. 73). Mang (2005) terms such self-generated songs as 'referent-guided improvisation', which use source materials derived from a repertoire that is familiar from a child's musical culture.

Finally, typically (though by no means always) from around the age of four, two advances occur, which pertain to *frameworks*. First, children develop the capacity to abstract an underlying pulse from the surface rhythm of songs and other pieces (meaning that they can perform 'in time' to a regular beat that is provided). Second, they acquire 'tonal stability', with the clear projection of a key centre across all the phrases of a piece (Hargreaves, *op. cit.*, pp. 76 and 77; Welch and Preti, 2018). As we have seen, these abilities imply a cognisance of repetition at a deeper structural level in the 'background' organisation of music.

22   Adam Ockelford and Angela Voyajolu

Again, this literature supports the notion of three phases of development in music-structural cognition, though, once more, without specifying how each kind of mental processing arises and how the different levels are connected.

A new study: *Sounds of Intent in the Early Years*

The new study reported here, the first phase of *Sounds of Intent in the Early Years*,[2] takes the exploration of the zygonic hypothesis in the context of the musical development of young children a stage further. The research was undertaken at an integrated children's centre, nursery school and crèche in south-west London that offers early years education and care to local families. The facility is inclusive, providing services to children irrespective of any special educational needs or disabilities they may have, and reflects a wide social and cultural demographic characteristic of many urban settings in the UK. As a consequence, the children's experiences and expectations of life at home are very diverse, and for many, English is an additional language.

The main aim was to ascertain whether children in the early years follow the same or a similar music-developmental path to that set out in the original *Sounds of Intent* project. It was expected that there would be at least some points of connection, since the design of the *Sounds of Intent* framework took account of previous research into the nature and level of young children's engagement with sound and music. However, it was not known whether the extant *Sounds of Intent* framework would be sufficient to offer a comprehensive description of early years' musical development, or, conversely, whether there were elements that played a part in the musical lives of children and young people with learning difficulties that would not typically figure in the growth of 'neurotypical' musicality. A related objective was to ascertain the extent to which any phases of musical development that formed part of the original *Sounds of Intent* framework, where they were not age-related, would be so in the case of able-bodied children in the early years.

The method adopted was observational, with the second author attempting to capture, through video recording, a broadly representative sample of individual children's forms of musical engagement that occurred during their days spent at the early years' centre, for subsequent analysis by the research team as a whole. Preliminary work had suggested that the majority of musical activities happen frequently and spontaneously throughout the day, so children were observed in a range of contexts, including not only adult-led activities in which singing and playing were the primary foci, but also free-flowing musical interactions with peers and self-directed play in which music was sometimes incidental. With around two hours of observation time available per week over a period of six months, it had been hoped to gather data on at least 50 children. In the event, 125 discrete episodes of musical engagement were identified involving 25 boys and 33 girls, aged from 0 to 4 years. The mean number of observations per child was a little over 2, with a mode of 1 and range 1–8. These data pertain to 86 separate events; hence the mean number of observations made per activity was around 1.5.

The children were used to being videoed as part of the day-to-day assessment procedures in the centre, and they soon became accustomed to the presence of an additional adult observing them. As far as it was possible to ascertain, this potential distraction did not have a significant impact on the children's typically spontaneous music making, occurring as it did in an already busy environment. It is of interest to note that 87 observations (69.5%) pertained to child-led musical activity, of which 44 (35%) were of children on their own, 35 (28%) were with another child or other children and eight (6.5%) were with an adult – in six cases with the child alone (5%) and on two occasions (1.5%) as part of a group. Of the 38 adult-led episodes of musical engagement (30.5%), most of which were planned, although some arose spontaneously, 13 (10.5%) were with an adult alone, and 25 (20%) were in a group with other children. See Figure 2.3.

The recordings, which ranged in length from around 30 seconds to three minutes, were analysed by the research team through viewing (repeated as often as necessary) and discussion, to ascertain whether the musical engagement that each showed was reflected in one or more of the elements that make up the *Sounds of Intent* framework. Given the exploratory nature of the research, no attempt was made to gauge the levels of musical

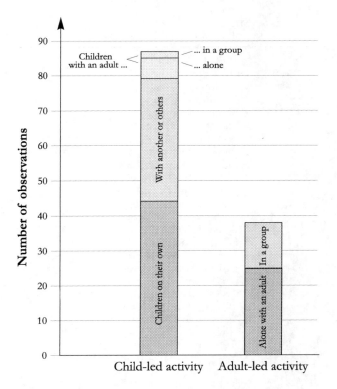

Figure 2.3 The social contexts of the *Sounds of Intent in the Early Years* observations.

24   *Adam Ockelford and Angela Voyajolu*

engagement *within* elements, since the experience of data gathering in the original *Sounds of Intent* project involving children with learning difficulties had suggested that to make such refined judgements required each child to be observed on a number of observations at different times (Cheng, 2010; Ockelford *et al.*, 2011; Ockelford, 2012b). Table 2.2 shows a range of examples taken from the assessments that were made.

Table 2.2 A range of examples from the *Sounds of Intent* assessments that were made in the early years research project

Child	Age (months)	Sex	Description of musical engagement	Sounds of Intent assessment		
				Domain	Level	Element
1	4	F	Appears transfixed as the recorder is played to her.	R	2	B
2	12	M	Explores the small keyboard in different ways, playing clusters of sounds with his right hand and individual notes using his index finger.	P	2	A
3	12	M	Strikes the keyboard with the flat of his hand in response to the clusters of notes made by Child 2.	I	2	A
4	14	M	During an impromptu music session in the baby room, an adult starts a chant about a bubble growing bigger and bigger before it pops. She repeats the word 'bubble' each time getting louder and louder, before clapping loudly once, simultaneously exclaiming 'pop!' With each repetition of the word and increase in dynamic level, Child 4 gets more excited, jumping up and down, then clapping and squealing with the final 'pop!'	R	3	C
5	38	F	Plays the snare drum in the garden, creating different beats, alternating with two sticks.	P	3	C
6	17	M	Copies another child by making sounds with his voice through a tube that he holds to his mouth.	I	3	B

Child	Age (months)	Sex	Description of musical engagement	Sounds of Intent assessment		
				Domain	Level	Element
7	14	M	An adult spontaneously sings a short song made up of repeated phrases: 'I can shake, I can shake, and I'm having lots of fun. I can shake, I can shake, can you?' Child 7 copies her shaking movement with each phrase and smiles.	R	4	B
8	42	F	Repeats a short musical motif after reading the lyrics to a song that she learnt during Black History Month.	P	4	B
9	31	F	A practitioner plays a descending scale on the white notes of a keyboard, and Child 9 copies, changing the sequence from slow to fast. This interaction continues in a pattern of turn-taking.	I	4	D
10	18	F	A practitioner sings the song *Roly Poly* for the children, which they know well. The second time though, it is performed very quietly. Child 10 listens through the whole of the first verse and joins in the actions the second time around. She appears to understand the structure of the song, sometimes anticipating what is coming next.	R	5	B
11	42	M	Sings *Happy Birthday* as part of a game after making a cake with candles out of clay. His singing is in time and largely in tune.	P	5	A
12	36	M	During a music session, a group of children is hopping along to a recording of a song. Child 12 spontaneously sings along with the female vocalist.	I	5	A

26   *Adam Ockelford and Angela Voyajólu*

No observations were made that were gauged to be at Level 1 or Level 6 of the framework. However, within the remaining 2–5 range, it was quite common for a child to exhibit musical engagement at different levels within a single observation period – even within the same activity. For example, a three-year-old girl, playing outside with a boy of similar age who was on the autism spectrum and non-verbal, demonstrated a regular beat on the drum that she intended the boy to emulate (Level 3, interactive), subsequently using their playing as an accompaniment to a vocal rendition of *Twinkle, Twinkle, Little Star* (Level 5, interactive). The boy copied the beat (Level 3, interactive) and attempted to imitate the song as well, managing to vocalise the contour of the descending pattern of the fourth line ('Like a diamond in the sky') using the consonant 'd' and different vowel sounds (Level 4, interactive) – see Figure 2.13.[3]

The complete set of observations was distributed across the *Sounds of Intent* domains (R, P and I), levels (2, 3, 4 and 5) and elements (A, B, C and D) as illustrated in Table 2.3. The frequency with which each was observed is shown per element, per level and per domain. So, for example, there were no recorded instances of musical engagement at R.2.A, two at R.2.B, none at R.2.C and four at R.2.D, meaning that there were observations pertaining to 50% of the four available elements, which together yield a total of six cases at R.2. As Table 2.2 shows, 28 observations were made across Level 2 as a whole, with 75% of elements represented, while the entire reactive domain ('R') had 23 observations, amounting to 50% elemental representation. Because of the relatively small number of cases per element, in the analyses that follow, the potential developmental differences *between* elements at the same level (shown in Figure 2.4) are disregarded, although their importance will be picked up again in later discussion (see Figures 2.17–2.19).

It was found that the essence of each of the 125 observations could be encapsulated in one of the *Sounds of Intent* descriptors, and all three domains (R, P and I) across Levels 2–5 featured in one observation or more, in a distribution whose irregularities are not statistically significant: χ^2 (6, $N = 125$) = 4.18, $p = 0.65$). Clearly, the evidence provided by this preliminary study is limited in size and scope, and so it could be that other forms of musical engagement exist in the early years that the framework does not capture. Moreover, data pertaining to 15 elements out of 48 (31%) are absent, and around 40% of the remainder are attributable to just five elements as follows: P.2.A 'makes sounds intentionally, potentially through an increasing variety of means and with greater range and control' at 10.4%; I.3.D 'imitates simple patterns in sound made by another through repetition, regularity and/or regular change' at 9.6%; P.4.B 'makes musical motifs by repeating or varying them' at 8%; P.3.A 'intentionally makes simple patterns through repetition' and P.5.A 'performs short and simple pieces of music, potentially of growing length and complexity, and increasingly "in time" and [where relevant] "in tune"' both at 6.4%. Nonetheless, the findings

Table 2.3 The complete distribution of *Sounds of Intent* assessments

Domain	R				P				I				*n*
Level/element	A	B	C	D	A	B	C	D	A	B	C	D	
2	0	2	0	4	13	0	0	0	2	3	0	4	**28** (50%)
2	**6** (50%)				**13** (25%)				**9** (75%)				
3	1	1	1	1	8	2	5	1	1	6	0	12	**39** (92%)
3	**4** (100%)				**16** (100%)				**19** (75%)				
4	0	5	1	1	5	10	1	0	0	5	3	4	**35** (75%)
4	**7** (75%)				**16** (75%)				**12** (75%)				
5	3	2	0	1	8	1	0	0	6	2	0	0	**23** (58%)
5	**6** (75%)				**9** (50%)				**8** (50%)				
n (% elements represented)	**23** (75%)				**54** (63%)				**48** (69%)				**N = 125** (69%)

The emboldened numbers are totals in each category.

28   Adam Ockelford and Angela Voyajolu

suggest that, in broad terms, the *Sounds of Intent* framework offers a credible first iteration of a model of musical development in the early years.

The distribution of observations is skewed towards the proactive domain (43%), with 38.5% classed as interactive, and only 18.5% reactive. Since music is so prevalent in the auditory environments of young children (Lamont, 2008), the latter may well be an under-representation, reflecting the fact that reactive musical engagement, potentially requiring musical significance to be attributed to non-musical behaviours, may be more difficult to isolate than activity that has overtly musical outputs.

Implications of the *Sounds of Intent in the Early Years* findings for the zygonic model of musical structure

How can we use the data obtained from the *Sounds of Intent in the Early Years* study to test the conjecture that the three-level model of musical structure (which, as we have seen, identifies imitation operating at the level of events, groups and frameworks) may have psychological relevance and validity?

We have argued that if there are indeed cognitive correlates of the postulated structural levels then they must emerge as aspects of a child's musical development, and, given the assumption that these make successively greater demands on an individual's capacity for processing auditory stimuli, we would expect their emergence to be sequential. However, as the *Sounds of Intent in the Early Years* project was able to observe children in action for only a limited period of time, no longitudinal data pertaining to individuals were generated, just as they had not been in the original *Sounds of Intent* investigation into the musical development of children with learning difficulties.[4] With the cross-sectional findings pertaining to children in the early years, though, it is possible to adopt a *proxy* longitudinal approach, by considering the ages at which given music-developmental phases are reached across the research sample (something that would not have been practicable with the children with learning difficulties due to their varying profiles of developmental delay).

To this end, for the purposes of age/phase analysis, children were assigned to six-month age bands centred on 0, 6, 12, 18, 24, 30, 36, 42 and 48 months (each therefore extending ±3 months). Figure 2.4 shows the range of *Sounds of Intent* levels recorded for each child, irrespective of domain (since reactive, proactive and interactive engagement with music are believed to provide equally valid evidence of cognitive activity). In 36 out of the 58 cases (62%), only one level was observed; two adjacent levels were logged in the case of 13 children (22.5%) and the musical engagement of nine participants (15.5%) was found to span three. None of the profiles extended across four levels. In Figure 2.4, each child's rating is recorded as a single dot (where only one level was observed) or two dots connected with a line (showing ranges of two or three levels).

A perspective from the Sounds of Intent *model* 29

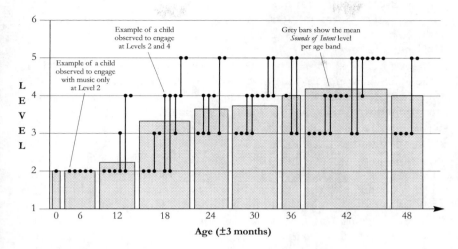

Figure 2.4 Graph showing the range of *Sounds of Intent* levels observed in each child by age.

In seeking to analyse the data, it is important to remember the exploratory nature of the research from which they derive. The observations were not made with aim of providing comprehensive accounts of each child's capacity for musical engagement. Rather, as we have seen, they were intended to provide a range of ecologically valid snapshots of a demographically mixed population of young children reacting to or participating in musical activity, based on what the observer found to be salient at any given point in the naturalistic, protean context of an early years centre. This proviso notwithstanding, the data do nevertheless offer a preliminary indication of how musicality may develop across a group of socially and culturally diverse children in such an early years context.

Babies from 0 to 9 months were all observed to be at Level 2, which is concerned with children becoming aware of sound and the range of sounds that exist, including those pertaining to music; with developing a notion of agency in being able to make sounds themselves in an increasing variety of ways and with having an emerging sense of self and other in the context of interaction through sound. From 9 to 15 months, engagement with sound and music at Level 2 persists, and is supplemented with an awareness of – and the capacity to produce – repetition and regular change involving individual sounds (Level 3), and the recognition and creation of imitation and transformation pertaining to clusters of notes (Level 4). The period from 15 to 21 months is additionally characterised by engagement with music at Level 5, which involves the awareness and, potentially, the production of a more abstract level of structure over time: here, children are likely to sing songs increasingly in time and in tune. From 21 months,

30   Adam Ockelford and Angela Voyajolu

musical engagement at Level 2 is no longer reported, and the three higher levels (3, 4 and 5) remain functional at least as far as 51 months (although in the current study no instances of activity at Level 4 were reported in the 45–51 month range).

It is of interest to note that Levels 3–5, which persist in the observations of the older children, are those that pertain to the cognition and production of musical structure, whereas the acquisition of abilities at Level 2 (which is not acknowledged from children's third year) is regarded as a necessary step *en route* to subsequent music-structural understanding and generation. Furthermore, in terms of zygonic theory, we have seen that the individual music-structural relationships that pertain to Level 3 are predicted to work together to produce the cluster characteristic of Level 4, whose internal and external connections are in turn thought to underpin the creation of abstract frameworks of pitch and time at Level 5. Hence, the observation that musical engagement at Levels 3 and 4 continues alongside attainment at Level 5 is consonant with the zygonic conjecture. Moreover, the notion of a sequence of increasingly complex types of musical structure being matched in the trajectory of a child's early music-cognitive development is supported by the rising value of the mean of *Sounds of Intent* levels over time (shown as grey bars in Figure 2.4). As one would expect, given the move to simultaneous processing at Levels 3–5, the tendency is towards average values around Level 4.

A further way of capturing the development of the music-processing abilities evinced by the 58 children involved in the project is through taking into consideration only the highest *Sounds of Intent* level of functioning that was recorded for each (see Table 2.4). This offers a clearer picture of how the 'leading edge' of a child's music-structural cognition advances through the early years. The data are presented visually in Figure 2.5.

Table 2.4 Highest recorded *Sounds of Intent* levels per 6-month age band

Age band (±3 months)	Level				n	Mean level
	2	3	4	5		
0	1	–	–	–	1	2
6	5	–	–	–	5	2
12	4	1	1	–	6	2.5
18	2	3	4	2	11	3.5
24	–	1	3	2	6	4.2
30	–	2	3	2	7	4
36	–	1	1	3	5	4.4
42	–	2	4	6	12	4.3
48	–	3	–	2	5	3.8
n	12	13	16	17	N = 58	3.7

A perspective from the Sounds of Intent *model* 31

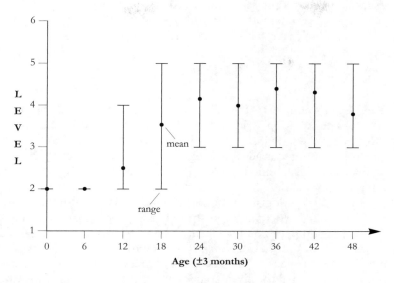

Figure 2.5 Mean highest *Sounds of Intent* levels by age.

Although 125 observations over an age range of four years is a relatively small number on which to attempt to model a developmental trend, the pattern of data indicates that mean highest *Sounds of Intent* levels achieved by children grow as they move through the early years, corroborating the upward trajectory observed in Figure 2.4. However, it is also evident that there is a wide range of individual differences. Hence, it would appear too simplistic to say that the *Sounds of Intent* level of a child, L, can simply be expressed as a function, f, of their age, a:

$$L = f(a).$$

Rather, it would seem more appropriate to consider a model in which children's progress is related to both their age and current level of music-cognitive development. These two elements are captured in the dynamic systems model, which was first introduced to the field of developmental psychology by Van Geert (1991). In mathematical terms, if x_t is taken to specify the value of variable x at time t, then a dynamic model takes the form

$$x_{t+1} = f(x_t)$$

which reads 'the value of x at time $t+1$ is a function (f) of the value of x at time t' (van Geert and Steenbeck, 2005).

But what is the nature of f? Visual inspection of Figure 2.5 suggests that the relationship between level L and age a may resemble a logistic function, in which the rate of change approximates to a period of exponential increase, followed by a phase of linear growth, and then an inversely symmetrical stage of exponential retardation, which together are representable as a sigmoid (or 's') curve. This is commonly expressed as

$$y = \frac{1}{1 + e^{-x}}$$

where 'e' ('Euler's number) is the base of the natural logarithm, approximating to 2.718. The equation yields values of y between 0 and 1, and a point of inflection where $y = 0$ (and $x = 1$); see Figure 2.6. This distinctive profile of growth has been used to model individual development in areas such as cognition (Eckstein, 1999) and language (Robinson and Mervis, 1998; de Bot, Lowie and Verspoor, 2007).

Here, we will use a logistic function to model the set of data from our group of research participants (illustrated in Figure 2.5), which requires that the lower and upper bounds of the codomain be specified (in our case, the highest and lowest relevant *Sounds of Intent* levels), the rate of change be defined (here, the pace of music-cognitive development) and the point of inflection be prescribed (in the current context, the age at which the rate of change moves from increase to decrease). These four variables are captured in the following equation:

$$L = l_{max} - \frac{l_{max} - l_{min}}{1 + \left(\dfrac{a}{c}\right)^i}.$$

Here, L is the *Sounds of Intent* level, $l_{max} = 6$ and $l_{min} = 2$; a is a child's age in months and the rate of change, c, and the point of inflection, i, are unknown. Using the data from Table 2.4 to inform an iterative process of nonlinear least squares regression, the values that provide the best fit are $c = 34.67$

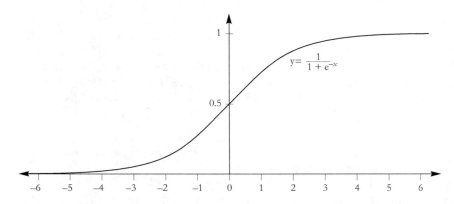

Figure 2.6 Visual representation of the basic logistic function.

A perspective from the Sounds of Intent model

($p = 0.00$) and $i = 1.15$ ($p = 0.03$), giving $R^2 = 0.75$. That is to say, the logistic equation that is most consistent with the data is

$$L = 6 - \frac{4}{1+\left(\dfrac{a}{34.67}\right)^{1.15}}$$

producing a curve as follows (see Figure 2.7).

It may seem surprising that, within the data range given, the function exhibits no period of stasis (modelling the position before development begins) nor, beyond the first five postnatal weeks, a period in which cognitive abilities grow at increasing rate, since one would expect both to feature in a sigmoidal model. It should be remembered, however, that the point in children's lives at which observations began had been preceded by several months of musical development, extending back to a time before the end of their mothers' second trimester of pregnancy – that is, before their hearing first started to emerge *in utero* (see Birnholtz and Benacerraf, 1983; Lasky and Williams, 2005), and to Level 1 of the *Sounds of Intent* framework.

It is informative to compare the findings from the *Sounds of Intent in the Early Years* project with those reported in the established music-developmental literature. It was noted above that the latter broadly accord with the three phases of music-structural cognition suggested by zygonic theory, and Figure 2.8 shows how they relate to the *Sounds of Intent in the Early Years* data. With the

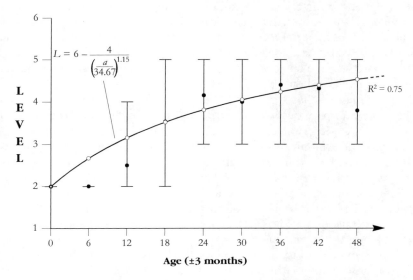

Figure 2.7 A logistic regression accounts for 75% of the variance in the data pertaining to the mean highest *Sounds of Intent* levels by age.

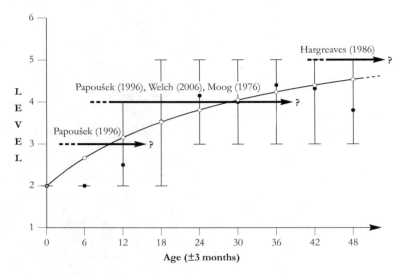

Figure 2.8 Graph comparing the findings of the current project with previous observations of musical development in the early years.

exception of Papoušek's (1996) assertion that infants at only two months have the ability to match certain features of their mother's vocal sounds (implying interaction at Level 3) – a form of proto-musical engagement that was not seen at this age in the current study – all other documented accounts fall within the age ranges pertaining to music-developmental levels that were observed in the *Sounds of Intent in the Early Years* project. Nonetheless, the distribution of reported observations suggests that the previously identified phases of music-cognitive development may occur earlier in a child's life than the new data indicate. Why should this be the case?

First, it may be that some of the forms of engagement with music and sound that have previously been recorded do not correspond to the *Sounds of Intent* level descriptors as satisfactorily as may initially have been supposed. For example, it may be that a child's early – and so, inevitably, limited – vocal repertoire could give a misleading impression of imitation through a mother's empathetic restriction of her own vocal efforts to the relatively small range of sounds that her son or daughter was capable of making (Ockelford, 2012a, sets out a method for evaluating such interactions probabilistically). Similarly, experience suggests that repeated syllabic patterns such as 'ma, ma, ma, ma' may on occasion be more about children's physical enjoyment of their capacity for duplicating sounds than conscious imitation in the context of potential acoustic variety. And, as far as very young children are concerned, making series of vocal whoops and glides may have less to do with deliberately imitating patterns of regular variation

A perspective from the Sounds of Intent *model* 35

in sound than relishing the repeated excitement of stretching newly discovered vocal cords. That is to say, activities that were thought to be at Level 3 on the basis of a short verbal description could in fact be representative of Level 2. Likewise, sequences of sounds may be grouped not in accordance with gestalt principles (as at Level 4 of *Sounds of Intent*) but in line with the constraints of what is possible with one breath from a small pair of lungs (suggesting engagement at Level 2 or 3).

Second, the observations made in the *Sounds of Intent in the Early Years* project did not seek to show what children may be able to achieve in optimal conditions (for example, alone with a parent at home), but the levels and types of musical engagement that they typically display amid the hubbub of an early years centre, often on their own or with peers and so unscaffolded by adults. In this context, certain abilities may manifest themselves later than in the intimacy and security of the family environment.

Third, it is evident that each level potentially covers a wide developmental range in the early years (something that, as we have seen, the original *Sounds of Intent* project acknowledged in the context of children and young people with learning difficulties). Consider, for example, that proactive engagement at Level 4 may potentially extend from canonical babbling (Papoušek, 1996, p. 106) (though see the caveats discussed above), through spontaneous melodic production that involves the repetition of a single phrase (Dowling, 1982, pp. 416 and 417; Welch, 2006, p. 318), to the creation of 'pot pourri' songs, which utilise different fragments culled from familiar material (Moog, 1968/1976, p. 115; Hargreaves, 1986, p. 73; Mang, 2005). One could argue that such variety within levels is inevitable, since it is inherent in the zygonic model of structure. For instance, motifs, the stuff of Level 4, occur across musical styles with varying degrees of internal complexity, and the relationships between them range from simple repetition to complex non-isomorphic transformations (Ockelford, 2004). Hence, it seems inevitable that progression through each *Sounds of Intent* level should take significant periods of time related to individual biography and context, something that may be masked when modelling musical development as a simple mean value by age (as in Figures 2.8–2.10). Clearly, future models of development that seek to relate musical phases to children's ages reliably should offer broad bands of probabilistically based distributions of ability levels that are based on studies of large populations of youngsters growing up in different cultural and social environments.

* * * * *

To summarise our discussion up to this point: both the new *Sounds of Intent in the Early Years* data and the findings from the traditional Western music-developmental literature broadly support the notion that the three-level hierarchical model of musical structure postulated in the context of zygonic theory is mirrored in children's early cognitive development (with the addition

36 *Adam Ockelford and Angela Voyajolu*

of a preceding 'perceptual' level). Across the sample of 58 children in the current research, there was a general sense of moving up through the *Sounds of Intent* levels as participants' ages increased, and no instances were observed of youngsters functioning at Level 5 who did not show music-structural processing abilities at Levels 3 and 4, or of those at Level 4 whose music-cognitive capacity did not encompass Level 3 as well. Indeed, it was frequently a feature of the children's engagement with music that two structural levels or more were implicated at the same time; an example was given of a girl playing with a boy on the autism spectrum, who both produced a regular beat on their drums, while she sang *Twinkle, Twinkle, Little Star* complete (implying simultaneous activity at Levels 3 and 5) and he vocalised a version of the fourth line (entailing concurrent functioning at Levels 3 and 4).

Perhaps, we should not be surprised by this, since zygonic analysis shows that all but the simplest music is structured through imitation on several levels at once (Ockelford, 2005). Take, for instance, the excerpt from the first movement of Beethoven's 5th Symphony shown in Figure 1.7 in Chapter 1, and consider the case of an experienced listener who is familiar with the work and, more broadly, with the Western Classical style. We can assume that the three levels of structure drawn out in the analysis will all have cognitive correlates for the listener concerned, since it is only by acknowledging the connections between individual notes (Level 3) that the design of the ubiquitous four-note motif can be understood (Level 4), and a recognition of the differential transformations of the motif at different pitch heights is necessary to grasp the tonal framework of the movement (Level 5).

How a mature listener's attention is distributed across different structural levels is not known (Ockelford, 1999), nor (therefore) what young children may hear in music that includes forms of structure that they are not yet capable of processing. For example, what would children functioning at *Sounds of Intent* Level 2 make of the Beethoven symphony? Presumably, it would pass them by as an arbitrary flow of perceptual experience in the auditory domain. Whereas we can suppose that a child at Level 3 would be aware of 'surface' repetitions and regularity (between successive or nearly successive events) and, perhaps, a regular underlying beat; and we can imagine that a child at Level 4 would pick up on the moment-to-moment motivic relationships without having a sense of the larger structure and tonality of the piece.

Arguably, it is possible for an adult to glean some idea of what very young children's experience of music may be like by listening to a piece that is culturally and stylistically unfamiliar. For example, on a recent trip to Bangalore, the first author attended a concert of Indian (Carnatic) classical music for the first time. One item in particular made a vivid impression, partly, because the singer's subsequent explanation of how she had structured her improvisation showed her English guest how little he had actually understood of what had gone on. Here is an excerpt adapted from Ockelford's unpublished field notes, written after the event:

A perspective from the Sounds of Intent *model* 37

During the unmetered opening of the piece – the alapana – I could hear that the female vocalist was starting to introduce a raga against a drone of sa and pa (the first and firth notes of the scale). I quickly sensed the sa in the drone 'tugging' at the melody to return to its musical home, a metaphorical demand with which it unfailingly complied following each motivic excursion (in terms of zygonic theory, implicating an imitative relationship of pitch between two events, and thereby implying structural cognition on my part at *Sounds of Intent* Level 3). I was also aware of the evolving links between the singer's improvised melodic motifs as these gradually became more elaborate and used successively more notes from the raga (Level 4). However, I subsequently learnt that I had missed completely the deeper teleological organisation of this introductory section, which, as it unfolded, became more and more about 'teasing' the audience with the conscious avoidance of the raised form of Ni (the leading note), thereby delaying resolution to sa (the tonic) in the upper octave. (That is, I failed to detect a crucial structural feature of the first section of the piece at *Sounds of Intent* Level 5.) In the second part of the piece, the mridangam played a key role, providing a lively rhythmic accompaniment to the singer and other instrumentalists, and featuring a regular beat (which I could discern, Level 3) within a complex metrical framework (which I struggled to follow, Level 5). But I felt my ignorance most acutely at what was evidently a key moment in the musical narrative, when the audience suddenly cheered the female vocalist – a hearty outburst of approval that was followed by laughter and clapping, and the exchange of looks of shared understanding. Yet I had not been aware of a particularly salient event in the music. What had happened? I learnt after the concert that a new raga had been introduced (Level 5), and it was this that had produced the strong, communal emotional reaction in the evidently knowledgeable audience (Level 6). Yet despite my listening having been at *Sounds of Intent* Levels 3 and 4, indicating that I had been oblivious to much of the music's deeper structure and meaning, I nonetheless had been mesmerised by the driving, hypnotic pulse of the mridangam and had relished the chains of vocal and instrumental melodic motifs swirling by in a colourful wash of sound. That is to say, I may not have comprehended much of what the expert Indian listeners had so readily understood about the performance, but I had greatly enjoyed hearing it nonetheless. It seems that the musical message can be so richly structured, that grasping even part of its abstract, multi-levelled auditory narrative can be sufficient to make sense and even to offer an aesthetically satisfying experience.

This is surely a critical point to grasp in seeking to understand how very young children's engagement with much of the plethora of music to which they are exposed in the environment may work. The great majority of it will not be designed with them in mind: it will make use of probabilistically structured frameworks of pitch and time (Level 5), which may well be flexed, along with subtle variations in loudness and timbre, according to cultural and stylistic convention, to create affective narratives in sound (Level 6). But there will also be structures functioning at Levels 4 and 3, and it is to the latter that babies' attention will presumably initially direct itself as their developing brains search for auditory patterns of a type that they have the capacity to process, for, as we have seen, such patterns are underpinned by simple forms of repetition that can be processed in working memory alone. The important thing as far as musical development is concerned is that these basic forms of organisation are not an end in themselves, but constitute the building blocks from which deeper structural understanding is subsequently engineered.

The process through which the musical brain intuitively selects a processing strategy that best fits a given piece of music at a particular phase of cognitive development has resonance with Robert Siegler's 'overlapping waves' theory, which evolved in the context of microgenetic enquiry, in which the same children are studied repeatedly over a short period of time (Siegler, 2006). The theory assumes that 'development is a process of variability, choice and change', and that 'individual children use different strategies on different problems within a single session. ... With age and experience, the relative frequency of each strategy changes', with new strategies being discovered, 'and some older strategies abandoned' (Siegler, *op. cit.*, pp. 477 and 478). The data from the current study suggest that this process may be occurring, as observations of children functioning at Level 2 tend to peter out with age as their attention appears to be directed more to structures at Levels 4 and 5. And we noted an example of how a young girl's focus varied between Levels 3 and 5 within the space of a few moments of musical interaction, as she produced musical structures ranging from a simple beat to a complete song.

The very capacity of music, though, to bear multiple structural interpretations also presents a danger for those researching music in the early years, since it is difficult (if not impossible) to avoid hearing things through adult ears and so potentially over-intellectualise children's engagement. Watching a group of young children hearing a piece is rather like seeing a number of light bulbs of different wattages in the same electrical circuit. The bulbs may all be illuminated, just as the children all appear to be listening, but what each bulb draws from the energy source, and what each child takes from the music, may vary tremendously according to individual disposition. The risk for the musically experienced observer is to focus too much on the input (the piece of music, to which they will inevitably have a personal reaction) rather than the outputs: the children's responses, which may be difficult to ascertain. It may be a question of seeking corroboration of a given level of understanding by observing children in different musical contexts to know just what it is that they are attending to. For instance, in an action song, children may be seen to anticipate the chorus (Level 5?), but is their expectation built on an awareness of the musical structure or of the associated sequence of words and movements? One way to find out would be to see whether they

A perspective from the Sounds of Intent *model*   39

can grasp comparable forms of organisation in other, purely musical contexts. Or a child playing a xylophone made up only of a diatonic major scale (equivalent to an octave of the 'white notes' on a keyboard – C, D, E, F, G, A, B, C) may seem to improvise a tonal melody (Level 5). But this impression could merely be a result of the constraints of the pitch universe that is available, and a tendency of the child to conclude what she is doing at one end of the instrument of the other (either of which may be heard to function as a tonic) for physical reasons (*cf.* Ockelford, 2012a, pp. 37–85). To know for sure, the child would need to be given other improvisational opportunities with different arrangements of notes. Similarly, very young children may be observed to produce regular beats on instruments (Level 3?), but these may stem not from the imitation of inter-onset intervals (the times between the beginnings of notes) but from the natural speeds of movement of the children's arms going up and down. Again, the key to knowing is to change the context – to provide a pulse for them to emulate, for example.

It goes without saying, of course, just because children may have the capacity to extract surface patterns from deep and complex auditory textures, that sophisticated pieces of music – mature artistic products of the culture in which they were generated and which they help to define – should be all that they are exposed to. As Colwyn Trevarthen and Stephen Malloch have so persuasively shown, parents and other caregivers intuitively engage in non-verbal, proto-musical dialogues with their children, using their voices to match the simple patterns in sound that babies make (at Level 3 of the *Sounds of Intent* framework) and enticing them to make more – in effect providing an auditory sandpit in which the youngsters can safely play and practise their early musical skills (Malloch and Trevarthen, 2008). And it is a central longer-term aim of the *Sounds of Intent in the Early Years* project to set out musical activities that correspond to children's assessed phases of music-cognitive development to enable adults to scaffold their progress to the greatest effect. But, in the view of the authors, such interactions should merely constitute the key features in an extensive, rich and alluring musical environment.

* * * * *

We now move on to consider how the cognitive correlates of the three structural *Sounds of Intent* levels may interact as they develop over time in an individual, and what the implications of this are for zygonic theory. What does the evidence tell us directly, what can we infer and what can we postulate?

First, we have already observed that just as all types of musical structure can vary in complexity so, it appears, the acquisition of knowledge and skills pertaining to each level is incremental rather than binary, and occurs over a period of months (if not years in some cases). Hence, one possibility is that the different phases of music-structural cognition exist on a continuum, whereby children become wholly competent at one level before development starts at the next. This scenario is illustrated in Figure 2.9.

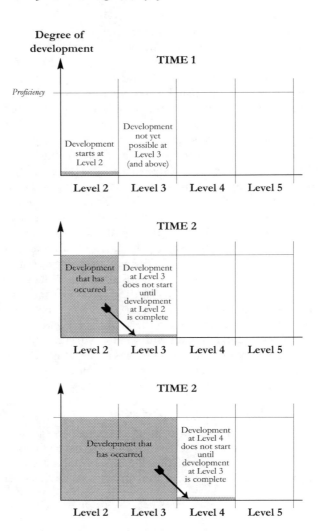

Figure 2.9 Illustration of the scenario in which development at a given level does not start until development at the previous level reaches a state of proficiency.

Another way of conceptualising this situation is to make the assumption that the logistic growth function, which was adapted above for use with our set of research participants as a whole, offers a reasonable approximation to the rate at which individual development in a given area of cognition occurs (*cf.* van Geert, 1991). For now, in order to make theoretical headway, we will represent the entire, multidimensional stream of musical development as a single sigmoidal curve per level, recognising that this is an oversimplification – a matter to which we will return in due course. The resulting developmental trajectory is continuous, with spells of growth alternating with periods of stasis

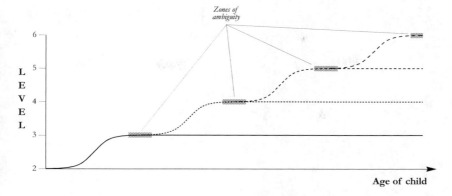

Figure 2.10 A sequential model of music-structural cognitive development.

(see Figure 2.10). Observe that the acquisition of abilities is assumed to be cumulative, whereby capabilities at one level are maintained as others at higher levels develop. The top line depicts the most advanced music-structural cognitive skills that are deemed to be in operation at any given point.

Support for this model is to be found in examples of children's musical engagement that appear to move seamlessly from one level to the next, where the point at which activity testifies to competence at Level *l* merges into the beginnings of achievement at Level *l*+1. Here, a portion of a child's music making will fall within what may be termed a 'zone of ambiguity'. This is depicted in Figures 2.11 and 2.13.

Three examples of this shift occurring between different levels are provided in Figures 2.12–2.14. In the first, a baby aged around six months is lying contentedly, face-to-face with his older sister (aged eight). The baby is vocalising, largely short descents in pitch using different vowels of varying lengths, with periods of silence between, apparently enjoying the experience of exploring what his voice can do (an activity at *Sounds of Intent* Level 2). The girl starts to copy her brother (see Figure 2.12), and he soon becomes more animated, vocalising more loudly, anticipating one of his sister's responses, and then appearing

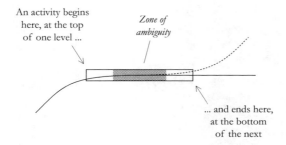

Figure 2.11 Representation of activity that shifts between one level and the next.

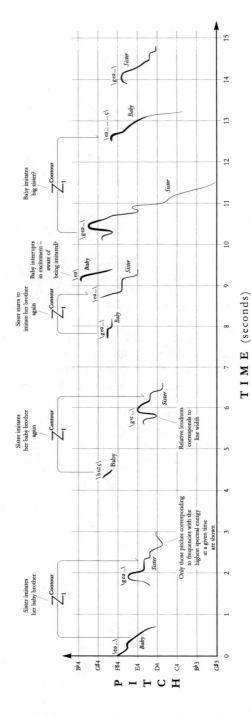

Figure 2.12 Interaction between a baby and his older sister, showing a possible transition from Level 2 to Level 3.

A perspective from the Sounds of Intent *model* 43

to imitate her, delighting in the give and take of this new game (Level 3). Just where the shift from Level 2 to Level 3 occurs, though – the point at which the baby becomes aware that he is being imitated – one cannot be sure.

Second, we return once more to the boy on the autism spectrum making music with a friend, banging a drum and singing a fragment of *Twinkle, Twinkle, Little Star*. We have already noted that he was engaging in activity at both Level 3 (the regular beat) and Level 4 (the motif from *Twinkle*). However, there was also a *transition* between the two levels within the drum beat, in that the continuous pulse (Level 3) broke off at the end of his vocal phrase, implying a simple form of grouping (Level 4). Ambiguity arises since the point at which he starts (intuitively) to consider the beat as a group is not clear, and is in any case only evident to observers in retrospect (see Figure 2.13).

The third example of a transition between levels is provided by a three-year-old girl, playing outside on her own, who is singing fragments of songs that she has learnt with the other children in a group. She starts with the first phrase of *Roly Poly* (which goes 'Roly, poly, roly, poly, up, up, up'), half-singing, half-speaking it a number of times, producing clusters of vocal sounds that only approximately correspond to the pitch intervals of the original, and without a particular sense of pulse (indicative of engagement at Level 4). After several repetitions, the girl hesitates, and the last 'up' becomes the first word of the second half of line one of *The Wheels on the Bus* (with the words 'up and down' replacing 'round and round' – Level 4). This motif is also repeated (Level 4), before a clear rendition of the song appears – recognisably conforming to the major scale and binary metre of the standard version (Level 5). Again, it is difficult to determine where engagement at Level 4 ends and Level 5 begins, and there is a 'zone of ambiguity' between the two (Figure 2.14).

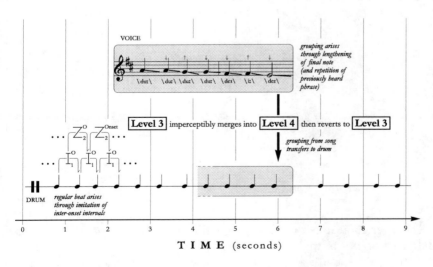

Figure 2.13 Example of seamless transition from Level 3 to Level 4.

44 *Adam Ockelford and Angela Voyajolu*

Figure 2.14 Transition from Level 4 to Level 5, with a 'zone of ambiguity' between the two.

However, there are other examples within the *Sounds of Intent Early Years* data that do not fit this model so well. Consider, for instance, the scenario in which an 18-month-old boy and two friends, supported by an early years practitioner, are playing with some pieces of Lego, exploring the range of

A perspective from the Sounds of Intent model

sounds that can be made by banging them together on the table. The practitioner shows the boy how to produce a rasping noise by rubbing a brick on a baseboard, first by modelling the action for him, and then helping him to do it, hand over hand at first, before he has a go on his own. Despite finding the level of coordination required to rub the pieces together difficult to achieve, the boy manages to make some gentle scraping sounds. Picking up two more pieces of Lego, the practitioner sets up a regular beat, scraping her block to and fro on a baseboard. The boy tries to emulate her, with limited success. So here we have an example of a Level 2 activity (exploring new ways of making sounds), which is in the early stages of development, juxtaposed with a form of engagement at Level 3 (imitating a regular beat), in which, again, full competence is not yet attained. That is to say, musical behaviour at Level 3 occurs before proficiency at Level 2 is reached.

Similar forms of transition (from 'mid'-Level *l* to 'lower'-Level *l*+1) were observed at later phases in children's musical development too. Take, for example, the following account of a small group of boys and girls aged around 18 months, who are seen playing with short lengths of cardboard tube that is wide enough for them to use as pretend loud hailers. The children make siren sounds, made up of motifs largely resembling a descending minor third, from F to D, although there is marked pitch variation in the second note. That is, we find musical activity at Level 4 getting underway (the children attempting to copy groups of notes) before development at Level 3 is complete (since they are still learning to imitate intervals) – see Figure 2.15.

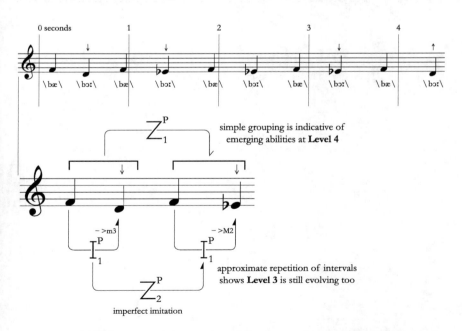

Figure 2.15 Abilities at Level 4 emerging while those at Level 3 are still evolving.

46 *Adam Ockelford and Angela Voyajolu*

An extension of this phenomenon can be seen in a further example of a girl aged 24 months, who is playing outside on her own with some wooden blocks. As she builds a tower, she sings to herself, initially a repeated two-note descending motif (approximating to a minor third between F and D). The motif then becomes part of a longer sequence of notes that form a short, two-phrase song, which is underpinned by a pitch framework resembling that of the major scale. So here we have musical engagement at Level 5 existing alongside activity at a still-developing Level 4 (and, indeed, Level 3); see Figure 2.16.

These examples indicate, contrary to the position shown in Figures 2.9 and 2.10, that different *Sounds of Intent* levels can overlap in a child's evolving musicality, whereby a more advanced phase of development can get underway before a lower level is complete (a phenomenon that has been found in differing aspects of language development – see Robinson and Mervis, 1998). Figure 2.17 models this principle in a simple way, whereby it is

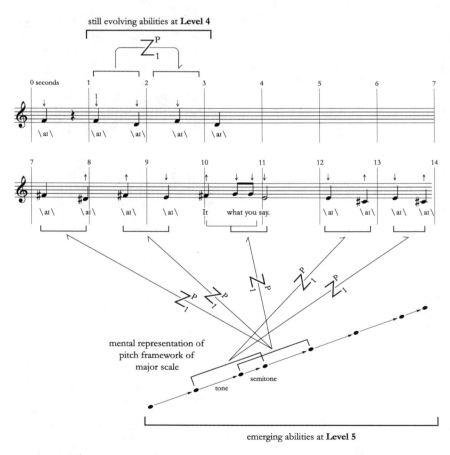

Figure 2.16 Abilities at Level 5 emerging while those at Level 4 are still evolving.

A perspective from the Sounds of Intent model   47

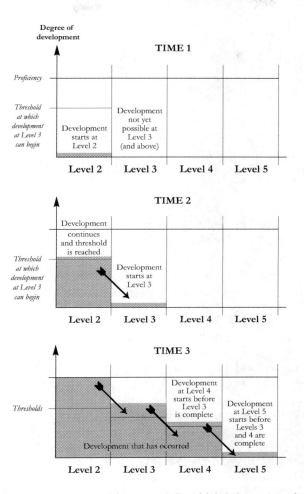

Figure 2.17 Model of music-cognitive growth in which it is proposed that *Sounds of Intent* levels may overlap in development.

assumed that a single threshold of less than complete competence at a given level is sufficient to enable a child to move on to the next. Three different points in a child's music development are shown. In the first, an awareness of cause and effect in the domain of sound is just emerging (Level 2) – as yet insufficient for the child to create patterns through imitation. In the second, later, scenario, the threshold at Level 2 has been reached at which the growing capacity to make sounds is sufficiently advanced to enable deliberate pattern-making to occur, and development at Level 3 begins. The third example shows cognitive abilities at Level 2 to be almost complete and moderately advanced at Level 3, with evidence of emergent processing abilities at Level 4 and incipient music-structural comprehension at Level 5.

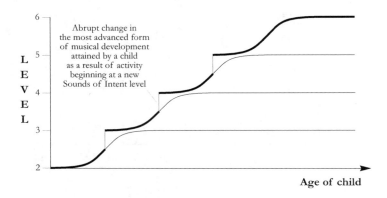

Figure 2.18 The effect of overlapping *Sounds of Intent* levels on the developmental trajectory of musical abilities.

Again, this process can be conceptualised using the logistic function to build a hypothetical model of music-cognitive development. Here, we will assume a 50% overlap per level. This produces the effect of discontinuities in a child's music-developmental trajectory that delineates his or her most advanced level of accomplishment at any given point (see Figure 2.18).

But how does this model account for the uninterrupted transition from one level to the next within a single musical activity modelled in Figure 2.11 and illustrated by the examples shown in Figures 2.12–2.14? The answer lies in the data set out in Figure 2.6 showing that children do not function only at their most advanced level of musical development, and the observation that, within each phase identified in the *Sounds of Intent* framework, different degrees of engagement are possible. So a child who is developmentally at 'mid'-Level 3 may nonetheless exhibit musical behaviours that are less advanced, and activities that manifest continuity between Levels 2 and 3 are conceivable. For example, it could be that the baby shown interacting with his sister in Figure 2.12 (by being aware of her copying his vocalisations) was himself capable of imitation (a more advanced stage at Level 3, shown in Figure 2.2b) – see Figure 2.19.

To conclude this discussion of how the cognitive correlates of the three structural *Sounds of Intent* levels may interact in a child's development, we rehearse some of the limitations of the modelling that has been undertaken. First, rather than the single threshold per level suggested in Figure 2.17, it seems that *multiple* thresholds must exist in relation to the distinct dimensions of ability that pertain to each phase of development. For example, in the proactive domain, it is evident that a child needs to be able to control when sounds are made (Level 2) in order to produce a regular beat (Level 3). However, to make a pattern in sound that varies regularly over time (also a Level 3 attribute) demands a further ability at Level 2: the capacity to produce a range of sounds in at least one auditory dimension (pitch, timbre or loudness). Then,

A perspective from the Sounds of Intent *model* 49

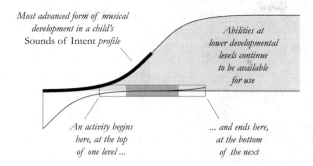

Figure 2.19 Activities that involve a continuity of engagement between levels are conceivable within the 'overlapping' model shown in Figure 2.17.

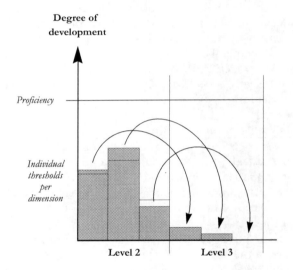

Figure 2.20 The existence of different dimensions of ability within *Sounds of Intent* levels implies the presence of multiple thresholds at which different forms of higher-level development can be triggered.

to imitate someone else's vocalisation (an interactive skill at Level 3) requires a child to be able to make a mental representation of a sound that is perceived from an external source, and to exercise the necessary physical coordination to replicate it. This principle is modelled in Figure 2.20. Clearly, more extensive research is required to ascertain where the thresholds that pertain to each *Sounds of Intent* level occur in all the dimensions of musical ability.

Second, it may well be the case that development at one level interferes with that at another, due to competition among finite cognitive resources. In the related context of language, Robinson and Mervis (1998, p. 371) model

50   Adam Ockelford and Angela Voyajolu

how lexical growth slows at the point where the acquisition of plural forms of words takes off, and one can envisage that a similar thing may occur in the domain of music. For example, it may be that when pattern detection starts at Level 3, the evolving capacity of the auditory system to make fine discriminations between sounds at Level 2 (see, for example, Buss, Hall and Grose, 2012) is inhibited. Indeed, it is well established in both language and music (Kuhl, 2004, pp. 832–833 and Siegel and Siegel, 1977) that listeners tend to categorise aspects of sounds (such as phonemes or melodic intervals) according to culturally determined frequencies of exposure, rather than hear them on continua. Clearly, further research is required to ascertain the impact of such phenomena on the development of music-structural cognition as set out in the *Sounds of Intent* model.

Third, it is self-evident that the logistic function (or any other mathematical formula) can only ever provide a notional representation of the music-cognitive developmental trajectory that relates to given child in the early years, and, more generally, to populations of such children. It seems reasonable to assume that intellectual growth of any type must ultimately proceed in finite increments (rather than the continuous change that characterises the logistic model; *cf.* Eckstein, 2000), though these tiny differences are in any case likely to be eclipsed by the impact of the different contexts in which the observations of a child engaging with music inevitably occur. Circumstances may vary for a host of reasons, including internal factors, such as a child's state of mind, health and motivations of the moment, and external forces, such as the nature of the environment in which the child is operating, the (musical) resources that are available, the existence of potential distractions and the presence of other children or adults. Hence, reliable assessments of musical development in the early years are likely to make use of the information available from a number of observations made in differing situations.

Although no such data currently exist in relation to the current project, the previous use of the *Sounds of Intent* framework with young people with learning difficulties, such as Evangeline Cheng's three longitudinal case studies (Cheng, 2010), has indicated a considerable degree of day-to-day (and even moment-to-moment) variability, and, as we shall see, there is no reason to suppose why a broadly similar situation should not apply in the case of 'neurotypical' children in the early years (Wu, 2017). For example, Cheng monitored 'J' in 16 of his class music sessions over a period of around six months. When the research began, J was 11 years old, and was reported to have severe learning difficulties, with expressive language limited to a few single words, visual impairment and cerebral palsy, which meant he had restricted movement in his arms and legs. He was known to be prone to epileptic seizures, which led to marked fluctuations in his sense of well-being. During the research period, Cheng recorded 543 separate observations across the three *Sounds of Intent* domains, and overall means were calculated for each of the 16 sessions. The results are shown in Figure 2.21.

A perspective from the Sounds of Intent *model* 51

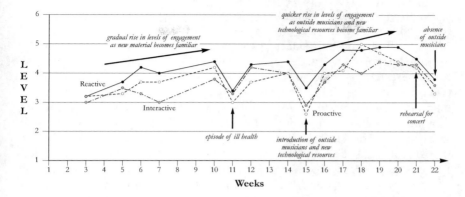

Figure 2.21 The influence of internal and external factors on J's recorded levels of musical engagement.

Although the general trend is upwards, there is a wide range of values, equivalent to 1.7 *Sounds of Intent* levels. Cheng's field notes offer some insights as to why the variation may have occurred.

The first observations were made near the beginning of term, when new material was being introduced. J's proactive and interactive contributions appeared in the form of vocalisations, through using a switch, which triggered pre-recorded sounds, and by playing small percussion instruments such as the cowbell, a task in which he required physical assistance. Reactively, his responses ranged from passivity and thumb-sucking, which staff interpreted as meaning a lack of interest or dislike, to smiling, laughing and screaming, which were taken to be signs of pleasure or excitement. Predictably, perhaps, as the material that had been presented at the beginning of term became familiar over the coming weeks, the nature and degree of J's engagement increased rapidly, from around Level 3 to Level 4 (a much greater rate of change than would usually be expected in a child with severe learning difficulties; *cf.* Ockelford, *et al.*, 2011). However, in the sixth week that observations were made (Week 11), this fell back sharply, and Cheng's notes indicate that J's health was poor: he was sleepy and found it difficult to concentrate. Weeks 7 and 8 saw a return to a higher level of engagement, before a further sudden decline in Week 9. According to Cheng, in this session a project involves three outside musicians commenced, who introduced new musical materials and music technology resources, which evidently had a deleterious effect on J's musical engagement, falling to its lowest recorded point. However, in the sessions that followed, the ongoing presence of the musicians appeared to have a positive effect, with J's mean *Sounds of Intent* level rising consistently to 4.7. Session 15 (Week 21) was a rehearsal for an end-of-project concert, which saw J's level of engagement fall back somewhat. However, it is most telling that in the final session in which observations were made – at which the visiting musicians were not present – a further significant decline was recorded.

Hence, both internal factors (J's well-being) and external considerations (repeated exposure to particular materials, resources and personnel) appear to have exerted a significant effect on his levels of musical engagement. These two types of influence can be modelled by applying the variables k_i (denoting internal agencies) and k_e (representing external forces) to the basic logistic function in the manner shown below (Equation 2.6), in which the notional rate of musical development is modified for specified lengths of time. Observe that L represents the resultant *Sounds of Intent* level, a is the child's age, and t_1 and t_2 are the points in time between which either factor or both are in play. The constants 2 and 4 arise since 2 is the first level at which musical engagement can be discerned and 4 is the number of potential levels of progress:

$$L = 2 + \frac{4}{1 + e^{-(a \cdot k_i \cdot k_e)}} \quad \text{where} \quad t_1 < a < t_2.$$

The theoretical impact of favourable and adverse intra-personal and environmental factors over different periods of time is illustrated in Figure 2.22.

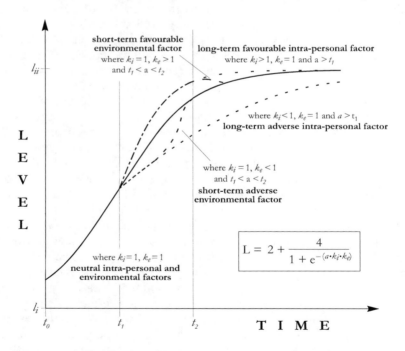

Figure 2.22 Modelling the impact of adverse and favourable factors on the development of music-structural cognition through the addition of variables to the standard logistic function.

A perspective from the Sounds of Intent *model*   53

For children in the early years, the importance of an environment conducive to general learning and development, and, conversely, the dangers of deprivation to emerging brain architecture are well known (Fox, Levitt and Nelson, 2010). There has been some systematic research in this area specific to music, showing the potential significance of rich experiences to the nature and level of children's evolving abilities (Hannon and Trainor, 2007; Tafuri, 2008), though much remains to be done. Two examples from the current study are worth pointing up: one showing the importance of short-term scaffolding for musical achievement and the other indicative of the possible impact of longer-term support.

The first (short-term) case is of a three-year-old girl whose singing of Line 1 of *Roly Poly* is transcribed in Figure 2.14. Here, she is playing outside on her own, and repeating fragments of songs (indicating proactivity at Level 4). However, on another occasion, she is observed joining in the entire song with the other children in an adult-led group (interactivity at Level 5). That is to say, she seems able to perform at a higher level when provided with the necessary musical scaffolding (to extend the metaphor coined by Wood, Bruner and Ross, 1976, p. 90): a framework of relative pitch and time, and prompts as to the transitions between groups of notes. In Vygotskian terms, the girl's zone of proximal development ('ZPD') – the distance between the level of musical production that she is capable of achieving independently and that which she can attain with adult guidance or in collaboration with more advanced peers (Vygotsky, 1978, p. 86) – lies between *Sounds of Intent* domains P.4 and I.5. What is the nature of this musical ZPD? For Vygotsky, it is not that the girl's participation in a singing activity with an adult and older children has changed the rate at which her musical development occurs (as was the case with 'J' above), but rather that the repeated experience has enabled her skills to flourish earlier than would otherwise have been the case. As Vygotsky puts it (*op. cit.*, p. 87): 'The zone of proximal development defines those functions that have not yet matured but are in the process of maturation, functions that will mature tomorrow but are currently in an embryonic state'. This state of affairs can be modelled in a simple way in the interactive domain by incorporating a 'scaffolding' variable – 'k_s' – in the logistic function as follows, effectively bringing forward the age at which given abilities manifest themselves:

$$L_{interactive} = 2 + \frac{4}{1 + k_s \cdot e^{-a}}.$$

Hence, the extent of the ZPD is given by the difference between a child's interactive level and proactive level of musical development. That is:

$$\text{Extent of ZPD} = L_{interactive} - L_{proactive}$$

$$= \left(2 + \frac{4}{1 + k_s \cdot e^{-a}}\right) - \left(2 + \frac{4}{1 + e^{-a}}\right) = \frac{(1 - k_s) \cdot 4e^a}{(k_s + e^a)(1 + e^a)}.$$

54 Adam Ockelford and Angela Voyajolu

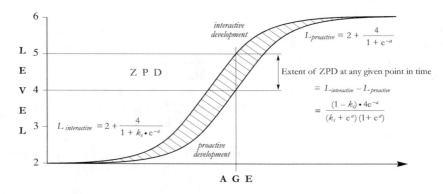

Figure 2.23 Modelling the zone of proximal development in music using the logistic function.

This is represented graphically in Figure 2.23.

If we assume that ZPDs function in a comparable way at all *Sounds of Intent* levels, and that, as in language, musical reactivity precedes proactivity and interactivity, then we can postulate a trajectory of the development of music-structural cognition illustrated schematically in Figure 2.24. Here, elements of knowledge and understanding are first acquired and internalised in the reactive domain, through listening experiences, before being externalised initially through interactive engagement, where a child's first efforts at production are stimulated and supported through others, and subsequently realised proactively, by a child with the ability and confidence to generate

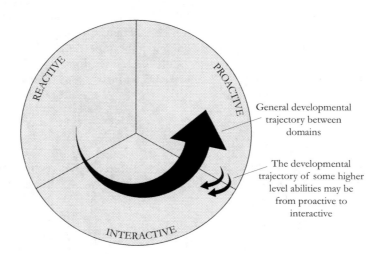

Figure 2.24 The postulated trajectory of musical development across domains.

or replicate material alone. However, data from the *Sounds of Intent* project with young people with learning difficulties suggest that there may be some aspects of performance at higher levels, which may involve the conscious practice of skills, where shifts are more likely to occur in the opposite direction, from proactive to interactive. For example, improvising in ensembles by maintaining an independent part (I.5.B) is an advanced ability that builds on the capacity to improvise on familiar pieces of music in simple ways – something that may well be tackled first in isolation (P.5.B).

The second (long-term) case of a child's environment appearing to have an impact on musical development is provided by boy of 21 months, who was observed on his own in the baby room of the nursery, playing with 'Stickle Bricks'. He spontaneously started singing *Twinkle, Twinkle, Little Star*. Although many of the words produced were just approximations in sound (the effect being rather like a continuous stream of changing timbres that only partly resembled the customary pattern of vowels and consonants), the melody was sung largely in tune and in time. It was known that at home the boy's life was particularly rich with musical experiences, having a mother who was passionate about making music with her children. Here, it seems, the scaffolding provided by sustained musical interactivity with a parent was so effective that it catalysed inner musical growth to such an extent that it became self-supporting, and it appears that the course of the boy's musical development in all domains was permanently advanced compared with many other children of his age (see Figures 2.5 and 2.22). This implies that Equation 2.7 can be generalised to all three *Sounds of Intent* domains (Figure 2.25):

$$L = 2 + \frac{4}{1 + k_s \cdot e^{-a}}.$$

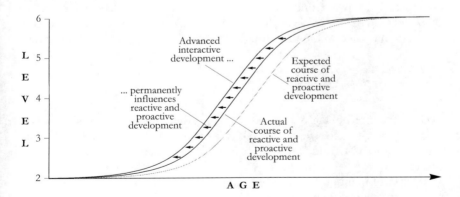

Figure 2.25 The postulated impact of sustained musical interactivity on development in the reactive and proactive domains.

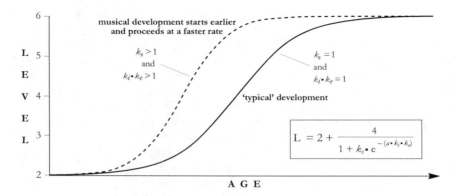

Figure 2.26 The impact on musical development of scaffolding and positive other environmental and internal factors.

Scaffolding may work together with other positive external and internal factors to produce a music-developmental trajectory that is not only advanced from the outset, but whose rate of change is also elevated. In terms of the logistic function, this can be modelled as follows:

$$L = 2 + \frac{4}{1 + k_s \cdot e^{-(a \cdot k_i \cdot k_e)}}.$$

This is illustrated graphically in Figure 2.26.

The analysis and models set out above take no account of what might be termed an individual child's *potential* to develop music-structural cognition (on the assumption that latent abilities are subject to individual differences), and, with that, a broader appreciation and understanding of music and the skills to perform pieces and create new ones. Hence, it would seem appropriate to add a further variable to the equation – 'k_p' – such that both the onset of an area of musical development and the rate at which it grows may be affected:

$$L = 2 + \frac{4}{1 + k_p \cdot k_s \cdot e^{-(a \cdot k_i \cdot k_e)}}.$$

Just how the internal factors k_p and k_i (that is, the predisposition of the infant or foetal brain to acquire musical abilities and skills, and the individual inclinations and motivations that drive it to do so) relate and how these in turn interact with the external agencies k_e and k_s (positive or negative influences in the environment and scaffolding) have long been a matter of debate (see, for example, Howe, Davidson and Sloboda, 1998; Winner, 2000; Gaser and Schlaug, 2003; Norton *et al.*, 2005). In this respect, it is illuminating to consider research with certain groups of outliers, such as children who are blind from birth, whose atypically developing neurological architecture produces what Ockelford (2013) terms an 'exceptional early cognitive environment' ('EECE'). One of the potential music-developmental consequences of EECEs is emergence from around 24 months of universal absolute pitch ('AP'), whose prevalence is estimated to be between 38% and 65% among those who are congenitally blind (Ockelford, 1988; Welch, 1988; Hamilton, Pascual-Leone and Schlaug, 2004; Ockelford and Matawa, 2009), compared with around 1 in 10,000 of 'neurotypical' Westerners (Takeuchi and Hulse, 1993). Since children may be born blind for a host of different genetic reasons or, very often, none, these data suggest that a child's environment must play a crucial role in the development of exceptional musicality and so (it seems reasonable to assume) in the evolution of musical abilities more generally. However, the fact that not *all* congenitally blind children develop AP indicates that there may be a genetic component too that is not shared by everyone.

Conversely, it may be the case that some children's learning difficulties, as the original *Sounds of Intent* study showed (Ockelford and Welch, 2012), restrict achievement beyond a certain level. For example, impaired working memory in the auditory domain may make the processing of clusters of sounds that is characteristic of *Sounds of Intent* Level 4 impossible. Or it may be that a child has the capacity to remember and reproduce short series of notes – say, three or four – but a child cannot retain and cognitively manipulate sequences of events that are longer than this. Hence, progress within levels may effectively be capped through internal constraints. Such ceilings of musical attainment may be modelled logistically as shown in Equation 2.12, where 'k_r' is a variable of cognitive restriction (see Figure 2.27). Observe that caps on development brought about through learning difficulties are likely

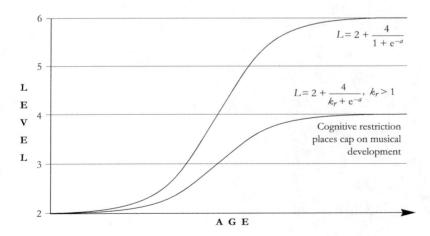

Figure 2.27 Model of cognitive restriction placing an upper limit on musical development.

to go hand in hand with musical progress that is relatively delayed and proceeds at a slower pace than would otherwise be the case:

$$L = 2 + \frac{4}{k_r + e^{-a}}, \quad k_r > 1.$$

It is also possible, with some neurodegenerative conditions, such as the neuronal ceroid lipofuscinoses (NCLs), in which children's cognitive abilities are gradually lost (see, for example, Mole, Williams and Goebel, 2011), that musical development may effectively go into reverse. However, to date no research has been undertaken to establish whether, and if so in what way, the capacity of a child with chronic mental deterioration to engage with music degrades, nor how this may relate to (or contrast with) general patterns of cognitive atrophy, though work with adults with dementia (for instance, Dassa and Amir, 2014) suggests that elements of musical ability such as singing may persist while spoken language declines. If the diminishment of a child's powers of musical engagement were to occur as a reversal of his or her music-developmental trajectory, then this could be modelled logistically by introducing the variable 'k_d' as a measure of music-cognitive decline, as shown in Equation 2.13 and Figure 2.28:

$$L = 2 + \frac{4}{1 + k_d \cdot e^{-a}}, \quad \text{where} \quad k_d < \frac{1}{e}.$$

However, the limited evidence that is available suggests that things are probably far less straightforward than this. For example, long-term memories of complete and potentially complex songs may endure in children with NCL (*Sounds of Intent* Level 5) (Bills, *et al.*, 1998; von Tetzchner, Fosse and

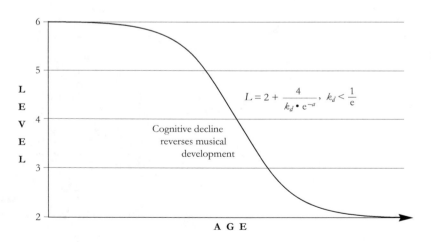

Figure 2.28 Model of cognitive decline in which musical development is simply reversed.

A perspective from the Sounds of Intent *model* 59

Elmerskog, 2013) while auditory attention and working memory (required to process short and relatively simple chunks of music, as at Level 4) wane (Lou and Kristensen, 1973; Adams *et al.*, 2007). Hence, children may display the ostensibly incongruous effects of possessing a residue of advanced skills and knowledge that were built up in the past (and that rely on long-term memory), while more basic abilities (that rely on processing new material in the moment) no longer exist. Lou and Kristensen (1973, p. 318) found this to be the case in relation to language and general cognitive capacity in their study of 28 children with NCL (then classed as a form of 'juvenile amaurotic idiocy'). In an 'information' test, they discovered that children 'often manage to answer relatively difficult questions and cannot reply to simple ones ... [probably] due to their short memory span for immediate detail'. The children continued to have extensive vocabularies, learnt at earlier age, but did not seem to be able to add to them. Although there is currently no comparable research with a cohort of children with NCL in relation to music cognition, one can speculate, in terms of the *Sounds of Intent* model, that higher-level music-cognitive functions may persist while the lower-level building blocks of musical processing upon which they were originally erected disappear. This 'bottom-up' disintegration may be represented visually as follows (see Figure 2.29).

However, a case study that bears directly on this issue suggests that patterns of decline such as that illustrated in Figure 2.29 may not be inevitable. Ockelford (2012a, pp. 75–84) gives an account of a young person, Abigail, in the final stages of Juvenile Tay-Sachs disease, a condition similar to NCL

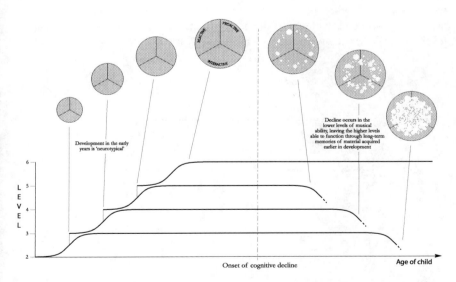

Figure 2.29 Model of cognitive decline in which musical development is lost from the lower levels.

60 *Adam Ockelford and Angela Voyajolu*

(see Haltia, *et al.*, 2011, p. 4). Although unable to speak and with virtually no capacity for facial expression, it seemed that Abigail enjoyed listening to songs that she had learnt earlier in her life, particularly *Raindrops Keep Falling on My Head* by Burt Bacharach (*Sounds of Intent*, Level 5). Given her profound intellectual and motor impairments, though, it was very difficult to know the extent to which she was able to engage with new material. However, through the use of interactive light beam technology, created by Optimusic®, which, through MIDI, can convert even the tiniest movement into any sound, Abigail showed that actually she was able to join in an improvised piece with her class, largely in time with the beat (Level 3) and with a degree of melodic imitation (Level 4). One explanation is that there may be a discrete 'music module' in working memory, which could conceivably be spared in some cases of neurodegeneration in which elements of executive function pertaining to other domains were compromised (Ockelford, 2007).

Finally, and briefly, we consider the potential effect of children's gender on the development of their music-structural processing abilities. As noted above, there were 33 girls and 25 boys in the *Sounds of Intent in the Early Years* sample. Girls' mean age was 25 months (*SD* = 13.8), and boys' was 30 months (*SD* = 13.5). The age ranges were virtually identical, from 0 to 4 years, with just one girl (and no boys) in the lowest age band (0–3 months). The mean *Sounds of Intent* levels are shown in Table 2.5. Taken as a whole, these were judged to be the same for each group: girls, *M* = 3.46, *SD* = 0.97; boys, *M* = 3.45, *SD* = 0.95; in both cases, with a range from Levels 2 to 5. However, the girls were on average five months younger, and using the same iterative process of regression to identify the best-fitting logistic curve as before (see Figure 2.7), we can see that, following the first year of life, their music-developmental trajectory was somewhat ahead of the boys – by just under half a *Sounds of Intent* level by the time they were four years old; see Figure 2.30.

Table 2.5 Mean levels of music-cognitive development in the *Sounds of Intent in the Early Years* sample by age and gender

Age band (±3 months)	Means	
	Girls	Boys
0	2	–
6	2	2
12	2.17	3
18	3.5	3
24	4	3.5
30	4.25	3.25
36	4	4
42	3.9	4.1
48	4	3.5
Means	3.46	3.45

A perspective from the Sounds of Intent *model* 61

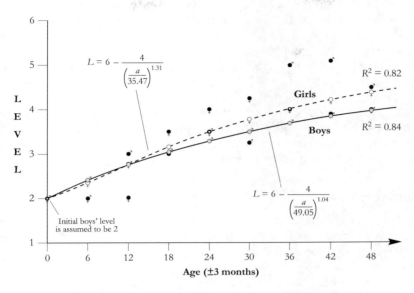

Figure 2.30 The different rates of music-cognitive development in girls and boys in the *Sounds of Intent in the Early Years* sample.

Clearly, a number of factors may potentially have played a part in this outcome. For instance, it may be that musical development in girls and boys typically proceeds at the same rate, and that the relatively small sample was unrepresentative of the wider population due to its demographic particularities. Observer bias (albeit non-conscious) may have had an impact on the results too. However, it may also be the case that the course of music-cognitive development is indeed more rapid in girls and boys, on account of either (unwitting) socio-cultural partiality in the way that they are treated by the adults around them (implying a gender-based differential in values of k_e and k_s) or biological differences (entailing a sex-induced imbalance between values of k_i and k_p), a view that is increasing supported by psychological and neuroscientific research. For example, Koelsch *et al.* (2003) measured the event-related electric brain potentials elicited in children aged five and nine while they listened to tonal chord sequences that occasionally contained stylistically improbable harmonies. These anomalies induced negative brain responses that were bilateral in girls but left-predominant in boys (a lateralisation that apparently changes with the transition to adulthood; see Koelsch, *et al.*, 2003). Welch *et al.* (2012) in a study of around 10,000 children in the UK found that girls tend to be me accomplished than boys at singing at an earlier age. Thorpe, Ockelford and Aksentijevic (2012) found that men's and women's predicted continuations of an unfamiliar melody at any given point differed significantly, suggesting

62 Adam Ockelford and Angela Voyajolu

that alternative strategies for processing musical structure may be adopted by males and females. In terms of our affective response to music, Hunter, Schellenberg and Stalinski (2011) found that the accuracy with which children identified the emotions conveyed by unfamiliar pieces of music was higher for girls than boys aged five, although both sexes reached adult-like levels by the age of 11. In any event, perhaps we should not be surprised if, for whatever reason, the paths of musical development in girls and boys do subtly differ; both the general developmental statistics pertaining to the children's centre from which the participants were drawn and national early years data in England (Department for Education, 2018) show girls leading boys in all of the early learning goals.

Conclusion

This chapter investigated for the first time whether musical structures at the level of events, groups and frameworks that are identified in zygonic theory have developmental correlates. Data were obtained through observation of a sample of 58 children attending a culturally and socially diverse early years centre in south-west London, as part of the *Sounds of Intent in the Early Years* project. Exhaustive analysis of the children's engagement with music, reactively, proactively and interactively, with peers, adults and – very often – on their own, broadly supports the notion that the three levels of music-structural understanding are indeed linked to identifiable phases in young children's cognitive development. However, it seems that the emergence of music-structural processing abilities, while sequential (events, groups and then frameworks), is complex (with fuzzy, overlapping boundaries between one level of engagement and the next) and is critically dependent on environmental factors, in particular the willingness of adults to engage consistently with children in musical activities.

Much work remains to be done. For example, in psychological terms, the validity of the music-developmental model that is sketched out needs to be tested with greater numbers of children in a wide range of different contexts – and this task is underway with Angela Voyajolu's doctoral studies at the Applied Music Research Centre, University of Roehampton. Neuroscientifically, it will be key to ascertain whether areas of the brain can be isolated that correspond to the three different levels of structural hearing, and, if so, how these emerge in development. Educationally, the findings suggest that while intuitively driven adult-directed musical activities seem to bring benefits to some children, it may well be the case that targeted forms of interactive engagement may promote development more efficaciously – particularly in those children whose capacity to process and make music appears to be relatively delayed (whether for internal or external reasons). Above all, the findings of the *Sounds of Intent* and *Sounds of Intent in the Early Years* projects, which together indicate an apparent universality of musical potential, irrespective of genetic factors (or neurological trauma), should be taken on board by all those working with or caring for children in early years, since this is the period in which the majority of the music-cognitive strata that will serve us for the rest of our lives are laid down.

Notes

1 Other children's names mentioned in the text are pseudonyms to ensure their anonymity.
2 The core research team had three members: Adam Ockelford, Angela Voyajolu (University of Roehampton) and Lavina Boothe (Eastwood Nursery School: Centre for Children and Families, Roehampton, London, UK).
3 It seems as though the words were treated as an additional feature of the music (*cf.* Ockelford, 2012b).
4 The current doctoral research of the second author addresses this issue by consciously adopting a longitudinal approach. See also Wu (2017).

3 Extending the *Sounds of Intent* model of musical development to explore how people with learning difficulties engage in creative multisensory activities

Adam Ockelford

Introduction

The original *Sounds of Intent* ('SoI') project (as set out, for example, in Ockelford *et al.*, 2005, and Vogiatzoglou *et al.*, 2011, and available at www.soundsofintent. org) was intended to map purely *musical* development in children and young people with learning difficulties. In part this was meant to be an antidote to the tendency of practitioners, education managers, policy-makers and others (including, in the UK, Ofsted school inspectors) to conceive of musical engagement among pupils and students with special educational needs in other than musical terms – a notion that has a long pedigree. For example, at the turn of the century, the UK Government's own documentation (Qualifications and Curriculum Authority, 2001, p. 6) asserted that music is particularly valuable for pupils with learning difficulties since it offers opportunities for them to 'experience a sense of pride and achievement in their own work ... choose, discriminate and justify decisions ... develop coordination and functional fine motor skills', as well as purportedly fostering the development of movement and mobility, encouraging cooperation, tolerance and a willingness to work with others and helping to develop self-discipline and self-confidence.

To a certain extent, this strangely biased (not to say discriminatory) view – that music is primarily of importance to people with learning difficulties since it is somehow good for them for extra-musical reasons – may have been a reflection of the fact that the predominant paradigm in the field of music and special needs was in the past a therapeutic one (Ockelford, 2000; Welch, Ockelford and Zimmermann, 2001; Markou, 2010), in which music is deployed as a means of achieving other than musical ends, such as promoting well-being, enhancing communication skills and nurturing social engagement. It is also the case that most of those responsible for coordinating and delivering the music curriculum in special schools were, and continue to be, non-music specialists (Ockelford, Welch and Zimmermann, 2002; Welch, *et al.*, 2016), who tend to lack the expertise or confidence to analyse their pupils' musical engagement in musical terms. Hence, they often resort to observing and recording extra-musical behaviours as more or less unwitting proxies for descriptions of truly *musical* engagement (Ockelford, 2008).

Extending the Sounds of Intent *model*   65

However, a focus only on sound and music led some to criticise the *Sounds of Intent* approach for being unhelpfully constrained (and constraining), since in many 'real-life' situations, music does not exist in isolation from other sensory input or, indeed, other activity in the domain of sound (notably language). Besides (people argued), it is an artificial exercise to extract one strand of children's development from the rest. In acknowledgement of these concerns, this chapter takes the first steps towards setting out, theoretically, how the *Sounds of Intent* music-developmental framework may be extended to embrace other forms of sensory engagement that may occur in multisensory environments and in arts activities with children, young people and adults with learning difficulties. The practical application of the conceptual framework is already being tested in some special schools in London.

The senses, and the potential impact of learning difficulties and autism on sensory perception

An immediate challenge is to identify which forms of sensory input may be of relevance in creative contexts, and to define what these domains of perception tell us about ourselves, the environment in which we are situated and our relationship to it. The taxonomy presented in Table 3.1 attempts to summarise current psychological thinking in relation to the eight main sensory areas that pertain to the outside world. They are:

- the auditory domain, which is concerned with hearing, and provides the listener with information about sound – specifically pitch, timbre and loudness (see, for example, Warren, 2008);
- the visual domain, which pertains to sight, and informs the observer about the qualities of light, which may be conceptualised as hue, saturation and brightness (Davis, 2000);
- the tactual domain, which relates to touch, and is concerned with the perceived attributes of the surfaces of things, including texture (roughness, stickiness and hardness – see Hollins *et al.* (1993, 2000)), pressure and vibration (Plumb and Meigs, 1961);
- the haptic domain, which, though touch and proprioception, provides information about the three-dimensional nature of things (their size and shape) – Grunwald (2008);
- the proprioceptive domain, which tells people where the parts of their bodies are in relation to one another – their vertical and horizontal angles and distance apart (Dickinson, 1976);
- the vestibular domain, which enables us to detect any change in bodily movement, and gives a sense of physical orientation in relation to the vertical, permitting us to balance (Goldberg, 2012);
- the gustatory domain, which bears on taste, and recognises five types of flavour: sweetness, sourness, saltiness, bitterness and umaminess (Engelen, 2012, pp. 20–22) and

Table 3.1 Taxonomy of the senses

Sense	Auditory	Visual	Tactual		Haptic	Proprio-ceptive	Vestibular	Gustatory	Olfactory
Common name	Hearing	Sight	Touch		Touch	Body awareness	Balance	Taste	Smell
General features that are gauged	Sound	Light	Attributes of the surfaces of things		The three-dimensional nature of things	Physical disposition of self	Physical orientation	Flavour	Odour
Specific features that are gauged	Pitch	Hue	Texture	Roughness	Size and shape	Horizontal angle Vertical angle		Sweetness	Camphoraceousness
	Pitch	Hue	Texture	Stickiness				Sourness	Muskiness
			Texture	Hardness				Saltiness	Floralness
	Timbre	Saturation	Temperature			Distance apart		Bitterness	Saltiness
			Pressure					Bitterness	Bitterness
	Loudness	Brightness	Vibration					Umaminess	Pungency
									Putridity
	Position in the environment/change of position = movement								
	Position in time/extent in time = duration								

Extending the Sounds of Intent *model*   67

- the olfactory domain, which concerns smell, and acknowledges seven potential types of odour: camphoraceousness, muskiness, floralness, peppermintiness, ethereality, pungency and putridity (Amoore, 1970).

Perceptual data from each sense can usually be contextualised in relation to its source (its position in the environment) and, potentially, a change in position (which equates to movement), and its relative position in time and duration.

Inevitably, this taxonomy represents something of a simplification, since perceptual input typically interacts and overlaps in complex ways, both within and between sensory domains. For example, within domains, changing the loudness of a sound alters our perception of its pitch; the perceived hue and brightness of a patch of colour will depend on its surroundings and the nature of the light in which it is viewed and how hot or cold an object feels to be will vary according to what was touched immediately before. Instances of between-domain interaction include the fact that our perception of the shape of something is likely to be informed by how it looks, that vision typically works alongside proprioception in determining how we sense our own physical disposition and that the taste of a food depends to a great extent on its smell. Beyond this, some people report having 'synaesthesia', a neurological phenomenon in which the stimulation of one sense leads to involuntary experiences in another (Baron-Cohen *et al.*, 1996; Harrison, 2001; Cytowic and Eagleman, 2011). A number of well-known musicians working in a variety of cultures, eras and genres, including Duke Ellington, Billy Joel, Nikolai Rimsky-Korsakov and Olivier Messiaen, have reported seeing different colours in response to particular pitches, harmonies, tonalities or timbres. However, synaesthesia is not confined to elite composers and performers, with prevalence estimates among those on the autism spectrum of approximately 20% (Baron-Cohen, *et al.*, 2013), around five times higher than in the population as a whole (Simner, *et al.*, 2006).

In any case, in most day-to-day situations, more than one sense will be activated at the same time. Getting on a train, for example, is likely to engage hearing, sight, touch, smell, body awareness and balance. Having a meal with friends may well utilise *all* the senses. In short, life is multisensory, and would be overwhelming were it not for the fact that adults are typically 'exquisitely skilled at selectively attending to specific features or aspects of objects and events, picking out information that is relevant to their needs, goals, and interests, and ignoring irrelevant stimulation' (Bahrick and Lickliter, 2012). Such selectivity is possible since different forms of sensory input arising from a single object or event are initially processed discretely in the brain, before being cognitively reunited through 'binding' (Roskies, 1999; Barnard and deLahunta, 2017). Typically, this integration of sensory information is unthinking, and apparently so effortless that it is difficult to imagine how it could be otherwise. However, there is a mounting body of evidence that perceptual experiences and the way they are connected to

68   *Adam Ockelford*

form 'gestalts' (or fail to be) may be atypical among those on the autism spectrum (see, for example, Shalom, 2005; Iarocci and McDonald, 2006; Caldwell and Horwood, 2008). Furthermore, our perception of things is informed by our understanding of an object's function and its connotations learnt through experience and cultural immersion (see, for instance, Nisbett and Miyamoto, 2005; Miyamoto, Nisbett and Masuda, 2006; Davidoff, Fonteneau and Fagot, 2008). Inevitably, those whose learning difficulties constrain functional and cultural comprehension may quite possibly perceive things in a more naïve, naturalistic way – uncluttered by too much understanding and untrammelled by social prejudice.

Creative multisensory environments

Given these issues, for those working with people who have learning difficulties or autism (or both), there are clearly advantages to having access to environments in which sensory input can be controlled, more or less precisely, in terms of domain, position and timing. Moreover, two forms of sensory modification are possible that may be of particular benefit: *simplification*, through the removal or suppression of potential distractions, and *amplification*, by increasing the intensity of a given stimulus, in absolute terms or relative to others. Such control enables people's reactions to a range of discrete (or carefully integrated) stimuli to be observed, helping practitioners to build up a picture of an individual's sensory understanding, interests and preferences. And in theory, at least, armed with such information, it will be possible for those facilitating the use of specialised environments to move beyond offering the merely experiential (as valuable as that may be in some cases) to devising programmes of learning that build on a person's sensory abilities and motivations to promote perceptual and cognitive development. Beyond this, specially tailored, shared sensory experiences can foster communication, interaction and social understanding. And paradoxically, through limiting the universe of sensory possibilities, individuals may be freed from a feeling of being overwhelmed by a seemingly infinite range of options and given the confidence to express themselves creatively through music, drama, art or movement, encouraging a sense of personal and artistic identity, and nurturing well-being.

Given these possibilities, it is little wonder that creative multisensory environments, in one form or another, have become an established part of special-educational practice, also featuring in some recreational and artistic programmes for adults with learning disabilities and older people with dementia (Hope, 1998; Staal, Pinkney and Roane, 2003). This is a field that is very much led by practitioners, and characterised by a plethora of imaginative ideas (Fowler, 2008; Davies, 2012) but evaluated, if at all, with little or no rigour (Mount and Cavet, 1995; Pagliano, 1999; Hogg *et al.*, 2001; Stephenson, 2002; Stephenson and Carter, 2011). There are a number of reasons for this.

Extending the Sounds of Intent *model*   69

First, the design of some environments appears to be driven primarily by the aesthetic predilections of their creators, using fantasy themes such as 'under the sea', 'the haunted house' and 'outer space'. However, this approach can be problematic if the people for whom they are intended are not yet at the stage of symbolic understanding. For sure, participants may derive pleasurable sensory experiences from the blooming, buzzing sources of light and sound and the artefacts that are provided, but what criteria are being used to assess their levels of engagement? To what extent is it feasible for a practitioner caught up in role-play as a diver, a ghost or an astronaut to adopt an objective stance in appraising someone's purely sensory reactions to these imaginary characters?

Second, the sheer complexity of what is typically on offer makes meaningful research very difficult, since it is almost impossible to isolate correlations between stimuli and responses, let alone assign causal connections between them. Add to this the idiosyncratic nature of the individuals involved (participants and practitioners alike), and, beyond individual accounts of 'success' (see, for example, Slevin and McClelland, 1999), there is typically little that can be said is of relevance or value beyond a particular context – no sense of *why* a particular approach may have proved effective, since the necessary abstraction of general perceptual and developmental principles from a range of comparable scenarios has not been undertaken.

Third, the commercial imperative of manufacturers to persuade schools and centres to purchase particular items of technology, ranging from the Snoezelen to the Soundbeam and, more recently, the Skoog, can lead to claims of efficacy that a more dispassionate perspective would be unlikely to support (Lotan and Gold, 2009). That is not to say that these and similar devices may not potentially be of value – even in some cases offering a unique channel of artistic expression to those with limited voluntary movement – but unless their utilisation is ultimately subservient to an understanding of an individual's levels of sensory and cognitive functioning, the engagement they stimulate is likely to be superficial rather than the heuristic, observational rather than developmental and recreational rather than therapeutic. That is to say, their potential for scaffolding personal growth will likely remain unfulfilled.

These three issues beg the question of why creative multisensory work is not better informed by an understanding of aesthetic development among those with learning difficulties and autism. The answer is, I believe, straightforward: because, with the exception of music (due in large part to the *Sounds of Intent* project), the necessary conceptual frameworks of artistic maturation, embedded in the relevant developmental sensory domains, do not currently exist. Hence, there is no defined theoretical space in which creative multisensory work can notionally be situated, through which different approaches could be contrasted and compared, and their relative effectiveness properly evaluated.

70 *Adam Ockelford*

This chapter seeks to take the first step towards plugging that gap in our understanding. It is based on the thinking set out in *Sounds of Intent*, which, as we have seen, in turn derives from zygonic theory. The question here is whether the zygonic conjecture can theoretically – and usefully – be extended into other areas of artistic endeavour. It is to these that we next turn our attention.

The arts

Just as the senses are conceptually complex, so too are the arts, as Table 3.2 shows. This sets out putative relationships between the media through which performances can occur (music, art, dance and language) and examples of artistic genres (which in actuality may be blended). Here, 'art' is used in a limited sense to mean painting and sculpture, and 'dance' refers to all forms of performance movement.

Table 3.2 The relationship between genres of the performing arts and the media through which they are expressed

	Medium			
Genre	*(Sound and) Music*	*(Fine) Art*	*(Movement and) Dance*	*(Language and) Drama*
Play	Possible (foreground or background)	In the set design	Possible	✓
Radio play	Possible (foreground or background)	–	–	✓
Film	Possible (foreground; very likely background)	In the composition of shots	Possible	✓
Silent movie	Yes – background	In the composition of shots	Possible	–
Opera	✓	In the set design	Possible	✓
Musical	✓	In the set design	Possible	✓
Ballet	✓	In the set design	✓	–
Modern dance	✓	In the set design	✓	–
Mime	–	In the set design	Possible	–
Instrumental concert	✓	–	–	–
Vocal concert	✓	–	–	✓
(Narrated) story	Possible (background)	–	–	✓
(Declaimed) poem	–	–	–	✓

Table 3.3 Music and language share a special relationship in the domain of sound

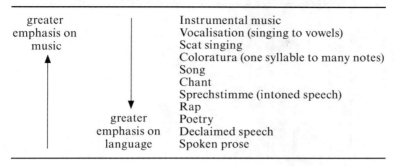

The connections between medium and genre are by no means straightforward. For example, a play will invariably involve language but may also (though need not) make use of music and dance, and art (in the set design). A radio play, however, is not likely to include art or dance, but will utilise language and may well incorporate music (as a 'foreground' entity in its own right, or in the 'background', typically affecting audience members without their being aware of its presence).

It is worth noting that music and language share a special relationship in the domain of sound. It is possible for either to exist in the absence of the other (as in instrumental music and speech), though these are extremes on a continuum in which the balance between the two varies (see Table 3.3).

The relationship of the senses to the arts

Sensory input relates in a complex way to the arts, as Table 3.4 shows. For example, while listeners typically engage with music by attending to its sounds (thereby acting in a 'reactive' way), other sensations may form part of the aesthetic experience too, including, for example, *seeing* the performers in action and (particularly in the case of loud music, or where deaf or hard of hearing audience members are concerned) experiencing vibration somatically. In the case of players or singers (who will be behaving 'proactively' to produce the necessary sounds), movement of some form will also be required. With regard to 'fine' art (here referring to genres such as painting, sculpture, photography and printmaking), the principal sense through which reactive engagement occurs is typically sight, though touch through movement may be involved too (notably in the case of sculpture, and blind people). Proactively, movement is invariably implicated in artistic production. Dance and other types of performative movement are usually experienced visually in the reactive domain, and proactively through proprioception and the haptic and vestibular senses. Drama normally (though not necessarily) entails audience members hearing and seeing what is going on, and actors will often call

Table 3.4 The relationship of the arts to the senses.

Art form	'Reactive' or 'proactive'	Sense					
		Hearing	Sight	Body awareness and/or balance	Touch	Taste	Smell
(Sound and) **Music**	R	**Usually the principal sense**	Usually	–	Could be vibration	–	–
	P			Yes	Usually	–	–
(Fine) **Art**	R	–	**Usually the principal sense**	Yes (for sculpture)	Yes (for sculpture)	–	–
	P	–		Yes	Yes	–	–
(Movement and) **Dance**	R	When with music	Yes	–	–	–	–
	P	When with music	Usually	**Usually the principal sense**	Could be	–	–
(Language and) **Drama**	R	Usually (though could be mime)	Usually (though could be radio play)	–	–	–	–
	P			Usually (though could be radio play)	Usually (though could be radio play)	–	–
Cuisine	R	–	Usually	Yes	Yes	**Usually the principal sense**	Yes
	P	–	Usually	Yes	Yes		Yes

upon their body awareness and sense of touch as well. Insofar as cuisine can be regarded as an art form, vision, proprioception and the tactual, haptic, gustatory and olfactory senses are all likely to be brought to bear, proactively (in food preparation) and reactively (in consumption).

Extending zygonic theory from music to other domains

In this section, we take the first steps towards extending the principles of zygonic theory from music to other domains. First, let us summarise the assertions of zygonic theory as they stand (Ockelford, 2009, 2017).

All music comprises perceived sounds (that exist directly in response to physical stimuli, or may be remembered or imagined), which have *per*ceived a*spects*, referred to as 'perspects'. Perspects constitute the dimensions along which variation within a given subdomain of sound, such as pitch, timbre, loudness, time of onset and duration, can occur (see Figure 3.1). Zygonic theory holds that every perception of a sound evokes a swift, unthinking emotional response, however slight (Bigand, Filipic and Lalitte, 2005).

The disposition of a perspect at a given point in time is termed its 'perspective value'. Perspective values are normally perceived non-consciously. However, musicians can conceptualise and label them, with varying degrees of precision. In the British-English-speaking tradition, for example, a pitch may be identified as 'C in the 4th octave' or 'middle C' – its timbre as a 'Steinway concert grand', its dynamic as 'forte' and its duration as a minim at ♩ = 60 (see Figure 3.2).

Perspective values may be compared through mental constructs termed 'interperspective relationships', which have 'interperspective values' (see Figure 3.3). The process of comparison typically occurs rapidly and

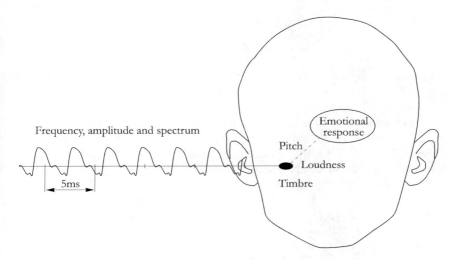

Figure 3.1 The 'perspects' (*per*ceived a*spects*) of a sound.

74 Adam Ockelford

Figure 3.2 The 'perspective values' pertaining to a note represented in Western musical notation.

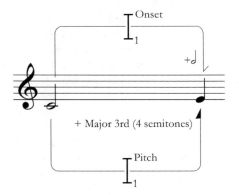

Figure 3.3 Examples of 'interperspective relationships' between values of onset and pitch.

unthinkingly, although musicians may reflect on what occurs in order to make small adjustments in timing, tuning or dynamic, for example. Where values differ, this will entail a change in emotional response. When they are the same, the response may be reinforced.

Interperspective relationships may be of different ranks. 'Primary' relationships (see Figure 3.3) are the vehicle through which perspective values are compared. Some can be conceptualised according to the perceptual domain in which they operate. For example, in the West, musicians term the differences between pitches 'intervals', and classify them using labels such as 'major' and 'minor thirds', which bear emotional connotations that are more or less culturally specific. 'Secondary' relationships gauge differences between

Extending the Sounds of Intent *model* 75

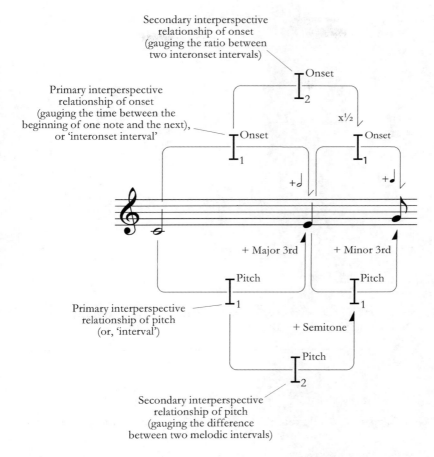

Figure 3.4 Examples of 'primary' and 'secondary' interperspective relationships.

primary interperspective values. Hence, they are more abstract than primaries (that is, further removed from the 'perceptual surface'). Again, these can be captured conceptually in musicological terms. For example, the *difference* between a major third and a minor third is a semitone. See Figure 3.4.

As we have seen, interperspective relationships between values that are the same or similar, and through which imitation is deemed to have occurred, are termed 'zygonic'. Figure 1.6 and Figure 3.5 provide examples of primary, secondary and tertiary zygonic relationships. This third level of cognitive abstraction from the qualia that are perceived directly (or remembered, or imagined) appears to represent a natural human processing limit in the auditory domain (in that no extant pieces of music use fourth level or 'quaternary' relationships; Ockelford, 2002). In Figure 3.5, the tertiary zygonic relationship of scale degree underpins a sense of rising intensity in the music as successive parts enter with melodic intervals of increasing size.

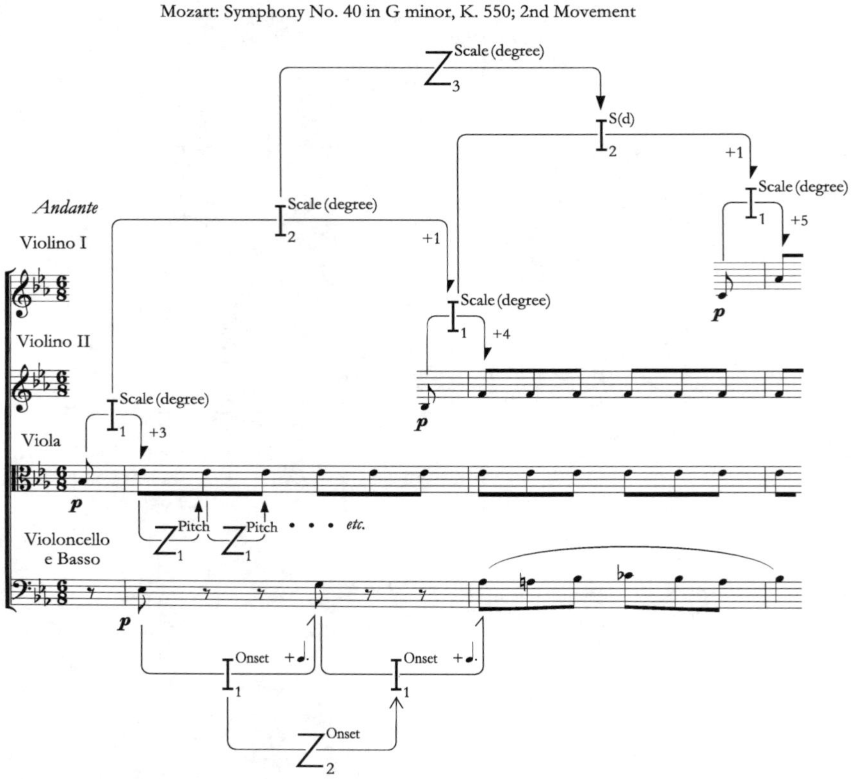

76 Adam Ockelford

Figure 3.5 Examples of primary, secondary and tertiary zygonic relationships.

Zygonic relationships are held to be the basis of all musical *structure*, in contrast to its *content*, which comprises perspective and interperspective values. So in Figure 3.5, for instance, the second note of the viola part has the 'pitch content' E flat in the fourth octave. The third note has the same content. The primary zygonic relationship – the mental construct – that is hypothesised to connect them cognitively constitutes the structural element of the music that is in play here. That is to say, through imitation, the musical content reifies its structure: structure can only exist (other than in a purely imaginary, conceptual way) when it is expressed through content. Is also follows that the same structure can have different content. For instance, in Figure 3.5, the second melodic entry (made by the second violins) is structurally identical to the first (in the violas), but its pitch content is different. It is this coexistence of similarity and difference, and the capacity of the brain to perceive structure divorced from content (and therefore to grasp the *transformation* of motifs), which enables music to convey a metaphorical and meaningful narrative over time when it comprises only of abstract patterns of sound.

Extending the Sounds of Intent *model*   77

Since music cannot exist without structure, since all musical structure is held to be zygonic and since zygonic relationships depend on a recognition of repetition and imitation, it follows that, in terms of the *Sounds of Intent* framework, an understanding of music can only occur in those who are functioning at Level 3 or above. As we saw in Chapter 2, to a child who processes sound at Level 2, a piece of music is likely to pass by as a series of unconnected auditory sensations, each capable of evoking an emotional response in its own right, though, inevitably, the whole experience will not add up to more than the sum of its parts. A child functioning at Level 3 may pick up on moment-to-moment regularities such as the immediate repetition of pitch of the uniform pulses of quavers in Figure 3.5. A child operating at Level 4 would be likely to appreciate that the opening motif is a distinct musical entity in its own right, and recognise the connection with this and the similar motifs that follow. A child functioning at Level 5 would be able to grasp the overall structure of the music in a simple way (albeit non-consciously), with its major mode and a sense of the motifs that are presented, changed and subsequently restated.

However, even for those who are operating at Level 5 (or 6), listening together to a given performance would by no means guarantee each had the same experience. Quite the opposite. It seems that we all pick up different things from a single performance. Why? Because music is typically supersaturated with far more repetition than is required for it to be coherent (Ockelford, 2005), which has two consequences. First, listeners do not need to hear all the available structure for a given musical message to make sense, and second, different listeners (or even the same listener on different occasions) can apprehend different structural elements, yet each can still have a coherent musical experience. Moreover (as we saw with children functioning at *Sounds of Intent* Level 3 or 4), a sense of derivation through imitation that was conceived by a composer need not be detected by listeners. (Note that the opposite scenario is also possible, whereby listeners hear structure in music that occurred as an unwitting by-product of the composer's efforts.) Nonetheless, there is normally enough common perceptual ground for pieces of music to exist as shared and meaningful cognitive enterprises, though since each structural interpretation will bear distinct affective correlates, everyone's emotional response to music will inevitably differ to a greater or lesser extent each time they hear a piece. However, to take this thinking a stage further, it means that the depth and sophistication of the emotional response to music experienced by those functioning at Level 3, 4 or 5 will necessarily be limited by their powers of structural processing.

The propensity of the brain to seek out structures in sound (and to impose them where none actually exists) has other consequences too, which are particular noticeable among some on the autism spectrum who have learning difficulties (Ockelford, 2013). For instance, pattern that occurs naturally in the auditory environment (or as a result of human activity) may be accorded the status of music. For example, Freddie, aged ten, enjoys emptying out flowerpots from the patio, arranging them rather like an earthenware gamelan in

78   Adam Ockelford

the kitchen, and then playing them with rapid finger-flicks; while Romy, aged eight, incorporates the sounds of mobile phone ring-tones into the pieces she plays by ear on the piano (Ockelford, *op. cit.*). Joseph, aged five, who is blind, indulges in so-called 'echolalia' – the repetition of words or phrases that often has no obvious semantic or pragmatic function (McEvoy, Loveland and Landry, 1988; Mills, 1993, p. 163; Sterponi and Shankey, 2014). In each case, it appears that ostensibly non-musical sounds are being treated as musical objects, and that the transformation that makes them 'musical' is imitation. The sounds of Freddie's flowerpots are musical (rather than horticultural) because he deliberately repeats the bell-like sound that each makes as it is flicked (an activity characteristic of *Sounds of Intent* Level 3). Romy's ring-tones are musical because she treats them not as sound symbols ('someone wishes to speak on the phone'), but as abstract musical motifs, to be repeated and transformed, and incorporated into fragmentary improvisations (*Sounds of Intent* Level 4). Joseph's words are musical because he reiterates them for the pleasure of the sound each makes rather than thinking about their potential semantic meaning (*Sounds of Intent* Level 3).

Composers, of course, have long done the same thing in rather more formal contexts: consider that Beethoven is reputed to have considered the opening motif of his fifth symphony as 'fate knocking on the door' (Fandel, 2006, p. 43), and recall the birdsong used in his sixth symphony, intended to enhance the pastoral conceit. The principle at work here, though, is just the same as the one that Romy adopts: a sound or sequence of sounds occurring extra-musically is transferred to a potentially musical context (for example, by being imitated on an instrument), and then is itself treated imitatively (through repetition or transformation) and thereby becomes music (Figure 3.6).

Beethoven's cuckoo (and the nightingale and the quail) is effective aesthetically, though, because sophisticated listeners (at *Sounds of Intent* Level 6) as well as hearing the new context, simultaneously, are aware of the old, and hence hear the stylised birdsong both as quasi-natural sounds *and* musical motifs: it is the blended meaning (Zbikowski, 2002, 2017) that is especially powerful.

A further level of abstraction is possible in which a (non-sounding) feature of an event or object is imitated in music. Although direct cross-modal mapping is possible (for example, all of us have the capacity to emulate, albeit approximately, the brightness of a light in the loudness of a sound we make, or to sing a pitch whose height will bear a more or less regular relationship to the vertical position of a dot on a piece of paper – see Thorpe, 2015 – while for synaesthetes, such relationships may be more consistent and involve other qualities such as colour), a more common form of relationship between different perceptual domains is to be found in terms of intra-modal change or difference. Since this will necessarily involve primary interperspective relationships in each of the sensory domains concerned, imitation inevitably involves zygonic relationships of secondary rank or higher. Consider, for example, how the speed of a funeral march reflects the slow pace of those walking on such occasions (which may be need not include the sound of boot on ground) – see Figure 3.7.

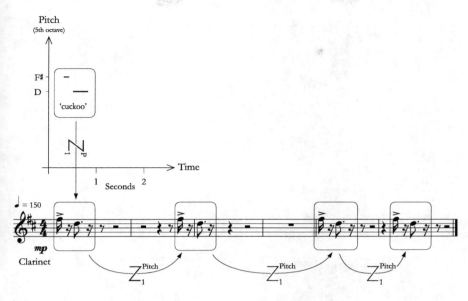

Figure 3.6 Imitation of natural sounds that become music.

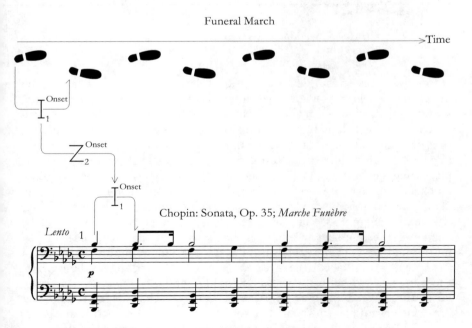

Figure 3.7 Imitation of a (non-sounding) feature in music.

80 Adam Ockelford

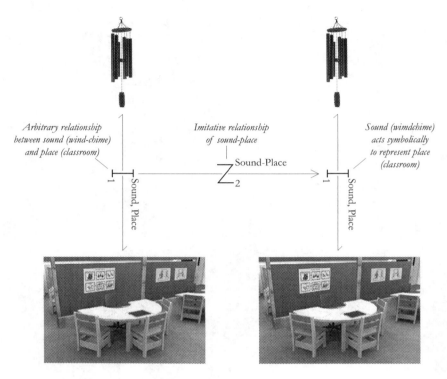

Figure 3.8 Arbitrary connection between sound and place is imitated, yielding symbolic meaning.

Finally, consider that wholly arbitrary relationships may occur between music and sensations or ideas generated in domains other than perceived sound – giving rise to *extra-musical* meanings. These occur when an experience in one other-than-auditory domain or more is encountered at the same time as a musical sound or structure, a relationship that is subsequently imitated. Through such means, a sound or fragment of music (or indeed a whole piece) may consistently bring something, someone or somewhere to mind, and hence come to represent it as an auditory 'object of reference' (Ockelford, 2001). For example, a child's classroom may be represented by a particular wind chime (Figure 3.8), a music session by a special bell and a key person by a jangly bracelet. Once the symbolic relationship is established, the sound or music and that which it represents may be separated in time and space.

Figure 3.9 summarises the three possible types of extra-musical imitation: those involving other categories of sound ('A' and 'B'), those utilising similar features from non-sonic domains ('C') and those cross-modal links that are arbitrary and learnt through association ('D'). These operate at *Sounds of Intent* Level 3, and demand increasingly advanced musical development.

As we shall see, these types of cross-modal relationships, which are peripheral in music, are far more important in other art forms.

Extending the Sounds of Intent model 81

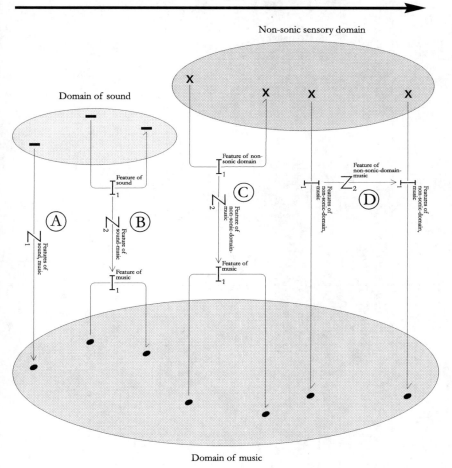

Figure 3.9 Visual taxonomy of extra-musical relationships.

Towards a general theory of zygonicity – extending the *Sounds of Intent* developmental framework into artistic engagement involving modalities other than music

Here, we extend the idea, first postulated by Ockelford (1993), that the forms of mental processing set out in zygonic theory need not be restricted to sound and music. As the data in Table 3.1 indicate, sensory domains each have a number of qualities (which, as we have seen, are termed 'perspects' in zygonic terminology), and these can be subject to variation (existing as

Table 3.5 Extending the *Sounds of Intent* principles through the generalisation of zygonic theory to perceptual domains beyond musical sound

Level	*Original* Sounds of Intent *description*	*Acronym*	*Core perceptual/cognitive ability expressed in terms not specific to a sensory domain*	*Zygonic implications*	*Symbolic understanding*
1	Confusion and Chaos	**C**	None: no perceptual awareness in any sensory domain	–	–
2	Awareness and **I**ntentionality	**I**	An emerging awareness of the perceived aspects of things and of the variety that is possible within each, experienced within the perceived present; a sense of agency, of intentionality	No cognition of repetition (and therefore no understanding of imitation)	No symbolic understanding
3	Relationships, repetition, **R**egularity	**R**	A growing awareness of how one perspective value may relate to another; a sense that one may replicate another	The cognition of repetition within working memory; initially simple primary relationships, with secondaries becoming possible	Early symbolic understanding – that one thing can represent another through imitation of one or more of its qualities, or through repeated association
4	Notes forming **C**lusters	**C**	The evolving notion of groups of perspective values as units of perception and meaning, and of the relationships that are possible between 'chunks', involving 'Gestalt perception'	The cognition of repetition within long-term veridical memory; chunks are defined internally and externally through imitation	More advanced symbolic understanding, through compound imitation or association

| 5 | Deeper structural Links | L | A growing understanding and appreciation of complete works of art (in any domain or domains), and the conventions of structure and content that underpin them | The cognition of repetition within long-term schematic memory (i): formal frames of reference; simple structural archetypes | The notion of a symbolic narrative over time |
| 6 | Mature artistic Expression | E | A growing awareness of the impact of artistic production on others; an evolving appreciation of culturally determined aesthetic values and the expressive nature of art; in the case of temporal art forms, an understanding of the 'narrative metaphor' that unfolds as works of art are perceived over time | The cognition of repetition within long-term schematic memory (ii): the imitation of expressive devices of creation or performance | Awareness of the impact of a symbolic narrative on others within a known culture |

84 *Adam Ockelford*

'perspective values'). For example, light has hue, saturation and brightness, while touch has roughness, stickiness and hardness (among others). And in everyday life, we use expressions that imply the presence of interperspective relationships, such as 'this colour is brighter than that one', or we may observe comment that one texture is rougher than another. Moreover, crucially, one perspective value can be perceived as being the same as or similar to another, and can be considered to be so through human agency – that is, through imitation.

As we have seen, the *Sounds of Intent* research sets out how the evolving capacity for mental processing indicated by zygonic theory underpins musical development (summarised in Table 2.1). Here, it is proposed that this may be generalised to other sensory and artistic domains as follows (Table 3.5).

Using these principles, there now follow the first outlines of developmental models in the domains of (fine) art (painting, drawing and sculpture); movement, gesture and dance; and language and drama. Because there is a substantial literature in relation to children's artistic development, this is considered in some depth. The frameworks pertaining to dance and drama are more preliminary in nature – even frankly speculative. But it is hoped that by setting out possibilities here, their usefulness will be tested in practical situations and through further research. Indeed, the first steps in this direction have already been taken with research conducted at The Village School in London (Cooper, 2016, 2017).

Art

Here, for ease of initial analysis, the term 'art' is used to refer to two of the 'fine' arts: painting and sculpture, though the thinking presented here could potentially be broadened in the future. There is a substantial literature on the development of drawing, painting and sculpting skills (and, more widely, on the emergence of creativity in the visual domain) in childhood, which reaches back as far as the late 1800s. However, until very recently, there was no formal research on artistic development in children with intellectual impairment. Cox and Cotgreave (1996) explored the human figure drawings of children with moderate learning difficulties and found them to be similar to those of 'neurotypical' children of the same *mental* age. Cox and Howarth (1989) had previously undertaken a comparable study with children with severe learning difficulties (SLD) and reached the same conclusion: the artistic output of those with SLD bears testimony to their substantial developmental delay, but there tend to be few, if any, qualitative differences to the products of their age-matched neurotypical counterparts. Indeed, as in music, children with learning difficulties who are on the autism spectrum may display exceptionally mature artistic skill (Selfe, 1977, 2011; Happé and Frith, 2010). Hence in searching for evidence on which to build a developmental model of the artistic development of those with learning disabilities, it seems appropriate to mine the literature pertaining to creative endeavour in the early years.

It is of interest to note that the venerable tradition of exploring children's art stands in stark contrast to the dearth of music-developmental literature until relatively recently, which began with the observations of Moog (1968/1976) and was first consolidated in a formal psychological context by Hargreaves (1986). Why should this be so? It may be because children's art with its tangible, fixed products is simply an easier area to study than music, which by its very nature is ephemeral and typically needs representing visually before it can be analysed – though standard Western notation struggles to capture the essence of children's early music-making with its fluidity of pitch and time.

A number of developmental stages in children's art have been proposed. These are almost entirely in the proactive domain, and are based on the analysis of what children produce, spontaneously or on request, with authors often amassing large collections of drawings and paintings, and then seeking to divine a developmental pattern in what goes on. According to Malchiodi (1998, p. 65), the first researchers, up until the beginning of the twentieth century, identified three main phases in children's artistic development:

1   A scribbling stage, which consists of both unsystematically scattered lines and later scribbling in the form of clustered lines and circular shapes.
2   A schematic stage in which children develop schemata to represent human figures, objects and environments.
3   A naturalistic stage in which there are more realistic, lifelike details.

Burt (1922) refined this taxonomy somewhat, and assigned an age range to each level of artistic accomplishment: scribbles (aged 2–3); single lines (aged 4); basic drawings of people and animals (aged 5–6); more realistic representations, incorporating spatial depth, motion and colour (aged 7–11). Burt noted that children tend to give up spontaneous drawing in their preadolescent years, perhaps through a lack of interest or confidence when they realise that their efforts fall some way short of picturing 'reality' as it is generally acknowledged to be.

Lowenfeld (1947) took a further step in asserting that children's artistic development was analogous to the process of organising thoughts and cognitive maturation. He identified six major stages of children's artistic development:

1   Scribbling (2–4): children's earliest drawings are often kinaesthetically based, and evolve from being disordered (implying no control of movement), to longitudinal (repeated movements) and circular (regular change in movement); in due course, scribbles have meanings assigned to them, shown by their being named (indicating a change from kinaesthetic to imaginative thinking).

86 *Adam Ockelford*

2 Preschematic (4–7): the early development of representational symbols, particularly rudimentary forms representing humans.
3 Schematic (7–9): continuing development of representational symbols, particularly a schema for figures, objects, composition and colour; use of a baseline.
4 Drawing realism (9–11): increasing skill at depicting spatial depth and colour in nature; increasing rigidity in art expression.
5 Pseudorealism (11–13): more critical awareness of human figures and environment and increasing detail; increasing rigidity; caricature.
6 Period of decision (adolescence): expression is more sophisticated and detailed – some children do not reach this stage unless they continue or are encouraged to make art.

A great deal more detail is added to 'high-level' taxonomies such as these by Kellog (1969), in her classic analysis of over one million drawings by children. For example, she identifies 20 'basic scribbles', which do not necessarily require hand-eye coordination and into which any drawing may ultimately be analysed. Next come the 17 'placement patterns', which determine where scribbles occur on the page, and therefore require children to attend visually to what they are doing. Then follow the 17 'emergent diagram shapes', which evolve into 'diagrams', of which there are six types (*op. cit.*, p. 45). Five of them are 'geometrically regular: the rectangle (including the square), the oval (including the circle), the triangle, the Greek cross, and the diagonal cross'. Kellog observes that children's versions of these lack geometrical precision. The sixth category is the 'odd shape', which serves as a catchall classification 'for any deliberate line formation that encloses an irregular area'. Next come the 'combines', which are two diagrams put together. Here, there are 21 possibilities (including the same diagrams being repeated) – 36 if 'asymmetry' is taken into account (where one diagram is more dominant than the other). The 'aggregates' follow: units of three or more diagrams that function as a repertory of visual ideas, whose possibilities are to all intents and purposes limitless.

Through these early stages of development, Kellog traces the importance of three shapes in particular, the 'mandalas' (*op. cit.*, pp. 64–73) – essentially circles with an inner cross; 'suns' (pp. 74–85), which are circles with lines emanating from them in the manner of rays and 'radials' (pp. 86–93), which are lines radiating in all directions from a common central point. In a similar way, Kellog traces the development of 'humans' (starting with the head) from particular types of scribble, to the oval 'diagram' and then the face 'aggregate', made up of different proto-shapes (*op. cit.*, p. 94). 'Humans' grow in complexity, sprouting arms and legs then hands and feet, and eventually fingers and toes. Kellog describes them as an example of 'early pictorialism' (*op. cit.*, pp. 114*ff*), of which other examples are animals, buildings, vegetation and transportation. This is as far as her taxonomy goes – which applies in a parallel way to children's work in clay.

Extending the Sounds of Intent *model*   87

An issue with Kellog's immensely detailed classification system is that by failing to take account of the limited universe of possibilities open to a child with a single mark-maker (such as a crayon) and a sheet of paper of limited size, she feels intellectually secure in ascribing significance to the commonalities that exist between different drawings, when some of these are in reality inevitable: there are only so many directions in which a line can be drawn, and only a limited number of places on the page where it can be placed. Hence, the similarities between children's early artistic efforts that an adult eye can detect may actually be artefacts of the physical and environmental constraints that acted on their creation, and in fact have no developmental consequence. This is similar to the problem that early years music specialists face in trying to analyse babies' first forays into sound-making. Is a repeated rising vocalisation intended to be imitative, or is it merely a result of chance, brought about by the fact that continuations in pitch can only exist in one of three forms (up, down or the same)? I deal with the probabilistic nature of the analysis that is necessary to tackle problems such as this at length elsewhere (Ockelford, 2012a; see Chapter 5, this volume).

A striking feature of the drawings that Kellog and others use to illustrate the stage of 'early pictorialism' is their lack of realism: they only partly resemble the objects and people that they are intended to represent. Arnheim (1974) puzzles over this characteristic of children's art: why is it that they do not reproduce what they can evidently recognise? As he observes (Arnheim, *op. cit.*, p. 168), at an age 'when they can easily tell one person from another and notice the smallest change in a familiar object, their pictures are still quite undifferentiated. The reasons must lie in the nature and function of pictorial representation'. He goes on (p. 169),

> image-making of any kind requires the use of representational concepts. ... [These] furnish the equivalent, in a particular medium, of the visual concepts one wishes to depict, and they find their external manifestation in the work of the pencil, the brush, the chisel.

In other words, children do not simply reproduce exactly what they see: in the language of *Sounds of Intent*, engagement in the reactive and proactive domains is out of kilter. This is because children's drawings are apparently informed as much by a functional and social understanding of objects and people in their environment as their visual qualities. This fusion of concepts and percepts seems to start in the scribbling stage, when children's first representations may be to imitate the properties of actions or things. For example, a mower may be represented as a whirling on the page – not because it *looks* like this, but because its blades *move* in circles that were emulated by the child's arm as she drew (Arnheim, *op. cit.*, p. 173). In fact, according to Arnheim, it is children's early expressive movements, indicative of their

88   Adam Ockelford

temperament and mood, which are the first source of emotional expression in art (*op. cit.*, p. 172).

This raises a further, crucial issue that must be addressed in seeking to understand children's art, including those with learning difficulties: although a completed drawing, painting or sculpture is static in time, and can be viewed as a whole (though one's eye may traverse an implied course through a fixed scene), the work in question will have been produced over time, and children's efforts may well form a narrative as they draw, paint or sculpt. As Arnheim says (*op. cit.,* p. 173):

> manual picture making ... comes about sequentially, whereas the final product is to be seen all at once. At the most elementary level this shows in the difference between the experience of drawing a line, of seeing it wind its way across the paper, like a growing line in an animation film, and the static final product, from which much of this dynamics has vanished. The circular path of a line is very different in nature from the centric symmetry of the two-dimensional circle, which remains as the final product.

Again, this shows an important difference in children's reactive and proactive engagement with their art.

Returning to his account of artistic development, Arnheim (*op. cit.*, p. 175) finds that the circle 'is the first organized shape to emerge from the more or less uncontrolled scribbles', and he contends that it is the circle that is the first thing to be representational: 'a young child in his drawings uses circular shapes to represent almost any object at all' (*op. cit.*, p. 176) – as do adult humans – the circle 'does not stand for roundness but for the more general quality of "thingness"'. The similarity between any solid object and its representation as a circle is that both are distinct units with a boundary that separates them from the 'other' beyond. And the circle is the shape of choice as it is conceptually the simplest to grasp: having no specific features beyond its perfect symmetry, it lacks attributes that could potentially conflict with the physical aspects of what it is intended to represent. As Arnheim puts it, we can be sure that a circle is intended to represent the same 'only when triangles are available as alternatives' (*op. cit.*, p. 181). This resonates with the principle in zygonic theory that imitation can exist only in the context of potential variety – if children have just a single chime-bar available to them, then, inevitably, all the pitches they produce will be the same. It is only when several notes are on offer, and children consistently choose to play the same one, we can be sure that the repetition is grounded in intentionality.

Arnheim's general caution as to the validity of any developmental model of children's art has resonances with the caveats surrounding the use of *Sounds of Intent* framework too (see Chapter 2, this volume). Arnheim states (*op. cit.*, pp. 181 and 182):

Extending the Sounds of Intent *model* 89

Only for the purpose of systematic theory can the development of form be presented as a standard sequence of neatly separated steps. It is possible and useful to isolate various phases and to arrange them in order of increasing complexity. However, this ideal sequence corresponds only roughly to what happens in any particular case. Different children will cling to different phases to different periods of time. ... The personality of the child and the influences of the environment will account for these variations. ... Earlier stages remain in use when later ones have been reached; and when confronted with a difficulty, the child may regress to a more primitive solution.

A comparable situation in the context of music would be the exposure of someone functioning broadly at *Sounds of Intent* Level 5 who was exposed to a new piece of music and being asked to join in. Since the melodic, harmonic and rhythmic detail will be unfamiliar, he or she would have little choice but to step backwards developmentally, as it were, and tap in time to the regular beat.

Finally, it is of interest to note that Arnheim dismisses claims that there is a 'fixed relation between the age of a child and the stage of his drawings' (*op. cit.*, p. 182). Again, this accords with the findings of the *Sounds of Intent* project and, subsequently, the *Sounds of Intent in the Early Years* project (Chapter 2, this volume), which found that age and stage of musical development have only the loosest of relationships.

Like many other writers and researchers, Arnheim's interest in children's art appears to be driven largely by seeking to understand its representational aspects. However, this is, of course, by no means the whole picture. Jolley (2010, p. 36), for example, reminds us of the importance of considering the expressive power in children's productions, and identifies three techniques that they use to convey meaning in what they draw or paint: literal, content and abstract expression (*op. cit.*, p. 37). In literal expression, mood is shown by 'the depiction of the facial expression in people, or through personification if shown on animals, other living things, or inanimate objects' (*ibid.*). In content expression, children use the subject matter to convey meaning. However,

without the appropriate use of what are called formal properties of the picture, such as line (its shape, thickness, direction, texture and shading), color and composition (the spatial arrangement of the elements on the page or canvass) much of the expressive potential of the chosen content would be lost.

These 'abstract' elements of art (that is, not derived through imitation of an external reality, but used on account of emotions they can evoke in viewers through their perceived expressive qualities, innate or learnt) appear to parallel the 'content' of musical sounds in zygonic theory. Hence, there is some overlap in the way that music and art work in zygonic terms, but the

90   *Adam Ockelford*

emphasis is different: in music, the *primary* source of meaning can be said to derive from its intrinsic content (the qualities of the sounds themselves) and structure (self-imitation of those qualities), while *secondary* meanings can arise through extra-musical imitation of sensory experiences beyond the piece itself (see Figure 3.9); whereas in representational art, the *primary* meaning arises as a consequence of imitation of sensations stimulated by the environment (or the imagination) of the artist, while *secondary* meanings come about through the imitation of internal features. The two may be perfectly in balance (as in Picasso's *Girl with a Mandolin* of 1910), for example. As more art becomes more abstract, so the internal content and structure assume greater importance (see Figure 3.10). As Jolley puts it (*op. cit.*, p. 38), 'if we looked at a painting that contained curved and uplifting lines, bright colors and a balanced composition we might interpret a positive mood'.

Jolley notes that while it is easy to find examples of expressive drawing such as this among children, it is not a simple matter to describe the underlying developmental pattern, on account of the subjective nature of abstract work and the differing values that may be employed in evaluating it (*op. cit.*, p. 65). However, I believe that a solution may be possible by borrowing ideas from the *Sounds of Intent* project, which, as we have seen, underpinned by zygonic theory, gauges music-developmental levels primarily by analysing abstract patterns in sound. A potential bridge between the *Sounds of Intent* approach and frameworks of artistic development is to be found in the work of Machón (2009/2013), who, in his exhaustive study of children's drawings, sets out a model that separates representational development from progress in the formal-graphic domain and shows how the two relate (Table 3.6).

We now consider these descriptors in more detail and consider how they may map onto the *Sounds of Intent* levels set out in Tables 3.1 and 3.5.

According to Machón (*op. cit.*, p. 130), a stage of 'pre-scribble' occurs around 11 months, when a child might

> 'grasp' a pencil or any other implement capable of leaving a mark and, by dragging it over a surface (the floor, a piece of paper, etc.), change the appearance of the latter with a mark or some lines. But this change will not initially be noticed by the child and, even if it is, she will not recognise it as the consequence of her own action.

This is similar to *Sounds of Intent* Level 1, which encapsulates a lack of perceptual awareness. The movement involved in producing the marks is more advanced than this, though, since it is intentional and may even, according to Machón (*ibid.*), originate in the imitation of an adult. But the 'artistic product' is produced non-intentionally and goes unrecognised by the child.

Next in Machón's taxonomy is 'uncontrolled scribble', which he contends is seen in children between 17 and 20 months, and represents the first stage of what might be termed 'artistic awareness' (Machón, *op. cit.*, p. 131). According to Read (1945, p. 126), scribbles of this type arise from the pleasure that children take in their arm movements *and*, subsequently, in the visible

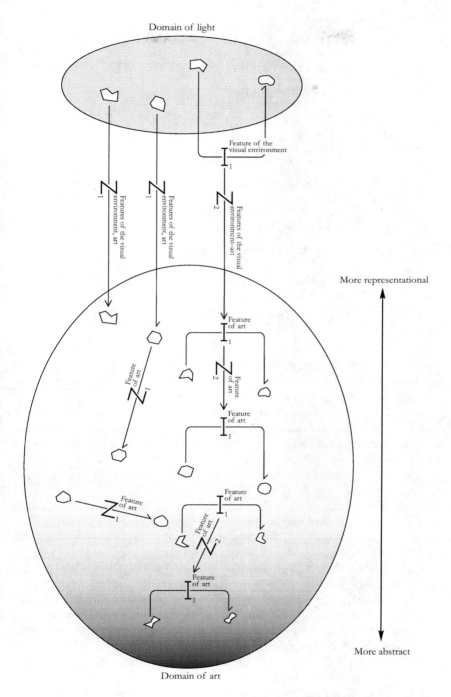

Figure 3.10 The balance between external relationships (between a work of art and the visual environment) and internal relationships (within the work of art itself) creates different degrees of representation and abstractness.

92 Adam Ockelford

Table 3.6 Framework of 'children's graphic development', from Machón (2013, p. 94)

Ages	Formal-graphic development		Representational development	
1–3		**I. Formless period** Scribbling		
0;11–1;04	0.	Pre-scribble		
1;05–1;08	1.	Stage of uncontrolled scribble		
1;09–2;07	2.	Stage of coordinated scribble	Graphomotor representations	
2;08–3;03	3.	Stage of controlled scribble		
3–4		**II. Period of form**	Graphic-symbolic representation	
3;03–3;09	1.	Stage of units	1.	The graphic symbol
3;09–4;03	2.	Stage of operations (combination)	2.	The ideogram
4–7		**III. Period of schematisation**	Figurative representation (The iconogram)	
4;03–5;03	1.	Pre-schematic stage	1.	The pre-schema
5;03–7;00	2.	Schematic stage	2.	The schema
8–10		**IV. Period of subjective realism**	Beginning of graphic notation	

traces of those movements that are left on the paper. Arnheim (1974, p. 171) describes children's interest in the marks that they leave at this developmental stage as 'simple sensory pleasure' (similar to that which is observed in primates that draw). These descriptions resonate strongly with the depiction of *Sounds of Intent* Level 2 as 'an emerging awareness of the perceived aspects of things and of the variety that is possible within each, experienced within the perceived present; a sense of agency, of intentionality' *but* with 'no cognition of repetition (and therefore no understanding of imitation)' and 'no symbolic understanding' (see Table 3.5).

Machón's 'coordinated scribble' (21–31 months) is characterised by a new 'continuity, fluidity and rhythm' of the arm movements through which children make marks. However, 'the perceptive function is [as with uncontrolled scribble, still] not yet actively involved in the configuration of the strokes ... and is limited for the time being to observing and noting the nascent graphic order' (Machón, *op. cit.*, p. 139). That is to say, in proactive terms, toddlers do not as yet attempt to imitate one mark with another. And reactively, they are not yet aware of the significance of increasingly ordered nature of what they produce – organisation that occurs accidentally. Hence, with regard to the *Sounds of Intent* framework, coordinated scribblers can still be said to be functioning at Level 2, though in a more advanced way than those whose mark-making efforts are wholly uncontrolled.

It is at this stage of 'coordinated scribble' that children first recognise that what they produce can stand for something else. However, according to Machón, toddlers at this stage of artistic development have no thought of

Extending the Sounds of Intent *model*   93

copying the features of things that they see around them, nor is there (intentional) consistency in their representations. In fact, children may well determine *post hoc* what it is that their scribbles stand for. It could be, of course, as Arnheim observes, that children's *movements* exist in imitation of what they see, and that orderly marks occur as a by-product – shown in his instance in the child's depiction of a mower cited above, and the examples of a 'wheel going fast' and a 'washing machine', drawn as circular scribbles, provided by Machón (*op. cit.*, p. 145). It is as though, in viewing the marks they have made, the child *plays* at them being representative (in the knowledge that the pictures adults make can perform this function). This is clearly a crucial stage on the journey to making 'true' representations, and one that adults instinctively encourage, pointing out features in the child's scribbles that bear a (chance) resemblance to the object that is notionally portrayed. There would appear to be a similarity here to certain activity in the domain of music, when children watch adults playing the piano or keyboard, and then bang it themselves with a regularity born of simple motor rhythms (rather than being driven through auditory considerations), and say that they are playing a familiar song. In either case (art or music), the activity would properly be characterised as being at Level 2 rather than Level 3, since imitation is not involved.

'Controlled' scribbling is said by Machón to occur between 32 and 39 months. This is the point in drawing at which 'a child's perceptive interests will take over from motor interests as a result of which the morphology of the traces of her drawing becomes the main focus of graphic activity' (Machón, *op. cit.*, p. 174). There is a problem here, though, since, as Machón concedes, the generally accepted definition of 'scribble' in the literature is of markmaking that is characterised by 'the predominance of action and motion and, therefore, to speak of "controlled scribble" [in the sense of it being directed visually] is paradoxical'. The difficulty of identifying 'controlled' scribbling as a distinct phase in children's art is compounded when one considers the developmental step that Machón next identifies, which he terms the 'stage of units' (the first part of the 'period of form'). This is distinguished by the 'making and recurring presence in children's drawings of a small group of more or less geometric shapes' which are tirelessly repeated. Yet, the supposed earlier stage of controlled scribbling appears to feature exactly this: according to Machón (*op. cit.*, p. 188), discrete shapes and patterns start to appear: strokes of various lengths, circles, spirals, zigzags and 'spots, dots and commas'.

However such shapes and designs are labelled, there is an evident affinity between artistic production of this type and *Sounds of Intent* Level 3: a 'growing awareness of how one perspective value may relate to another; a sense that one may replicate another' (see Table 3.5). But what is a 'perspective value' in the context of drawing or painting? Recall that, in music, a perspective value is the appearance of a perspect (an attribute of sound such as pitch, timbre or loudness) at any given moment in time. For simplicity's sake, in the musical analyses above, the unstated assumption was made that notes, generally thought of as the indivisible units of music (which, however,

94 Adam Ockelford

actually have a discernible duration in time), can be classed as 'values' (although strictly speaking they are 'constants', since they remain the same for a finite period, and therefore have an internal organisation of their own); see Ockelford (1999). The equivalent in art of a perspective value in music could be said to be a dot on the page, which in technical terms will have a hue, saturation and brightness (see Table 3.1), as well as a position relative to the edges of the sheet of paper on which it is drawn. In the interests of theoretical simplicity, though, it is helpful to regard the lines and circles that children make at this stage as indivisible units of their art (although, like notes, they actually have an internal orderliness). Hence, series of lines or circles that are drawn consciously with repetition in mind can be regarded as being configured both through primary zygons of 'shape' and secondary zygons of 'position' (see Figure 3.11). This accords precisely with the description of the nature and function of zygonic relationships at *Sounds of Intent* Level 3: the 'cognition of repetition within working memory; initially simple primary relationships, with secondaries becoming possible' (see Table 3.5).

What of symbolic understanding? The *Sounds of Intent* framework holds that, at Level 3, 'one thing can represent another through imitation of one or more of its qualities, or through repeated association'. As Figure 3.10 indicates, there are two possibilities here: a direct (primary or secondary) zygonic connection between an object and its representation, or a secondary zygonic link between two similar couplings of an object with an arbitrary mark (or shape) on a piece of paper (or other medium). The first of these scenarios is implicit in Machón's description of the 'stage of units' (Machón, *op. cit.*, p. 203):

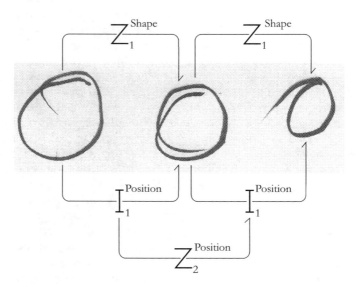

Figure 3.11 Zygonic relationships of 'shape' and 'position' thought to be at work in early children's drawing.

Extending the Sounds of Intent *model* 95

The names the child gives to them [the units] refer to the formal qualities of the strokes drawn: 'they're rounds', 'they're sticks', 'they're money' or 'they're aniseed balls'. These names ... tell us of the child's discovery of the first resemblances between the forms of drawing and those of the named objects that display these same basic formal characteristics'.

To find an account of the second type of symbolic representation (through association), we need to turn once more to Arnheim. Recall his analysis of children's early use of the circle (see above) as potentially representative of almost any object. To the extent that children, on a given occasion, use the circle consistently to represent an object or a class of objects, we can say that they are functioning at *Sounds of Intent* Level 3 in the domain of art.

Machón's 'stage of operations' (45–51 months) is chiefly about combining the units of the previous developmental phase, and creating links and connections between them (Machón, *op. cit.*, p. 209). As well as abstract patterns such as 'ladders' (a relatively long line or two parallel lines intersected at right angles with a series of shorter lines), children increasingly produce representative images, which Machón calls 'ideograms'. These are based on combinations of two units or more, and are likely to derive from functional or configural analogies – that is, representations that are based on the way something works or the topological disposition of its components (Machón, *op. cit.*, pp. 270–272). For example, ideograms may be founded on the notion of 'containment', as in the case of a large circle being made to enclose a series of smaller ones, which may held to represent a 'box of apples' or a 'bag of potatoes', for instance (Machón, *op. cit.*, p. 219). Another class of analogy, which Machón terms 'morphological', stems from 'fortuitous [visual] resemblances' (*op. cit.*, p. 276). In contrast, *intentional* similarities are held to be the province of the 'pre-schematic stage' (which is said to occupy artistic development from the age of four years three months to five years three months). Is this distinction sustainable, however?

Take, for example, children's first attempts at drawing humans, which, according to Machón, begin in the 'stage of operations' and end in the 'pre-schematic stage'. However, as we observed in relation to Kellog's taxonomy, children's representations of people gradually grow in complexity, with no obvious bipartite division. Rather, facial features are followed by arms, legs, hands and feet; and, as the child's artistic maturation continues, fingers and toes appear, during the phase that Kellog terms 'early pictorialism'. Hence, it seems more likely that what is happening here is the incremental development of combinations of 'units' that gradually acquire more verisimilitude, or, in terms of *Sounds of Intent* Level 4, 'the evolving notion of groups of perspective values as units of perception and meaning', implying the 'cognition of repetition within long-term veridical memory' with chunks 'defined internally ... through imitation', and 'more advanced symbolic understanding, through compound imitation or association' (Table 3.5).

However, there is another aspect of functioning at Level 4, and that is a growing awareness of 'the relationships that are possible between chunks',

96   *Adam Ockelford*

which may in part be defined externally through imitation (see Table 3.5). And indeed, we do find this occurring in the domain of art at Machón's pre-schematic stage, where 'we often find pages filled with drawings, accumulations of images that ... resemble samplers' (Machón, *op. cit.*, p. 335). Individual ideograms are more or less connected through their juxtaposition on the page and visual, functional or contextual similarities. However, there is no overarching coherence to what is produced, and the general effect brings to mind children's 'pot pourri' songs that are characteristic of *Sounds of Intent* Level 4, in which snatches of melody from different pieces are brought together in a musical patchwork that lacks overall tonal or metrical stability.

By contrast, Machón's 'schematic' stage (ranging from five years three months to seven years of age) sees the representation of space in two dimensions (height and width), which provides 'a link between images, relating them and making them mutually dependent, giving rise to the first scenes – coherent and unitary compositions that fill the whole sheet' (Machón, *op. cit.*, p. 335). Pictures become framed by a ground (the lower edge of the sheet of paper or sometimes a horizontal line) on which the subjects of the drawing stand (*op. cit.*, p. 369), and a sky, variously populated with the sun, moon, stars, and, nearer to earth, birds and aeroplanes. The fit with *Sounds of Intent* Level 5 seems irresistible, with its 'growing understanding and appreciation of complete works of art (in any domain or domains), and the conventions of structure and content that underpin them', underpinned by 'the cognition of repetition within long-term schematic memory [through] formal frames of reference [and] simple structural archetypes' (Table 3.5). That is to say, the convention of representing horizontality and verticality through height and width on the page provides an imaginary matrix (equivalent to pitch and time in music) upon which individual elements can be placed and related to one another. But what of the notion of a 'symbolic narrative over time'? Although, as we have seen, pictures are created in time, and children may well re-live narratives as they draw or paint, to the viewer, this sequence of events may be lost. However, representations of scenes from life often do capture a (short) period rather than a snapshot in time, when we can see things are happening that are contingent upon one another. And even where what is portrayed appears to be entirely static, the viewer's perception will not be, as the eye is drawn to rove from one element to another in a composition.

And so we reach the final stage of Machón's taxonomy: 'subjective realism'. Here, the picture plane becomes 'transparent', opening up a third dimension (foreground and background), and the narrative nature of scenes is enhanced by depiction of movement, gestures and attitudes in human figures (Machón, *op. cit.*, p. 380). Still, though, this could not be classed as the 'mature artistic expression' characteristic of *Sounds of Intent* Level 6. Hence, it appears that Machón's account of the development of children's drawings ends at Level 5.

To find accounts of young people, who, according to the *Sounds of Intent* Level 6 descriptor, show 'a growing awareness of the impact of artistic production on others', 'an evolving appreciation of culturally determined aesthetic

Extending the Sounds of Intent *model*   97

values and the expressive nature of art', 'imitation of expressive devices of creation' and an 'awareness of the impact of a symbolic narrative on others within a known culture' (Table 3.5), we need to return to Lowenfeld's sixth stage of artistic development, which occurs in adolescence. Here, as their technical skills evolve, so young people's artistic expression becomes more sophisticated and detailed, and, with appropriate support, embedded in their increased awareness of themselves as members of society, a mature sense of aesthetics will develop (Lowenfeld, 1947). However, young people typically do not reach this stage unless they are explicitly taught, although there are exceptions, both within the neurotypical and learning-disabled populations, as the well-known examples of Nadia and Stephen Wiltshire show (see Selfe, 1977; Wiltshire and Casson, 1987; Wiltshire, 1989, 1991), who both demonstrated prodigious talent at an early age. To what extent savants like Nadia and Stephen, as children, could possibly have appreciated the impact of their work in a wider cultural context is a moot point – just as it was with musical savants like Derek Paravicini, who could perform persuasively in adult contexts as a ten-year-old, despite having a severe, global developmental delay and little or no understanding of the wider world. However, it is also true to say that both Stephen and Derek, through being systematically taught and encouraged in their artistic endeavours as teenagers, and through the rich range of social contacts that their creative efforts brought them, matured socially and emotionally as young adults and, now in their late 30s, both have a sense of the value and place of what they do in the artistic communities to which they belong.

We are now in a position to map the general version of the *Sounds of Intent* levels shown in Table 3.5 onto Machón's developmental framework – see Table 3.7. This has a number of interesting features. The order in which stages occur fits without modification, although the 'boundaries' between them (which, reality, of course, are fuzzy) differ. That is to say, while the terminology, as a reflection of the way in which stages are conceptualised, may be dissimilar, the theorised direction of developmental travel is the same in each case. However, there is a major difference between the age ranges at which musical milestones are neurotypically met and their artistic equivalents, with musical development initially outstripping art, until the two converge again at Level 6 in adolescence. The extent to which learning difficulties impact on the age at which different abilities evolve is, as the original *Sounds of Intent* project and Maureen Cox's work (cited above) show, very variable. While there may be a delay in musical and artistic development in keeping with a child's global level of maturation, this need by no means always be the case – particularly with those who are on the autism spectrum in addition to having learning difficulties. Clearly, further research is required to ascertain how musical and artistic development relate among special populations.

Using this information, it is possible to postulate what a developmental model in the domain of art that uses the *Sounds of Intent* framework, with its three domains (reactive, proactive and interactive), may look like (see Table 3.8). The table includes sculpture, mentioned only peripherally

Table 3.7 The general *Sounds of Intent* framework mapped onto Machón's taxonomy

Ages	Machón's taxonomy	General Sounds of Intent level	Potential artistic descriptor	Musical descriptor	Typical age range for music
1–3 0;11–1;04 1;05–1;08 1;09–2;07 2;08–3;03	**I. Formless** 1. Pre-scribble 2. Uncontrolled scribble 3. Coordinated scribble 4. Controlled scribble	1	**Pre-scribble**	Confusion and chaos	Before –3 months
		2	**Scribble**	Awareness and intentionality	From –3 months
3–4 3;03–3;09 3;09–4;03	**II. Form** 5. Units; graphic symbols 6. Operations; ideograms; combinations	3	**Pattern** (and the beginning of representation and symbolism)	Relationships, repetition, regularity	From 12 months
		4	**Shape** (simple moving to compound)	Notes forming clusters	From 24 months
4–7 4;03–5;03 5;03–7;00	**III. Schematisation** 7. Pre-schematic stage 8. Schematic stage	5	**Composition** (schematic)	Deeper structural links	From 48 months
8–10	**IV. Subjective realism**				
	Arnheim	6	**Cultural schemata**	Mature artistic expression	From adolescence
Adolescence	'Period of decision'				

Table 3.8 Proposed framework of artistic development using the *Sounds of Intent* model

Genre		(Fine) Arts (painting, drawing and sculpture)					
Domain		Reactive		Proactive		Interactive	
Level 1	C	Encounters things that could potentially be seen (but does not process visual or tactual information)		Unknowingly does things and is unaware that others see or feel them		Relates to other people unwittingly through vision or touch	
Level 2	I	Shows an emerging awareness of visual images and tactual sensations		Deliberately does things for others to see (e.g., scribbles on paper, moulds clay)		Interacts with others using vision or touch (e.g., eye points to gain shared attention)	
		Abstract	**Representational**	**Abstract**	**Representational**	**Abstract**	**Representational**
Level 3	R	Is aware of simple visual and tactual patterns (e.g., repeated blobs of colour, balls of clay)	Is aware of the imitation of simple features of an object in a representation of it (e.g., colour, shape)	Creates simple patterns (e.g., repeated blobs of colour, lines that are intentionally more or less straight)	Copies simple features of things (e.g., blob of appropriate colour for tree, circle for face)	Engages with another to create simple visual patterns (through imitation)	Engages with another to imitate simple visual features of things

(Continued)

Genre		(Fine) Arts (painting, drawing and sculpture)				
Domain		Reactive		Proactive		Interactive
		The beginnings of Gestalt perception				
Level 4	C	Individual features of things are perceived together to form 'wholes' (e.g., dots forming a line; approximate shapes become 'corrected' in memory)	Is aware that whole objects can be represented (symbolically)	Creates whole shapes from two or more simple elements (e.g., a square comprising four straight lines)	Draws or sculpts entire objects (and can complete 'teapot with parts missing' puzzle and similar)	Engages with another to create simple visual or tactual wholes from parts	Engages with another to create representations of things visually or tactually
Level 5	L	Is aware of the composition of the whole of a work of art, abstract or representational, and basic conventions pertaining thereto (e.g., perspective), and the potential meaning of the art work as a whole		Creates art works comprising several elements that are coherently composed and have a meaning as a whole		Engages with others in creating art works comprising several elements that are coherently composed and have a meaning as a whole
Level 6	E	Is aware of styles of abstract or representative art (or both) and their social, cultural or historical contexts; shows mature aesthetic appreciation; understands *conceptual* art		Creates works of art, with an awareness of its potential aesthetic and cultural impact on others		Engages with others to create works of art with a shared awareness of their potential aesthetic and cultural impact

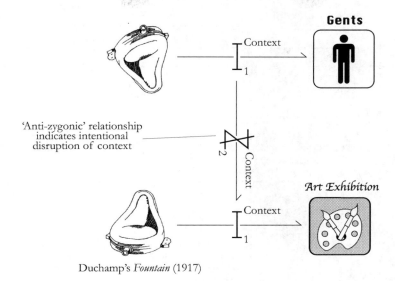

Figure 3.12 Duchamp's *Fountain* achieves its status as conceptual art by deliberately failing to imitate the culturally accepted context of a urinal.

above, whose descriptors work in parallel or are embedded in those pertaining to vision. An important distinction is drawn between representational art and abstract art, which, as the foregoing analysis suggests, are held to diverge at Level 3, before potentially converging at Level 5. Note that the 'interactive' domain is almost entirely theoretically driven, since there appears to have been little or no research on how children engage in artistic activity with others, although for those with learning difficulties, this is clearly a crucial area for further investigation.

Observe that 'conceptual' art, which is not mentioned in the developmental literature, is included at Level 6, since this requires an understanding of cultural expectations, which are consciously disregarded, implying 'antizygonic' relationships of association – see Figure 3.12.

Movement, gesture, mime and dance

There appears to have been no research undertaken into the development of what is termed here 'movement, gesture, mime and dance', the classic work of Laban (Newlove and Dalby, 2004) and Sherborne (1993/2001) notwithstanding, neither of which is truly developmental in its approach. Similarly, the more scientific approaches from the fields of the health sciences, with their focus on physicality, do not address issues of creativity or symbolism. Hence, the following framework is offered as an initial foray into the field, taking as its starting point the descriptors from Table 4.6. See Table 4.10.

Table 3.9 Proposed framework for the development of movement, gesture, mime and dance based on the *Sounds of Intent* model

Genre		Movement, gesture, mime and dance		
Domain		*Reactive*	*Proactive*	*Interactive*
Level 1	C	Is unaware of being moved or of movement in the external environment	Makes movements unwittingly (including reflexes)	Relates unwittingly through movement
Level 2	I	Is aware of being moved and movement in the external environment	Moves intentionally	Interacts with others using movement
Level 3	R	Is aware of simple patterns of abstract movement in people (e.g., 'to and fro'), that these can have meaning (as gestures), and how movements can imitate the simple movements of other people, animals or things and thereby symbolise them	Creates simple patterns of abstract movement intentionally (e.g., rocking to and fro); can use simple movements as gestures; and can imitate the simple movements of other people, animals or things, and is aware of their potentially symbolic import (i.e., by moving like someone else, you may indicate that you are pretending to be them)	Engages with others through imitating simple patterns of abstract, gestural or imitative movement
Level 4	C	Understands how individual movements can combine to form short abstract sequences, which may be abstract, gestural or imitative of external combinations	Creates or re-creates short, coherent abstract sequences of movements which may be abstract, gestural or imitative of external combinations; these may form fragments of mime or dance	Engages with another to create or re-create short, coherent abstract sequences of movements which may be abstract, gestural or imitative of external combinations; these may form fragments of mime or dance
Level 5	L	Understands and responds to short, simple, conventional routines of movement that may form mime or dance	Creates or re-creates short, simple, conventional routines of movement that may form mime or dance	Creates or re-creates short, simple, conventional routines of movement with other that may form mime or dance
Level 6	E	Appreciates extended and complex routines of mime or dance within cultural or stylistic artistic contexts, and potentially as metaphorical narratives	Creates or re-creates extended and complex routines of mime or dance within known cultural or stylistic contexts, and uses to express metaphorical narrative	Engages with others to create or re-create extended and complex routines of mime or dance within known cultural or stylistic contexts, and uses to express metaphorical narrative

Table 3.10 Proposed framework for the development of language and drama, based on the *Sounds of Intent* framework

Genre		Language and drama					
Domain		Reactive		Proactive		Interactive	
Level 1	C	Encounters vocal sounds		Makes vocal sounds unknowingly		Relates unwittingly through vocal sounds	
Level 2	I	Shows an emerging awareness of vocal sound		Makes vocal sounds intentionally		Interacts with others using vocal sounds	
		3rd person narrative	**1st person narrative**	**3rd person narrative**	**1st person narrative**	**3rd person narrative**	**1st person narrative**
Level 3	R	Understands the meanings of some sounds (made by humans and non-humans) and some individual words	Understands that hearing someone imitate a sound or word made by another person, an object or an animal; they can potentially pretend to be it	Uses some sounds and words to mean things	Imitates the sounds and words made by other people, animals or objects, to pretend to be them	Interacts through using sounds or words	Engages in interactive pretend play using sounds and words
Level 4	C	Understands the meanings of some short combinations of words	Understands that one person can pretend to be another (or a non-human) through imitating short combinations of words they use and vocal tone	Uses combinations of words with meaning	Uses short combinations of words to pretend to be someone or something else	Engages in dialogues using short combinations of words	Engages in imaginary play with another using short combinations of words

(Continued)

Genre		Language and drama					
Domain		Reactive		Proactive		Interactive	
Level 5	L	Intuitively understands syntax and form in simple speech, prose and poetry	Understands the meaning of short plays or narratives in which people take parts, pretending to be others	Speaks grammatically in sentences and connects these to create coherent meaning over time, factual or imagined	Acts simple parts (improvised or learnt) in monologues	Converses with others exchanging day-to-day ideas and feelings, and to tell or re-tell stories or poems	Acts with others in short, simple dramatic scenarios
Level 6	E	Has mature understanding of prose (fiction or non-fiction) and poetry and the narratives they create; has an aesthetic appreciation in cultural context in which materials were created	Has mature understanding of drama and the narratives it creates; has an aesthetic appreciation in cultural context in which it was created or is performed	Creates mature prose (fiction or non-fiction) or poetry, with an understanding of the potential impact on audiences	Performs or improvises drama in a mature way, with an increasing understanding of the potential impact on audiences	Creates mature prose (fiction or non-fiction) or poetry with others, with an increasing understanding of the potential impact on audiences	Acts maturely with others in plays, with an increasing understanding of the potential impact on audiences

Language and drama

At the first blush, 'language and drama' may appear to be an odd coupling, since there is so much more to drama than language, as Table 3.10 shows. However, given that language can be more than the recognition or production of words, and can also exist in media other than sound (for example, through sign), the model that follows is consciously limited for the sake of conceptual simplicity, and to serve as a potential starting point to permit wider interpretations to be developed in the future. Again, there appears to be little, if any, research that takes the creative-developmental perspective offered here, so what follows is necessarily conjectural. See Table 3.10.

Conclusion

This chapter has explored the possibility that the hierarchy of cognitive skills identified in relation to the development of musical understanding may have a broader applicability, extending across different perceptual domains, including vision and proprioception. These in turn underpin different areas of artistic endeavour. The new taxonomies that are presented appear to be theoretically persuasive and to accord with the findings of previous work in this field, insofar as any has been undertaken. Whether or not the surface commonalities arise from a single supramodal processor in the brain is a moot point (Thorpe, 2015). Clearly, this is an important area for future research, particularly from the perspective of practitioners working with those with profound intellectual impairments; for if the recognition of simple patterns at the highest level (irrespective of perceptual domain) is indeed the responsibility of a single region in the brain, then there is the real prospect of carefully coordinated multisensory work having an impact beyond the sum of its individual strands.

In the meantime, the first empirical work has been undertaken by Jenny Cooper, Head of Expressive Arts, and her team at The Village School, which is situated in the London Borough of Brent, UK. As part of her master's studies at the University of Roehampton, Cooper explored the potential of the *Sounds of Intent* framework being used in relation to art (painting, drawing and sculpture) for children with profound and multiple difficulties between the ages of 7 and 14. Twelve children were observed a total of 63 times. The headline descriptors shown in Figure 3.9 were found to offer a serviceable map of their engagement with art at Levels 1–3, although some simplification was felt to be desirable to make the framework more accessible for classroom practitioners (see Table 3.11). The project became known as 'Marks of Intent'.

The 'Marks of Intent' study raised a number of pedagogical issues in relation to art education for children and young people with profound and multiple learning difficulties, including:

- the value of appreciating *process* in the creation of *products*,
- the importance of interaction in experiential learning,

106   *Adam Ockelford*

- the crucial role of movement in early art development,
- the need to consider what constitutes appropriate tools, techniques and materials,
- the potential barrier to production that physical disability can cause,
- the high level of detailed assessment needed to understand children's engagement with art, and
- the fact that products may be intended to be representational even when we do not recognise them as such.

A further research project at The Village School investigated the framework set out in Table 3.9 – the possible read across from Sounds of Intent to the domain of movement, gesture mime and dance – for children and young people with profound and multiple learning difficulties. 'Movements of Intent', as the study was called, took 250 observations of 14 children, aged 5–14, in their dance sessions. The first three levels of the framework shown in Table 3.9 were found to be a usable and potentially powerful tool that practitioners could use to encourage the development of dance in those with the most complex disabilities. Conceptualising what the pupils did in terms of the framework demonstrated that those with profound and multiple disabilities can have their achievements recognised, and, in some cases, make progress in terms of their capacity for kinaesthetic and creative engagement. Cooper noted that the use of the framework gave a metaphorical voice to

Table 3.11 Simplified descriptors, Levels 1–3, of 'Marks of Intent'

Level	R, P or I	Descriptor
1	Reactive	Encounters things that could potentially be seen or felt
1	Proactive	Unknowingly makes changes in their visual, tactile or haptic environment
1	Interactive	Relates unwittingly with others through changes in the visual, tactile or haptic environment
2	Reactive	Shows an awareness of visual images and tactile sensations
2	Proactive	Intentionally makes changes in the visual, tactile or haptic domain
2	Interactive	Interacts with others by responding to changes in the visual, tactile or haptic domain or by changing something themselves
3	Reactive	Recognises simple visual, tactile or haptic patterns and/or realises that an element of art (such as a shape or colour) can stand for something else
3	Proactive	Intentionally makes simple patterns in the visual, tactile or haptic domain (for example, a series of indentations in clay) and/or copies simple features of things (as in colour matching, for example) which may but need not be understood as symbolising the object concerned
3	Interactive	Copies patterns in the visual, tactile or haptic domain and/ or is aware of own patterns being copied

Extending the Sounds of Intent *model*   107

pupils who were not previously able to show their preferred learning style. Listening to this voice and showing the children's achievements could be used to spread the belief that *all* learners can engage with dance, irrespective of the profundity of their needs.

Clearly, compared to the Sounds of Intent framework, 'Movements of Intent' is still in its infancy, with six broadly defined levels and no detailed 'elements' to cover the range of activities that might be on offer. Cooper's study fleshed out what needs to be incorporated into the framework in order for it to be used by professionals in the field and for it to be seen as sitting comfortably within the developmental movement context that they value. In particular:

- the use of touch needs to be embedded in the dance education for those with profound needs – touch of different qualities and styles, not just as gesture but also as a way to communicate, increase body awareness and interact with a partner;
- the use of props appears to foster progress, including, amongst other things, parachutes, lycra, sarees, musical instruments hanging from ribbons, feathers, ribbon sticks and bubbles;
- reactions, deliberate movements and interactions involving the developmental movement elements described by Laban need to be overtly present in the framework, including, though not limited to, movement involving the vertical, horizontal and sagittal planes, time, space, weight, shape, phrasing and flow.

These elements will be incorporated into the next iteration of the framework.

4 Expectations generated on hearing a piece of music on more than one occasion
Evidence from a musical savant

Adam Ockelford and Ruth Grundy

Introduction

This chapter builds on the research reported by Grundy and Ockelford (2014), which explored the expectations evoked on hearing a piece of music for the first time using data gathered from a musical savant (Derek Paravicini). The procedure was as follows: Derek was asked to play a newly created piece (the *Romantic Rollercoaster*) at the same time as he heard it for the first time. For him to succeed meant his being able to anticipate what notes were coming next at any given point. The probability of Derek predicting an event correctly was hypothesised to be a function of the number of zygonic relationships through which it was implied. This theory was supported by the data that were gathered. However, the experiment did not end after the first hearing. Nine further trials were conducted to ascertain how expectations developed with repeated exposure to the same material. It is the outcome of these that are reported here.

Zygonic theory and expectation in music

The capacity of music to communicate complex ideas and emotions through narratives in sound that unfold over seconds, minutes and even hours is particularly extraordinary given the fact that everything is perceived through the single, narrow slit of time that we think of as the 'present moment', producing a series of fleeting auditory sensations that subsequently have to be consolidated in the mind. This means that virtually all our experience of music actually arises from *memories* of events that have past. Accessing these memories, both short and long term, is an essential part of the listening process, enabling us to contextualise the new fragments of auditory data – notes and chords – that constantly assail us as we hear a work. However, by providing a frame of reference from the past, memory does more than allow us to make sense of the present: it means that, cognitively, we can escape the shackles of time in the other direction – the future – through fuelling imagination, and enabling us to anticipate what may occur next.

Evidence from a musical savant   109

But how precisely does this process work? What is it about the past and its relationship to the present that makes anticipation possible?

Zygonic theory offers a theoretical framework through which these questions can be answered. The line of reasoning goes as follows. Music makes sense since its elements are coherently organised. Such coherence demands that each musical event is perceived to be logically related to another or others. As we saw in Chapter 1, it is hypothesised that logical relationships in music – which are said to function 'zygonically' – occur through the perception of repetition that is imbued with a sense of intentionality, or *imitation*. Zygonic relationships may function *reactively*, in recognition of imitation that has past, or *proactively*, to predict what may occur in the future. It is through the second category – proactive zygonic relationships – that musical expectation is believed to operate.

To analyse possible scenarios, let us first (and hypothetically) imagine that the only musical experience available to a listener from which to project what may come next is that stemming from the perceived present. By definition, change is not possible within that experience (since that would imply the passing of time). Hence, in these circumstances, anticipation must occur from single appearances of the qualities of sound that are available in the moment (principally, pitch, loudness and timbre), and the only logical projection is for sameness or similarity in one or more of these domains (see Figure 4.1).

However, most musical structure involves the imitation of *change* in the domains of pitch and perceived time. Change requires that a musical element exist in two states at different times. Therefore, the logical anticipation of change, through *secondary* or *tertiary* zygonic relationships, necessarily involves memory. It can take three forms, occurring between *events*, *groups* and *frameworks* of pitch and perceived time (see Ockelford, 2006; Chapter 1, this volume). To hear these different forms of anticipation in action, and to understand the role that zygonic relationships are thought to play in them, we will take the opening motif of the theme from *Eye Level* by Jack Trombey. Imagine that a listener, new to the piece, has heard the second appearance of the opening melodic motif as far as the third note (see Figure 4.2). What is he or she likely to think will occur next?

First, at the level of *events*, it is hypothesised that the ascent of one scale degree and the inter-onset interval of around a quarter of a second, first heard between Notes 1 and 2, and imitated between Notes 2 and 3 through secondary zygonic relationships, will spawn further, similar imitation (see Figure 4.3).

Second, at the level of *groups*, it is suggested that hearing the opening of the motif will evoke a memory of the same thing heard moments earlier, leading to an expectation that the pattern will continue in the same way as before (see Figure 4.4).

Third, at the level of *frameworks*, it is postulated that hearing the leading note (7) will evoke memories of previous leading notes that generally rise

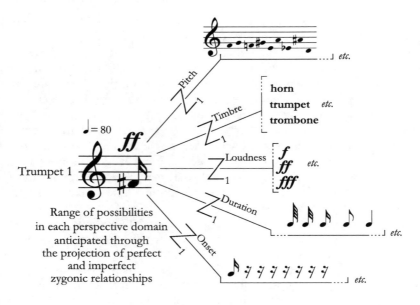

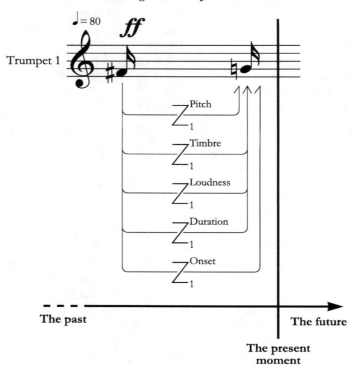

Figure 4.1 Range of continuations suggested by the opening note of *A Survivor from Warsaw* (1947), and the option selected by Schoenberg.

Figure 4.2 A fragment of the opening melody of *Eye Level*.

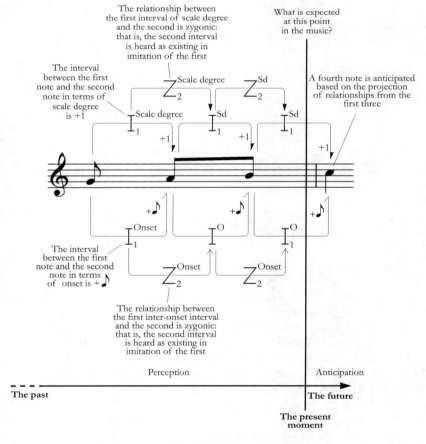

Figure 4.3 The projection of the fourth note of the second appearance of the opening motif of *Eye Level*, based on the patterning of pitch and perceived time set up by the first three notes.

112 *Adam Ockelford and Ruth Grundy*

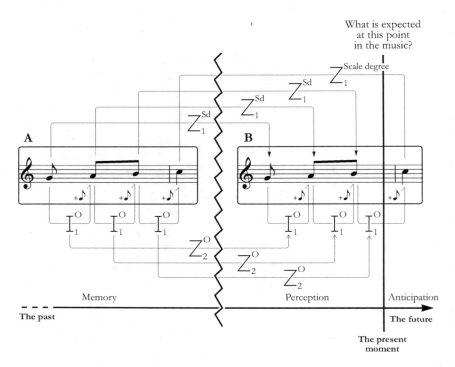

Figure 4.4 The projection of the fourth note of the second appearance of the opening motif ('B') of *Eye Level* based on the patterning of pitch and perceived time set up by the first appearance of the motif ('A').

to the tonic (1̂), fuelling the anticipation that this transition will occur once again through statistical learning (*cf.* Saffran, 2003; Aslin and Newport, 2012); see Figure 4.5.

These three forms of anticipation underpin the zygonic model of implication and expectation in music, the first version of which appeared in Ockelford (2006), which shows how they function *together* in the listening experience (see Figure 4.6).

All musical structures are initially perceived as part of a listening experience and are first encoded in working memory. Some are remembered longer term and are stored in one of two ways: 'veridically' or 'schematically' (Bharucha, 1987). A 'veridical' memory is the representation of a particular chunk of music, like the 'hook' of a familiar pop song, for example, while a 'schematic' memory arises from the consolidation of many musical experiences, deriving from the similarities that exist between them, such as the pattern of harmonies that make up the 12-bar blues. So veridical memories

Evidence from a musical savant 113

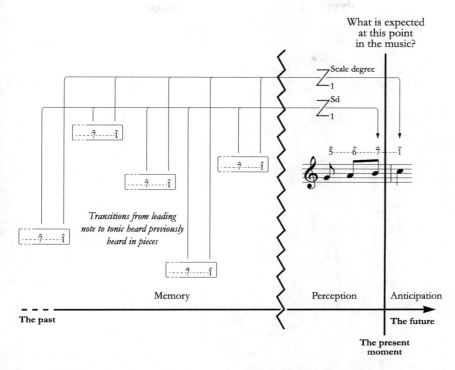

Figure 4.5 The projection of the fourth note of the second appearance of the opening motif of *Eye Level* based on previously heard transitions from the leading note to the tonic.

relate to particular *fragments* of music, while episodic memories pertain to more general *features*. There are parallels here with 'episodic' and 'semantic' forms of memory, which relate respectively to the *particular* and the *general*. Structures processed in working memory can function in relation to events (see Figure 4.3) or groups (Figure 4.4). Remembered structures pertain to frameworks (Figure 4.5) or groups. For example, a listener to *Eye Level* who was familiar with the piece before may predict what would happen after the third note of the melody based on the principle that the motif will follow the same path as in previous hearings (through a process similar to that set out in Figure 4.4).

The zygonic model further predicts that the balance of forms of expectation will change as a listener repeatedly experiences a piece on different occasions. It is postulated that, on a first hearing, *general* expectations will dominate, with *specific* projections being limited to groups of events (motifs, melodies, harmonic sequences and rhythms) that re-occur. As the listener

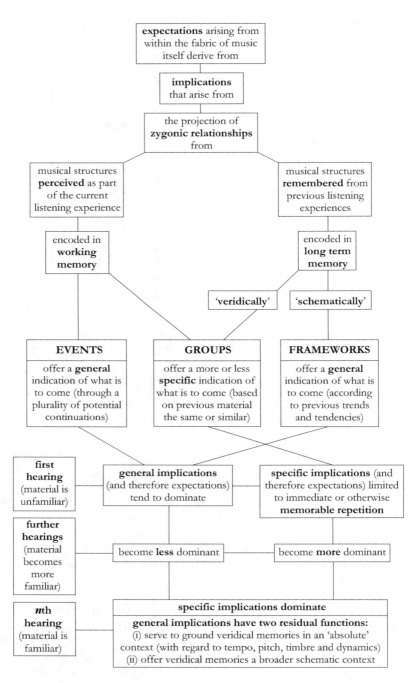

Figure 4.6 The zygonic model of implication and expectation in music.

Evidence from a musical savant   115

gets to know the piece better, *specific* forms of anticipation will become predominant, with *general* projections (at the level of frameworks) providing a backdrop that offers a broader context.

The origin of this thinking, like so many theories in contemporary cognitive musicology, lies in the pioneering work of Leonard Meyer (Meyer, 1956, 1967). Meyer's ideas sprang from two main sources: *Gestalt* perception and information theory, the former relating to what is termed in the zygonic model 'within-group' implication, and the latter to implications heard *between* groups of events, schematically encoded (Bharucha, 1987, p. 4) – that is, at a probabilistic level. Eugene Narmour incorporated both of these strands in his 'implication-realization' model (Narmour, 1977, 1990, 1992, 1996). This subsequently found some support in empirical studies (Schellenberg, 1996, 1997; Thompson and Stainton, 1996), which showed that simplification leads to little diminution of the predictive power of Narmour's model. Moreover, von Hippel and Huron's (2000) cross-cultural analysis of melodies indicated that Narmour's key principle of 'registral return' (a form of 'within-group' structure in the present terminology) could be explained as an artefact of constraints on range. Much of this work is consolidated and developed in David Huron's book *Sweet Anticipation* (Huron, 2006), which summarises his own thinking in this area and that of Bret Aarden (2003) and Elizabeth Margulis up to that point (2003, 2005). Here, there is an emphasis on the statistical modelling of expectation (broadly speaking, anticipating what will occur next on the basis of how frequently and in what contexts it has occurred in the past). In all this work, it is the expectations potentially generated between groups of musical events that are schematically encoded in memory that are downplayed (if not overlooked), and it is this lacuna in particular that the zygonically derived model was intended to fill.

A series of empirical studies, utilising different methodologies, have tested different strands of the model and explored in detail how they function. For example, Thorpe, Aksentijevic and Ockelford (2010) examined expectations in the domain of pitch at the level of *events* and *groups* in working memory during the first hearing of a piece (see Figure 4.7). Forty subjects were played a diatonic melody, starting with the initial note only, then the first two notes and so on. Each time, subjects were asked to sing what they considered to be the most likely continuation. The results were compared with the outputs of three algorithms derived from the zygonic model (using primary relationships only), which took into account adjacency ('Z1'); adjacency and recency ('Z2'); and adjacency, recency and between-group projections ('Z3'). Each algorithm modelled the perceptual responses with statistically distinct degrees of accuracy; Z3 was the most faithful to subjects' expectations, lending support to the hypothesis that projections at the level of events give only a general sense of what is to come, while expectations arising from the repetition of groups are specific, enabling listeners to anticipate *what* and *when* with a high degree of fidelity.

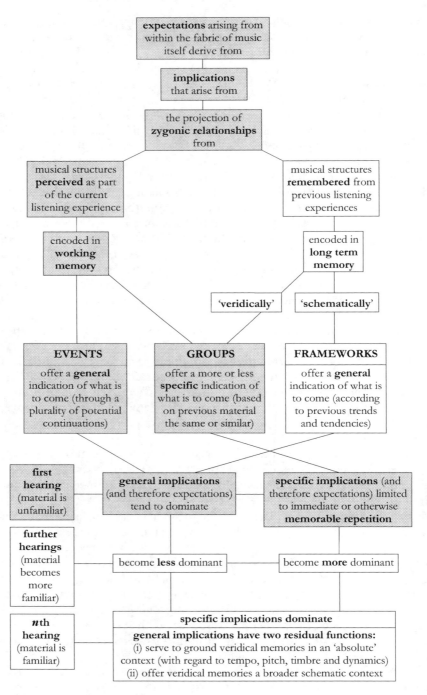

Figure 4.7 The elements of the zygonic model of implication and expectation investigated by Thorpe, Ockelford and Aksentijevic (2010).

Evidence from a musical savant   117

Hayley Trower (2011) undertook a preliminary investigation of a different aspect of the zygonic model – that pertaining to repeated hearings – using a different approach. The experiment is reported in more detail in Chapter 5 of this volume, but for now, suffice it say that her research subjects (N = 14) were presented with 16 pairs of short melodic sequences in the major mode. Subjects continuously evaluated the perceived predictability of each note in the sequences, which were presented in pairs separated by a distractor, using a proprietary device known as the 'Continuous Response Measurement Apparatus' or 'CReMA' (Himonides, 2011). This takes the form of a fixed ribbon, around 40 cm long, presented to subjects laterally. They place a finger on the ribbon, and move it left or right to rate what they are perceiving, in accordance with whatever instructions they are given. In Trower's case, the centre was said to represent a 'neutral' position with regard to melodic expectancy, with positions further to the left intended to indicate that a given pitch was perceived to be increasingly 'unexpected' or 'surprising', and locations further to the right showing a note pitch was more 'expected' or 'predictable'. The CReMA data are outputted in MIDI format, with a linear relationship between a subject's changing finger position and an assigned number. In Trower's experiment, the higher the number, the more expected a pitch was reckoned to be. For ease of analysis, the data were normalised, whereby the leftmost position on the CReMA (which equated to a pitch being 'totally unexpected') was assigned a value of 0, and the rightmost point (which corresponded to a pitch being 'completely expected') was allocated a rating of 1.

The zygonic model predicts that, during first hearing, when material is unfamiliar, *general* expectations will tend to dominate, based on any structural relationships that may exist between the events and the probabilities of pitch transitions deriving from their tonal implications. On the second hearing, subjects will have some memory of the melodic fragment concerned, though this, in tandem with a lack of contextual information, means that it will not initially be entirely clear whether this is 'the same thing again' or not (see Figure 4.8).

Hence, we would expect that the expectancies would generally be stronger than those felt in relation to the first hearing, and that they would rise as the segment progresses. Trower's data provide initial evidence that these predictions are correct. The mean predictability rating of the pitches following the first in the initial hearing of the short melodies was 0.58 and in the second hearing, 0.62; a statistically significant difference $t(47)$ = 7.03, $p < 0.001$. See Figure 4.9. The *differences* between the mean predictability ratings of the same three pitches in the initial hearing and the second were 0.028, 0.038 and 0.052, a consistent rise that reflects a statistically significant interaction between the hearing (first or second) and the sequential position of a pitch in the melody (second, third or fourth): $F(15,30)$ = 2.86, $p = 0.007$.

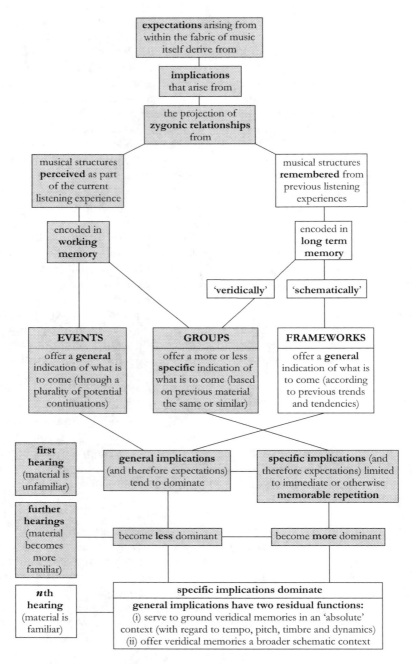

Figure 4.8 The elements of the zygonic model of implication and expectation investigated by Trower (2011).

Evidence from a musical savant 119

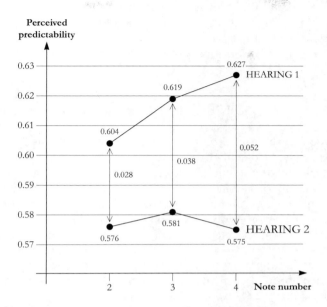

Figure 4.9 The changing predictability of pitches in the first and second hearings of a melodic fragment (after Trower, 2011).

The first *Romantic Rollercoaster* study

The current authors investigated the expectations evoked on hearing a piece of music for the first time (*cf*. Figure 4.7) utilising an entirely novel methodology (Grundy and Ockelford, 2014). This entailed asking the prodigious musical savant Derek Paravicini to play along with an original composition (the *Romantic Rollercoaster*), created especially for the experiment, at the same time as listening to it. Derek's goal was to produce, immediately and in real time, a synchronised replica of the unfamiliar piece to the best of his ability. Although this may appear to have been an impossibly contrived thing to expect of him, as far as Derek was concerned, the approach had a high degree of ecological validity, since it is typical of his preferred method of learning new material (and, indeed, is commonplace in aural traditions). But how could 'synchronous imitation' be possible on a first hearing?

Clearly, this could only occur where Derek was able to anticipate correctly what was coming next in *Romantic Rollercoaster*. And to the extent that his response accorded with a zygonic analysis of the piece (whereby elements that were theoretically predictable were, in fact, realised, and those that were reckoned not to be foreseeable were not anticipated), the experiment offered evidence of the validity of the zygonic model. But more than this, the methodology allowed Grundy and Ockelford to test the hypothesis that elements of a piece can be predicted with different levels of confidence, depending on the number of zygonic relationships from which they may theoretically be derived. That is to say, in formal terms, the probability ('P') of Derek anticipating an event correctly ('E_c') is held to be a function of the number of zygonic relationships through which it is implied ('$\#Z$'):

$$P(E_c) = f(\#Z).$$

Thus, $P(E_c)$ can reasonably be regarded as a *proxy measure* of structural strength.

The success of the *Romantic Rollercoaster* experiment was dependent on Derek finding the task neither too easy nor too difficult, since had he been able to anticipate all potentially predictable material through only one zygonic relationship, or had he been wholly unable to foresee what was coming (or only after a large number of hearings), then differentiation of varying structural strengths on the basis of his performance would not have been possible. Rather, what was needed, in terms of stimulus design, was a piece whose level of complexity was such that Derek would have a modest probability of anticipating material correctly through any one zygonic relationship. The likelihood of elements being predicted through two relationships or more could then be extrapolated from that.

The first eight bars of *Romantic Rollercoaster* are shown in Figure 4.10, annotated to depict the number of zygonic relationships through which

Figure 4.10 The opening eight bars of *Romantic Rollercoaster*, annotated to show the strength of structural derivation of each note.

each note derives from those that precede (where no number is present, the note cannot be considered to be generated structurally by any that precede).

Figures 4.11–4.13 provide examples of derivation from a single source, two sources and three sources, respectively. All of these occur between *groups* of notes, with the specificity that this allows. Potential connections between individual musical events and at the schematic level are minimised as far as possible to facilitate analysis. A fuller account is given by Grundy and Ockelford (2014).

Using this information, we were able to build a model that predicted the probability of Derek anticipating any given note correctly, based on its theoretically derived structural strength. To this end, certain initial assumptions were made. First, it was assumed that there was a constant

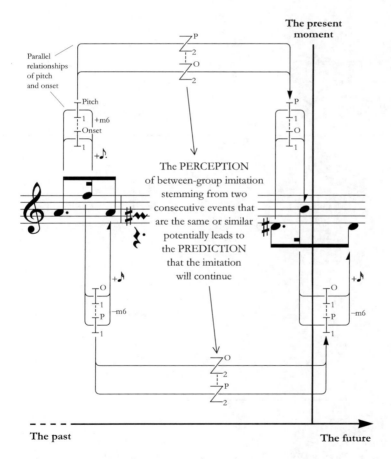

Figure 4.11 The first note in *Romantic Rollercoaster* that can be predicted on the basis of what has gone before (through single zygonic relationships in the domain of onset and pitch).

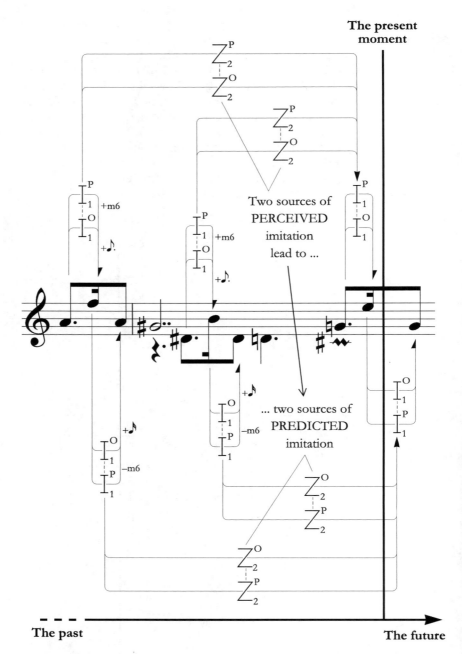

Figure 4.12 The first note in *Romantic Rollercoaster* that can be predicted on the basis of two zygonic relationships in the domain of onset and pitch.

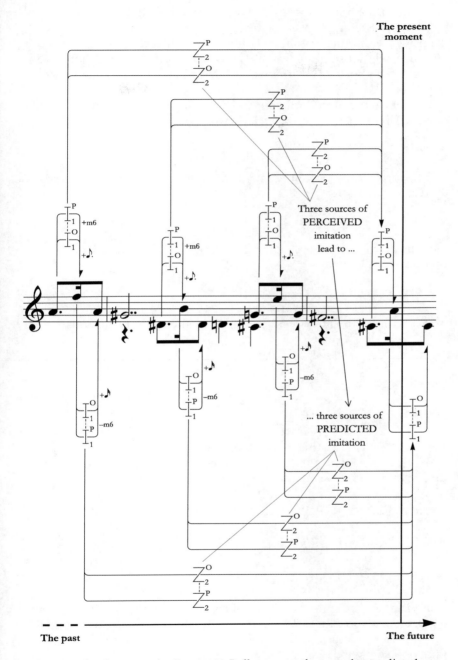

Figure 4.13 The first note in *Romantic Rollercoaster* that can be predicted at a given moment in time on the basis of three zygonic relationships in the domain of onset and pitch.

124 *Adam Ockelford and Ruth Grundy*

'baseline' probability of a single zygonic relationship being detected and acted upon. Second, it was supposed that this figure was not affected by the presence of other zygonic relationships: that registering and recalling one such relationship (or failing to do these things) would not have an impact on the success or otherwise of detecting and reproducing another or others.

This meant that if the probability of Derek anticipating an event correctly on the basis of a single zygonic relationship was

$$P(E_c)_{(\#Z=1)}$$

and the probability of him *not* getting it right (where the '¬c' means 'not correct') was therefore

$$P(E_{\neg c})_{(\#Z=1)} = 1 - P(E_c)_{(\#Z=1)}$$

then the probability of him making an accurate prediction where two relationships were present

$$P(E_c)_{(\#Z=2)}$$

would be the probability of either or both relationships being utilised

$$P(E_c)^2_{(\#Z=1)} + 2\left(P(E_c)_{(\#Z=1)} \cdot P(E_{\neg c})_{(\#Z=1)}\right)$$

That is,

$$P(E_c)_{(\#Z=2)} = 1 - P(E_{\neg c})^2_{(\#Z=1)}$$

Figure 4.14 illustrates this thinking in visual terms.

By extension, the probability of Derek anticipating an event correctly through three zygonic relationships (#Z = 3) was

$$P(E_c)_{(\#Z=3)} = 1 - P(E_{\neg c})^3_{(\#Z=1)}$$

And in general terms, if #Z = n, then

$$P(E_c)_{(\#Z=n)} = 1 - P(E_{\neg c})^n_{(\#Z=1)}$$

This yields an asymptotic trend as follows, in which the greater the number of zygonic relationships (#Z) pertaining to a given future event, the closer the probability with which it will be anticipated to 1 (that is, complete certainty) – see Figure 4.15.

$$P(E_c)_{(\#Z=n)} \to 1$$

Evidence from a musical savant 125

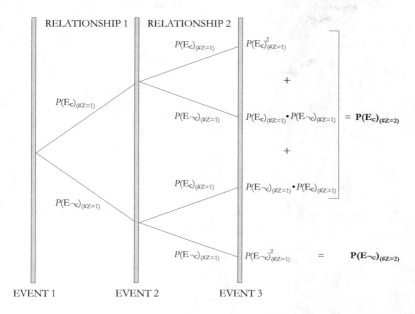

Figure 4.14 The theoretical probabilities of anticipating an event correctly based on one relationship or two.

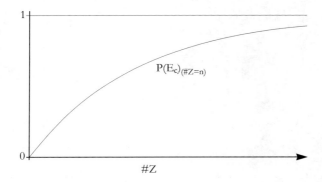

Figure 4.15 The asymptotic curve characteristic of $P(E_c)_{(\#Z=n)}$.

A preliminary mathematical analysis showed that the structural differentiation would have the greatest range of values when $P(E_c)_{(\#Z=1)}$ was close to 20%. The actual figure that Derek achieved on attempting to play along with *Romantic Rollercoaster* for the first time was 18%. The predictions of the model and the results of Derek's efforts (bars 1–8) were as follows (see Table 4.1). (Beyond bar 8, the low values of #Z meant that the few errors that Derek did make impacted on his scores disproportionately.)

126 *Adam Ockelford and Ruth Grundy*

Table 4.1 Comparison of the predicted probability of events being anticipated and the actual frequencies of occurrence, expressed as ratios of the number of events per value of #Z

#Z (the number of zygonic relationships through which a given event was implied), in Romantic Rollercoaster, bars 1–8	The number of events in Romantic Rollercoaster for each value of #Z	The number of events correctly anticipated by Derek	The proportion of events correctly anticipated by Derek	$P(E_c)_{(\#Z=n)}$
0	87	9	0.10	0.00
1	110	20	0.18	0.18
2	61	14	0.23	0.33
3	26	6	0.23	0.45
4	11	7	0.64	0.55
5	6	4	0.67	0.63
6	7	5	0.71	0.70
7	3	3	1.00	0.75
8	2	2	1.00	0.80
9	3	3	1.00	0.84
10	2	2	1.00	0.87
11	2	2	1.00	0.89
12	2	2	1.00	0.91
13	2	2	1.00	0.93

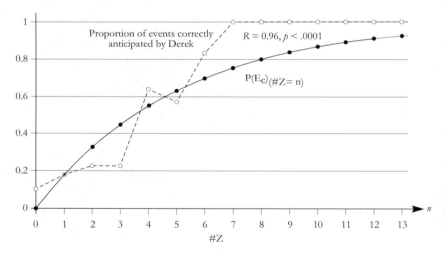

Figure 4.16 The relationship of $P(E_c)_{(\#Z=n)}$ and Derek's performance during his first attempt to play along with *Romantic Rollercoaster* (bars 1–8).

As Figure 4.16 shows, the outputs of the model and Derek's capacity to anticipate notes are highly correlated, lending support to the hypothesis that the number of zygonic relationships through which an event can be considered to be generated does indeed relate to its perceived

Evidence from a musical savant   127

'structural strength'. Moreover, the probabilistic nature of the proposed model appears to be robust.

The current study: expectations arising from hearing *Romantic Rollercoaster* during repeated hearings

This chapter reports on new data from the next stage of the *Romantic Rollercoaster* experiment, which occurred over a period of eight weeks, with a break of a month between Sessions 5 and 6. This entailed Derek making nine further attempts to play along with the piece at the same time as he heard it, thereby probing the final part of the zygonic model of implication and expectation in music (see Figure 4.8), which is concerned with repeated hearings. See Table 4.2.

As noted above, expectations at the level of events and frameworks were not considered to play a significant role, due to the lack of simple sequential patterns, and the constantly shifting tonal centre of *Romantic Rollercoaster*. Rather, it was expectations between groups of notes that were important, and in each trial following the first, these could stem from two sources: the recording of *Romantic Rollercoaster* being heard at the time or the long-term memories of it from previous sessions. This raised three questions.

1   How do repeated hearings of a piece work to form long-term memories?
2   What is the relationship between such memories and the expectations they can arouse in a further hearing of a piece?
3   How do long-term memories and the more immediate memories of a piece that are built up as it is heard interact to set up expectations?

In terms of experimental design, it was important that *Romantic Rollercoaster* was too complex a piece for Derek to memorise perfectly after the first few hearings, since faultless recall would not produce data that could be used to interrogate the three research questions (for it is where things start to break down that we can glean insights into *how* his musical mind works).

Table 4.2 The schedule of the *Romantic Rollercoaster* trials

Session	'Play along' trial	'Memory' trial	Day
1	1	–	1
2	2	1	3
3	3	2	8
4	4	3	10
5	5	4	18
6	6	5	43
7	7	6	45
8	8	7	50
9	9	8	52
10	10	9	57

Against this backdrop of Derek's fallibility, it was hypothesised that the relationship between long-term memory and expectation would function in a similar way to that between working memory and the capacity to anticipate what is likely to occur next, whereby the more times something has been heard in the past, the higher the probability that it will have been remembered and will be recalled to inform projections into the future.

As with the working memory, in order to make the model of long-term memory manageable, we needed to make the initial assumption that there is a single probability of any musical event that is heard being memorised during one trial and recalled subsequently in another. This can be expressed as

$$P(E_c)_{(\#T=1)}$$

where (#T=1) refers to the number of trials from which an event is remembered and reproduced correctly equals one. Hence, a probability tree for Trials 1, 2 and 3 can be constructed as follows (see Figure 4.17).

The probability of a musical event being recalled in Trial 3 is predicted to be

$$P(E_c)_{(\#T=2)} = 1 - P(E_{\neg c})^2_{(\#T=1)}$$

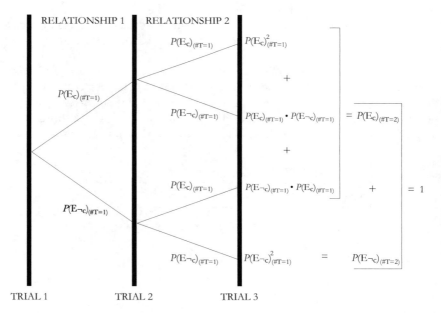

Figure 4.17 Model of the probabilities of musical events being recalled from long-term memory in the first three *Romantic Rollercoaster* trials.

Evidence from a musical savant

and after *m* trials,

$$P(E_c)_{(\#T=m-1)} = 1 - P(E_{\neg c})_{(\#T=1)}^{(m-1)}$$

It is possible to model how this fits with the probability of events being recalled *during* a trial as follows. Consider, for example, Trial 2. The long-term memory of Trial 1 provides what is effectively a 'background' level of probability that events will be remembered, upon which the efforts of working memory to identify structures during Trial 2 are superimposed. The probability tree shown in Figure 4.18 indicates the three ways in which an event in Trial 2 that is potentially generated from a single zygonic relationship may be anticipated:

- when it is recalled correctly from long-term memory alone (from Trial 1)

$$P(E_c)_{(\#T=1)} \cdot P(E_{\neg c})_{(\#Z=1)}$$

- when it is recalled correctly from long-term memory *and* working memory

$$P(E_c)_{(\#T=1)} \cdot P(E_c)_{(\#Z=1)}$$

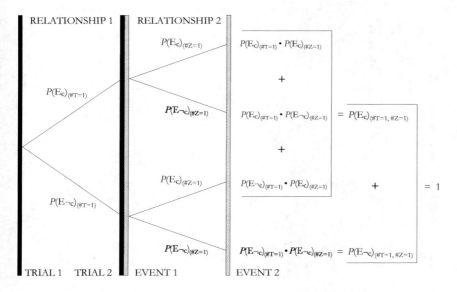

Figure 4.18 Model of the probabilities of musical events potentially being recalled from long-term memory and anticipated through a single structural relationship identified in working memory in the second trial of *Romantic Rollercoaster*.

- and when it is recalled correctly from working memory alone

$$P(E_{\neg c})_{(\#T=1)} \cdot P(E_c)_{(\#Z=1)}$$

The sum of these products yields the probability that an event will be anticipated correctly:

$$P(E_c)_{(\#T=1, \#Z=1)}$$

This can be expressed as

$$1 - P(E_{\neg c})_{(\#T=1, \#Z=1)}$$

which equals

$$1 - \left(P(E_{\neg c})_{(\#T=1)} \cdot P(E_{\neg c})_{(\#Z=1)} \right)$$

Extending this example to three events in Trial 2 (and therefore, potentially, two zygonic relationships) yields a set of probabilities as follows (see Figure 4.19).

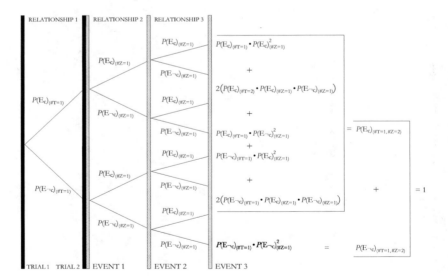

Figure 4.19 Model of the probabilities of musical events potentially being recalled from long-term memory and anticipated through two structural relationships identified in working memory in the second trial of *Romantic Rollercoaster*.

Evidence from a musical savant 131

Here, the probability of an event being anticipated correctly can be expressed as

$$P(E_c)_{(\#T=1, \#Z=2)}$$

which equals

$$1 - P(E_{\neg c})_{(\#T=1, \#Z=2)}$$

or

$$1 - \left(P(E_{\neg c})_{(\#T=1)} \cdot P(E_{\neg c})^2_{(\#Z=1)} \right)$$

Finally, consider the scenario in which an event is predicted in Trial 3 on the basis of two structural relationships (see Figure 4.20).

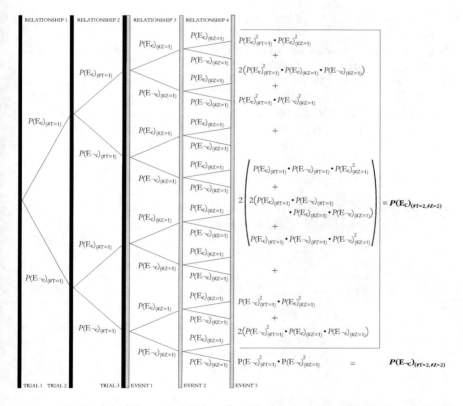

Figure 4.20 Model of the probabilities of musical events potentially being recalled from two previous trials and anticipated through two structural relationships identified in working memory in the third trial of *Romantic Rollercoaster*.

132 *Adam Ockelford and Ruth Grundy*

Here, the probability of an event being anticipated correctly can be expressed as

$$P(\mathrm{E_c})_{(\#T=2,\,\#Z=2)}$$

which equals

$$1 - P(\mathrm{E_{\neg c}})_{(\#T=2,\,\#Z=2)}$$

or

$$1 - \left(P(\mathrm{E_{\neg c}})^2_{(\#T=1)} \bullet P(\mathrm{E_{\neg c}})^2_{(\#Z=1)} \right)$$

So in general terms, we can hypothesise that the probability of an event being anticipated in Trial m through n structural relationships is

$$1 - \left(P(\mathrm{E_{\neg c}})^{(m-1)}_{(\#T=1)} \bullet P(\mathrm{E_{\neg c}})^n_{(\#Z=1)} \right)$$

How well does this equation model Derek's capacity to anticipate material in successive hearings of *Romantic Rollercoaster*?

To answer this question, we will confine our analysis of Derek's responses to $0 \leq \#Z \leq 6$, since in Trial 1, when $\#Z = 7$, Derek's performance had already reached a ceiling. The results were as follows (see Table 4.3).

The value of $P(\mathrm{E_c})_{(\#Z=1)}$ (and therefore that of $P(\mathrm{E_{\neg c}})_{(\#Z=1)}$, which equals $1 - P(\mathrm{E_c})_{(\#Z=1)}$ is already known from Trial 1:

$$P(\mathrm{E_{\neg c}})_{(\#Z=1)} = 1 - 0.18 = 0.82$$

But what of $P(\mathrm{E_c})_{(\#T=1)}$? At the first blush, it may seem that Derek's capacity to anticipate events in Trial 2, where $\#Z = 0$ (implying that there were no internal structural relationships of which he could avail himself, meaning

Table 4.3 The proportion of musical events anticipated by Derek in the range $0 \leq \#Z \leq 6$ across all ten trials of *Romantic Rollercoaster*

The proportion of events correctly anticipated by Derek

#Z	Trial 1	Trial 2	Trial 3	Trial 4	Trial 5	Trial 6	Trial 7	Trial 8	Trial 9	Trial 10
0	0.10	0.17	0.39	0.41	0.45	0.56	0.59	0.73	0.74	0.72
1	0.18	0.24	0.31	0.51	0.47	0.61	0.68	0.82	0.78	0.91
2	0.23	0.31	0.39	0.49	0.48	0.57	0.62	0.69	0.69	0.82
3	0.23	0.38	0.42	0.54	0.50	0.62	0.62	0.62	0.69	0.77
4	0.64	0.82	0.91	0.82	1.00	1.00	1.00	0.91	1.00	0.91
5	0.67	0.50	0.83	0.50	0.83	0.83	0.67	1.00	1.00	1.00
6	0.71	0.86	0.71	0.71	0.86	0.71	0.71	1.00	1.00	1.00

Evidence from a musical savant

that he had to rely entirely on his memory of Trial 1), would provide the answer: 0.17. However, the experience of Trial 1, in which Derek succeeded in anticipating 10% of events that were not predictable through structural relationships (and therefore occurred through chance), suggests that this may be an overestimate. This assumption is confirmed by comparing Derek's results for #Z = 0 for Trials 2–10 against the model (Figure 4.21):

$$P(E_{\neg c})^{m-1}_{(\#T=1)}$$

where

$$P(E_{\neg c})_{(\#T=1)} = 0.17$$

(see Table 4.4).

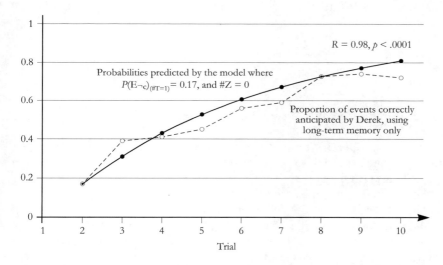

Figure 4.21 Visual realisation of the data in Table 4.4.

Table 4.4 The proportion of events with no structural antecedents that are anticipated by Derek compared to the model, where $P(E_{\neg c})_{(\#T=1)} = 0.17$

Trial	2	3	4	5	6	7	8	9	10
The proportion of events correctly anticipated by Derek (#Z = 0)	0.17	0.39	0.41	0.45	0.56	0.59	0.73	0.74	0.72
$P(E_{\neg c})^{m-1}_{(\#T=1)}$	0.17	0.31	0.43	0.53	0.61	0.67	0.73	0.77	0.81

134 *Adam Ockelford and Ruth Grundy*

While there is a high degree of correlation between the two series of figures – $R = 0.98$, $p < 0.0001$ – the model as a whole returns probabilities that are a little under 6% higher than the actual scores that Derek obtained.

Correcting for this gives $P(E_{\neg c})^{m-1}_{(\#T=1)} = 0.16$. Feeding *this* figure into the full model of expectation,

$$1 - \left(P(E_{\neg c})^{(m-1)}_{(\#T=1)} \bullet P(E_{\neg c})^{n}_{(\#Z=1)} \right)$$

means that the probability of an event being anticipated in Trial m through n structural relationships is

$$1 - \left(0.84^{m-1} \bullet 0.82^{n} \right)$$

For Trials 2–10, where $0 \leq \#Z \leq 6$, this yields a set of values that, on average, overestimate Derek's capacity to anticipate events correctly by around 16%. Correcting for this to give a global mean equal to Derek's across Trials 2–10 implies

$$P(E_{\neg c})_{(\#T=1)} = 0.14.$$

Hence,

$$P(\text{Derek anticipating an event correctly}) = 1 - \left(0.86^{m-1} \bullet 0.82^{n} \right)$$

That is to say, Derek's ability to anticipate events in *Romantic Rollercoaster* following the first trial was enhanced by around 14% through the operation of his long-term memory.

The full data set can be seen in Table 4.5.

The model's projections are represented visually in Figure 4.22. These predict that, trial by trial, Derek's capacity to anticipate events will come to rely less on the implications of internal structures and more on long-term memory, a trend expressed numerically as the probability of each and every event being anticipated correctly to rise towards the ceiling of 1.

The data pertaining to Derek's attempts are shown in Figure 4.23. Comparing these with the predictions set out in Figure 4.22 suggests that, in general terms, the model can account for what occurred with a fair degree of accuracy. This is confirmed with the correlation between predicted and actual values of $R = 0.86$, $p < 0.0001$.

Comparisons trial by trial enable a more detailed picture to be built up, including *systematic* differences (which occur more or less consistently in certain contexts, and which are therefore predictable) and *random* differences (which appear as 'one-offs', and could not be foreseen) – see Figure 4.24.

The principal systematic difference, where Derek invariably performs better than the model, occurs when $\#Z = 4$. This occurs ten times in *Romantic Rollercoaster*, and, invariably, as well as being predictable through

Table 4.5 The full data set across ten trials of the model and the proportion of musical events anticipated by Derek in the range $0 \leq \#Z \leq 6$

#Z	Trial 1		Trial 2		Trial 3		Trial 4		Trial 5		Trial 6		Trial 7		Trial 8		Trial 9		Trial 10	
	model	Derek	model	Derek	model	Derek	model	Derek	model	Derek	model	Derek	model	Derek	model	Derek	model	Derek	model	Derek
0	0.00	0.10	0.14	0.17	0.26	0.39	0.36	0.41	0.45	0.45	0.52	0.56	0.59	0.59	0.65	0.73	0.70	0.74	0.74	0.72
1	0.18	0.18	0.29	0.24	0.39	0.31	0.48	0.51	0.55	0.47	0.61	0.61	0.66	0.68	0.71	0.82	0.75	0.78	0.78	0.91
2	0.33	0.23	0.42	0.31	0.50	0.39	0.57	0.49	0.63	0.48	0.68	0.57	0.72	0.62	0.76	0.69	0.80	0.69	0.82	0.82
3	0.45	0.23	0.52	0.38	0.59	0.42	0.65	0.54	0.70	0.50	0.74	0.62	0.77	0.62	0.81	0.62	0.83	0.69	0.86	0.77
4	0.55	0.64	0.61	0.82	0.66	0.91	0.71	0.82	0.75	1.00	0.78	1.00	0.81	1.00	0.84	0.91	0.86	1.00	0.88	0.91
5	0.63	0.67	0.68	0.50	0.72	0.83	0.76	0.50	0.80	0.83	0.82	0.83	0.85	0.67	0.87	1.00	0.89	1.00	0.90	1.00
6	0.70	0.71	0.74	0.86	0.77	0.71	0.81	0.71	0.83	0.86	0.86	0.71	0.88	0.71	0.89	1.00	0.91	1.00	0.92	1.00

136 *Adam Ockelford and Ruth Grundy*

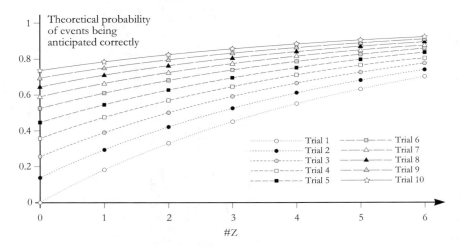

Figure 4.22 Visual representation of $1 - (0.86^{m-1} \cdot 0.82^n)$, where $0 \leq n \leq 6$ and $1 \leq m \leq 10$.

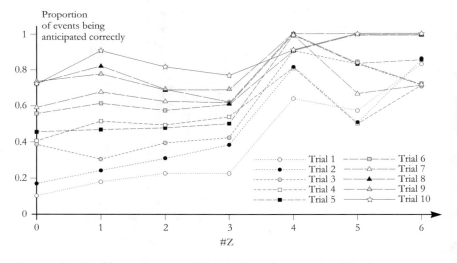

Figure 4.23 Derek's results across Trials 1–10, in the range $0 \leq \#Z \leq 6$.

between-group prognostication, the events are also part of sequences (*within-group structures*) – that were an inadvertent feature of the design of the piece. For example, see Figure 4.25.

Irrespective of these exceptions, the results provide evidence that the formula

$$P(\text{Derek anticipating an event correctly}) = 1 - \left(0.86^{m-1} \cdot 0.82^n\right)$$

Evidence from a musical savant 137

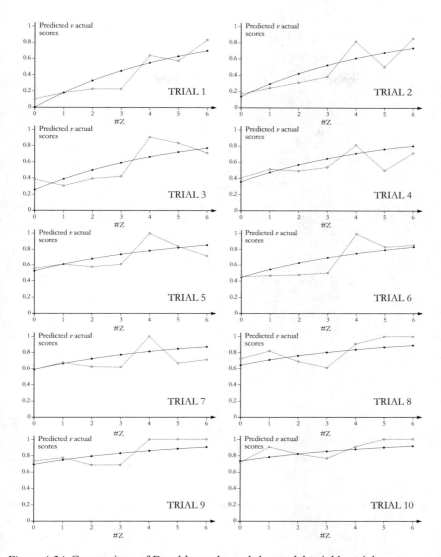

Figure 4.24 Comparison of Derek's results and the model, trial by trial.

(where *m* is the Trial number and *n* is the number of structural relationships) offers a fair model of Derek's capacity to anticipate events, including the interaction of zygonic relationships from within a hearing of *Romantic Rollercoaster* and long-term memories of it. The prediction of the model that, as long-term memory comes to figure more in Derek's mental processing, there will be a tendency for all events (barring the first)[1] to be anticipated correctly (causing all values to move towards 1) is borne out in the results.

138 *Adam Ockelford and Ruth Grundy*

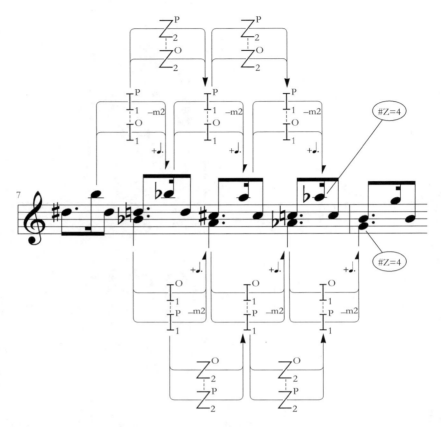

Figure 4.25 Examples of #Z = 4 being predictable through sequences as well as structural relationships existing between groups.

It is of interest to consider the status of the relationships that are retrieved from long-term memory as they interact with those derived from the current hearing of the piece. In terms of zygonic theory, from a musicological point of view, there would be an *indirect* relationship between music heard on one occasion and the same material heard on another, both considered to be derived from a (hypothetical) 'original' version of the piece in question (see Figure 4.26). However, it may be that as auditory images from previous hearings are brought forward into a 'musical executive' in working memory (Ockelford, 2007), these are treated in the same way as more recent recollections (from the current hearing), and material that is predicted is heard as deriving from it imitatively.

Finally, the data gathered enable other aspects of Derek's performance on the task to be interrogated too. For example, of the 308 notes in the piece,

Evidence from a musical savant 139

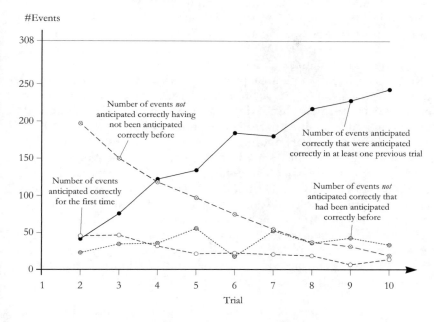

Figure 4.26 The efficiency of Derek's learning over time.

the total proportion that Derek predicted correctly having anticipated them at least once in the past was 80%, with only 3% never being successfully predicted again. This indicates that his learning of the piece was efficient. Only 5% of events were not anticipated at all, in any of the trials. These were predominantly at or near the beginning of the piece, when (observational evidence suggests) Derek was still orienting his hands in relation to the notes that needed to be played (and, as noted above, the presence of a preceding 'click track' could have obviated this difficulty). Trial by trial the results were as follows (see Figure 4.26).

Conclusion

The data and analysis presented in this chapter lie some way outside 'mainstream' music-theoretical and music-psychological thinking. The dominant paradigm in contemporary music theory is to explain musical structure and meaning idiosyncratically through the ears of elite individuals who have conceptual resources that are far beyond those typically acquired by listeners. Music-theoretic apologists claim that such individual perspectives can have a positive impact on the musical understanding of those who are prepared to make a commitment to the necessary advanced level of study. In contrast, music psychology (like cognitive psychology itself) tends to be

140 *Adam Ockelford and Ruth Grundy*

norm-related, driven by the search for an imaginary typicality that can be acquired by identifying and measuring group characteristics, from which it is all too easy to make the mistake of inferring individual abilities and traits. In reality, of course, the results of such analysis are very unlikely to reflect the experience of any given individual.

Research using the unique capacity of musical savants such as Derek Paravicini to reproduce on an instrument such as the piano the musical sounds he can hear in his head, that is at the same time uncontaminated by conceptual understanding, borrows from both paradigms. It uses a specific case to inform our understanding of the generality of human ability. Such an approach can be justified since Derek functions like most other people in that his grasp of music is implicit rather than explicit, perceptual rather than conceptual and intuitive rather than intellectual. And he frequently learns and practises pieces alongside other musicians, and engages with them in sophisticated improvisations, implying a commonality in the way that he and they are processing music. So the finding that Derek's way of perceiving and memorising a piece of music accords with a prediction of zygonic theory can be regarded as reasonable evidence for the generalisability of that aspect of the theory to other listeners. As Ockelford (2017, p. 9) asserts:

> The human tribe exists on continua of interests, abilities, propensities and traits, and, by observing people who function at the extremes of out species' natural neurodiversity, we can better understand the ordinary, everyday, musical experiences that are characteristic of us all.

Note

1 An introductory pattern of pulses (which would have enabled Derek to judge when the first note was due) was not provided.

5 Exploring the effect of repeated listening to a novel melody

A zygonic approach

Adam Ockelford and Hayley Trower

Introduction

This chapter further considers the topic of implication and expectation in music, specifically in relation to repeated hearings. The research that is reported here was initially informed by the zygonic model proposed by Ockelford (2006) and concludes by suggesting certain refinements to it. An important difference between this chapter and the previous one is that in this case expectations are judged *retrospectively*, through *reactive* zygonic relationships, rather than *prospectively*, through *proactive* connections. And here, rather than using purely *musical* responses to what is heard to evaluate what are typically intuitive cognitive processes, data are obtained through the use of a device that enables participants to register the perceived strength of expectation that a given musical event engenders in them by moving a finger left or right along a ribbon. The categorisation of musical structure as events, groups or frameworks, and identifying which of these different responses pertain to, enables sophisticated psychomusicological analyses to be undertaken. These provide insights into the evolving aesthetic response as a melody is heard repeatedly, both in the short term and over longer periods of time.

Expectation as an essential element in the musical experience

The emergence of analogue and subsequently digital recording has enabled modern populations to re-experience performances of music whenever they wish with ever greater ease (Lacher and Mizerski, 1994; North and Hargreaves, 1997), and songs that are already replete with repetition are encountered recurrently on the internet, television and radio (Margulis, 2014). Conversely, it is has been estimated that only 1% of musical experiences involve material that listeners have not heard previously (Huron, 2006). Despite this repeated exposure, it seems that listeners continue to be moved emotionally by the same pieces of music many times (Margulis, *op. cit.*). This is understood to stem from the complex and often conflicting implications that are set up through the multi-layered structures that characterise music: an irresistible soundscape that fuses predictability and surprise, and that draws listeners in, time and again.

142   *Adam Ockelford and Hayley Trower*

The primary motivation for the research reported in this chapter is to address the question: how is it that we can continue to be emotionally engaged by pieces of music, even when we have heard them many times? Surprisingly – and despite the fact, as we have observed, that pieces of music tend to be heard over and over again – the phenomenon of re-listening has received only scant theoretical and empirical attention. Meyer (1956, p. 49) speculates that musical repetition cannot exist psychologically, only physically, and that listeners engage a 'willing suspension of disbelief' when presented with familiar music (Meyer, 2001, p. 352). Building on the work of Eugene Narmour (1990, 1992), in which it is proposed that with each new hearing of a piece micro-adjustments to an individual's musical schemata result in different sets of expectations being aroused, Elizabeth Margulis postulates that for the first few hearings of a piece, listeners focus on different aspects each time. Margulis (2014, p. 109) contends that they shift their expectational set from a general idea of what will ensue based on previous knowledge of that genre or composer, to a more specific framework for that particular piece.

When different expectations collide

The thinking underlying Margulis's contention is that the expectations that patterns of notes trigger in the mind, consciously or non-consciously, are of two main types. As we saw on p. 114, *schematic* expectations (pertaining to 'frameworks') are relatively inflexible long-term memory ('LTM') constructs acquired from substantial exposure to music, and offer a *general* indication of what is to come that can be expressed as probabilities (Dowling and Harwood, 1986). They are rapidly activated and, metaphorically speaking, always 'hear music as though for the first time' (Jackendoff, 1991). In contrast, *veridical* expectations equip listeners (pertaining to 'groups') with *specific* knowledge about what will ensue. They can be retrieved from both LTM and working memory ('WM') and may arise between similar groups of notes occurring within a single piece as well as between corresponding groups of notes existing in different pieces (Bharucha, 1987). The length of groups is variable: listeners can have veridical expectations for an entire work.

It is believed that expectation continues to play a part in repeated hearings because these two processes – schematic and veridical – operate in conjunction, meaning that a particular chordal transition, for instance, can remain relatively unexpected (in the context of all possible chordal transitions) even when, on another level, a listener feels sure that it will occur (Dowling and Harwood, 1986; Bharucha, 1987; Jackendoff, 1991). The oft-cited example is of the so-called 'deceptive' or 'interrupted' cadence: from previous hearings of a piece, a Western-encultured listener may know that, at a particular point in the music, the submediant chord is going to follow the dominant (V–vi). However, on hearing the cadence, the listener may still feel a certain sense of surprise, since the transition V–I is stylistically far more common. See Figure 5.1.

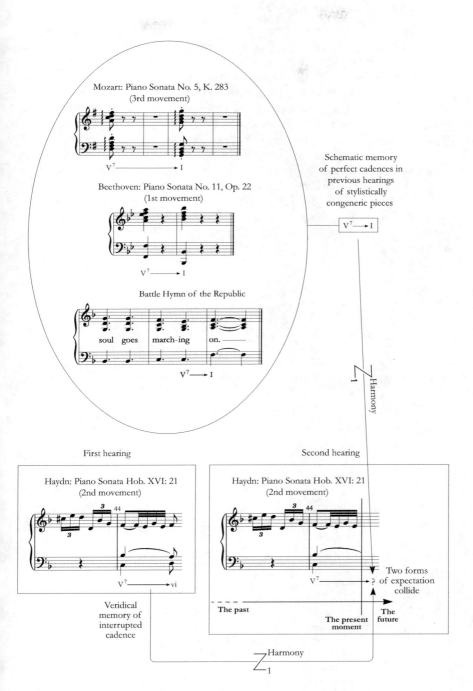

Figure 5.1 Theoretical explanation of the continued effect of an interrupted cadence when it is heard for a second time.

Is this the full picture, however? For instance, how are schematic expectations likely to be affected by repeated hearings? Take, for example, the case of the interrupted cadence in the Haydn piano sonata shown in Figure 5.1. Imagine listening to it many times. We would expect the schema V–vi to become more strongly represented in cognition, and so felt to be more probable than before. But how much more probable? Would there come a point when a sense of unexpectedness would disappear altogether? These questions are considered in some depth below.

For now, though, we raise another issue: that of veridical expectations that may arise through multiple hearings. How do those that may occur in the course of the second hearing of a piece, when a motif is repeated, interact with those from the first hearing, for example? Imagine, for instance, someone listening to a familiar children's song, *Frère Jacques*. Two forms of veridical expectation are likely to be in play (see Figure 5.2). How do they interact? Again, this question is one that will be addressed in due course.

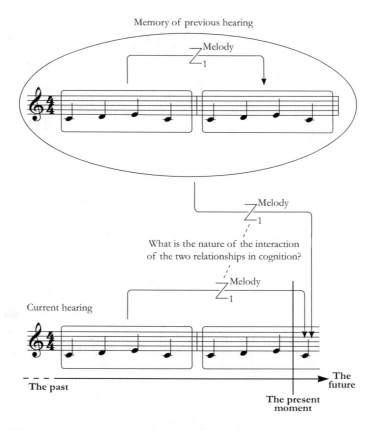

Figure 5.2 Two forms of veridical expectation occurring together as someone listens to *Frère Jacques* for a second time.

A zygonic approach 145

In addition to the schematic and veridical forms of expectation, as we noted on p. 115, there is a third type that pertains to 'events' as they unfold in the current music listening experience, and which operates adaptively *within* groups of notes as they unfold (see Huron, 2006; Ockelford, 2006, 2012a) Drawing on the work of Meyer (1956) and Narmour (1990), Huron theorises that such expectations, which he terms 'dynamic', derive from short-term patterns that update in real time, decay quickly and are salient when listing to novel or unfamiliar music. Ockelford (2006) postulates that these typically yield a *range* of values, since multiple regularities usually exist simultaneously in the domains of pitch and perceived time, giving rise to a plurality of logical continuations. Here, the important question is, how do these expectations at the level of events contribute to the mix in the repeated hearings of pieces?

Reviewing the zygonic model of implication and expectation in music: a reconsideration of Trower (2011)

The zygonic model of implication and expectation in music

As we saw in Chapter 4, a model of implication and expectation in music was constructed using zygonic theory that brought together the three strands of expectation, at the level of events, groups or frameworks (Ockelford, 2006, 2012a, 2017); see Figure 4.6. To reiterate: the model is founded on the notion that zygonic relationships can function *proactively* to anticipate, with varying degrees of certainty, what may logically occur next, and *reactively* to gauge the perceived expectedness of a note in retrospect. That is to say, patterns of notes are perceived to bear certain *implications* that in turn give rise to particular *expectations* in listeners.

As we observed in Chapter 4, empirical tests of the zygonic model show that it accurately predicts expectations experienced during the first hearing of a melody in the context of Western tonal music (Thorpe, Ockelford and Aksentijevic, 2012; Grundy and Ockelford, 2014). Moreover, by inverting the model's schematic assumptions, it can predict the 'anti-structure' that listeners come to expect when hearing atonal music too (Ockelford and Sergeant, 2012). In terms of repeated hearings, the zygonic model of expectation in music postulates, in a similar vein to Margulis, that the balance between general and specific expectations, which work hand in hand, gradually changes with each rehearing of a piece. Aside from the study reported in Chapter 4, this assertion has only previously been tested – and in a limited context – by Hayley Trower, who (as we observed in Chapter 4) undertook an exploratory investigation into the effect of tonality on memory for melodies using Lerdahl's (2001) theory of 'tonal pitch space' (Trower, 2011).

Trower's (2011) research

Trower's 14 research participants comprised nine females and five males, aged between 25 and 34, with differing levels of music education and a

146 *Adam Ockelford and Hayley Trower*

wide range of musical experiences within Western mainstream traditions. Nationalities included British, British-Indian, American and Japanese. Participants were presented with 16 pairs of slow-moving melodic sequences that used the framework of the major scale. Each consisted of five pitches of equal length, lasting 15 seconds in total, to enable ratings of expectedness to be made, and to minimise the potential impact of rhythm on the perception of expectancy (Schmuckler and Boltz, 1994). Eight pairs were of melodies the same, and eight differed in their final pitch, allowing every scale degree to appear once in a cadential function (with the tonic repeated at the higher and lower octaves). In each case, the first four notes formed a different, stylistically conventional pattern (see Figures 5.3a and 5.3b).

The stimuli were created using Sibelius music notation software, and converted from MIDI to audio files, using Logic Pro, to sound like a Steinway piano, rich in tone and with some reverberation. The order of sequences was randomised by participant. A distractor was played between each pair of sequences, comprising eight random tones of equal duration, lasting approximately seven seconds.

Trower's experiment comprised two conditions – 'listening' and 'rating' – and seven participants were randomly allocated to each. The rating condition required participants continuously to evaluate the perceived predictability of each note in the sequence, using a proprietary device known as the 'Continuous Response Measurement Apparatus', or 'CReMA' (Himonides, 2011), whilst the melody was played to them at a comfortable level through speakers. After 15 seconds (of which seven were taken up with the distractor), the second group of stimuli were presented, and the rating task repeated. In both listening and rating conditions, after each trial, participants had to judge whether the pair of sequences they had just heard was the same or different. Trower's hypotheses were that there may be correlations between tonal stability (as calculated using Lerdahl's model) and melodic memory, and expectancy ratings and memory. In the event, the data were inconclusive, but those from the participants who provided continuous ratings did provide a fascinating insight into how perceived melodic expectancies change with repeated hearings.

To understand how the data were gathered, it is important to know how the CReMA functions. It takes the form of a fixed ribbon, around 40 cm long, presented to participants laterally. They place a finger on the ribbon, and are instructed to move it left or right to rate what they are perceiving. In Trower's case, the centre was said to represent a 'neutral' position with regard to melodic expectancy, with positions further to the left intended to indicate that a given pitch was perceived to be increasingly 'unexpected' or 'surprising', and locations further to the right showing a note pitch was more 'expected' or 'predictable'. The CReMA data are outputted in MIDI format, with a linear relationship between a participant's changing finger position and an assigned number. In Trower's experiment, the higher the number, the more expected a pitch was reckoned to be.

Since Trower was interested in relative (rather than absolute) pitch expectancies, only responses provided after the second note in each sequence were

A zygonic approach 147

taken into account. Thereafter, the responses of longest duration were taken to be participants' definitive responses. In cases where no one, unequivocal response was apparent, the mean of the ratings following the event (up until the next one) was taken as the participant's response. Since half the stimuli pairs (each comprising five pitches) had different final notes, only the ratings

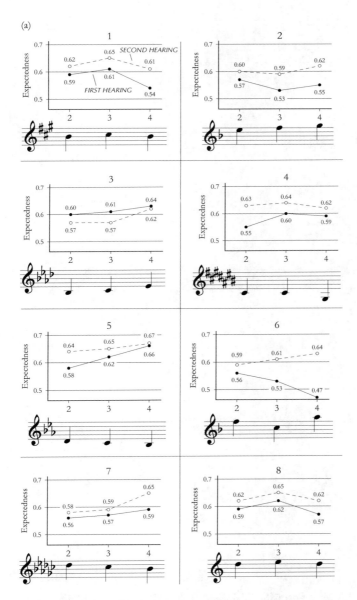

Figure 5.3a The mean normalised expectancy ratings on the first and second hearings of Trower's (2011) melodic stimuli (cont.).

148 Adam Ockelford and Hayley Trower

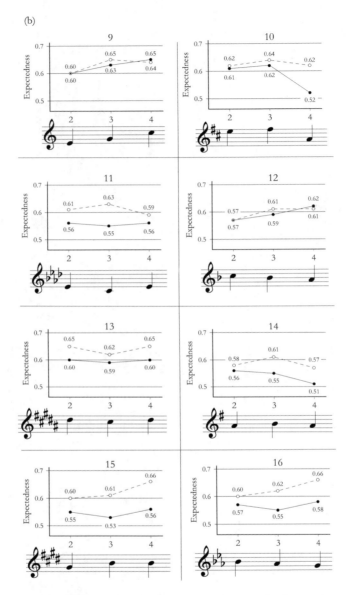

Figure 5.3b The mean normalised expectancy ratings on the first and second hearings of Trower's (2011) melodic stimuli.

pertaining to pitches 2, 3 and 4 will be considered here. So, in summary, we have seven participants' ratings of how expected or unexpected they found pitches to be in retrospect in relation to 16 (identical) stimuli pairs. These are normalised to a scale of 0 to 1, and shown in Figures 5.3a and 5.3b.

A zygonic approach   149

New perspectives on Trower (2011): the function of WM (events)

A fresh analysis presented here shows the extent to which these data accord with the zygonic model of implication and expectation in music. This predicts that, on a first hearing, when the material is unfamiliar, the only expectations present will be the *general* ones arising from implications at the level of events and frameworks, since Trower's miniature melodies are not structured in terms of groups. That is to say, the degree of expectedness of a particular note will be a function of the event-based and framework-based implications associated with it. Expectedness equates to the *perceived probability of occurrence.*

In formal terms, the perceived retrospective probability with which a note occurred in Hearing 1 (labelled 'N_{H1}') is a function of the implications, arising from zygonic relationships 'z' pertaining to events (E) (in the current hearing) and frameworks (F) (from previous hearings of other music):

$$P(N_{H1}) = f_{N_{H1}}{}^{z}(E, F)$$

where

0 (totally unexpected) $\leq P(N_{H1}) \leq 1$ (completely expected).

What could the neural correlates of this conjecture be? In order to address this question, we will consider the theoretical mechanisms through which zygonic relationships are postulated to engender different perceived probabilities of occurrence.

To return to first principles: we can assume that, as one of Trower's sequences is heard, the notes are encoded in WM. Seeking to make sense of this novel stimulus, the brain will search for structure in what has been perceived, through formulating zygonic relationships *reactively*. As the melodic fragment unfolds, these connections will be used *proactively* to anticipate what may occur next. In terms of Trower's experiment, these can then be drawn into consciousness and their potency gauged once the event in question has passed; thus the participants will be using representations of relationships in WM order to make their judgements.

The zygonic model predicts that listeners' expectations deriving from events are likely to produce a *plurality* of potential logical continuations, thereby offering only a *general* sense of what is to come. And not all continuations are perceived to be equally probable. Ockelford (2005, p. 125) proposes a set of 'preference rules' that set out how the brain is likely to interpret musical structures (which can typically be parsed in a number of ways) based on a psychological interpretation of 'Occam's Razor': namely, that the brain will prefer the simplest way of making sense of incoming perceptual data. There is no reason to think why these preference rules should not function proactively too in the process of anticipation, and they can be re-framed in the context of probable future occurrence, whereby, for example, expectations involving the simpler manipulation of data are felt to be more likely than those utilising more complex mechanisms.

There is another route, though, through which the expectations attached to different musical outcomes can vary, and that is according to the number of relationships that point to a particular future event. Previous work that tackled this issue, such as those by Thorpe, Ockelford and Aksentijevic (2012), Grundy and Ockelford (2014), and Ockelford and Grundy (Chapter 4, this volume), built on the traditional psychological view that the perceived probability of an event arising is based on the frequency of its past occurrence: that, other things being equal, the more often something has happened in the past, the more likely we believe it will happen again. This supposition will be tested at some length below. For now, an initial refinement to the thinking, derived from zygonic theory, is that *the more times a given future is predicted structurally, the more likely it will be perceived to be.* That is to say, the greater the number of zygonic relationships that lead the ear to a given musical outcome, *ceteris paribus*, the higher the perceived likelihood of that outcome occurring.

In the three research studies by Aksentijevic, Grundy, Ockelford and Thorpe cited above, the zygonic relationships in question functioned between *groups* (in a veridical rather than a schematic sense). But the principle can also apply to *events* and *frameworks*. First we will consider the position with regard to events.

Take, for example, two descending notes in a major scale: $(\hat{3}, \hat{2})$. A logical projection from this embryonic pattern is for the descent to continue to $\hat{1}$ through a single secondary zygonic relationship of scale degree (see Figure 5.4). (Note that, in the interests of simplicity, for the time being we will ignore the schematic expectations – pertaining to frameworks – that may also be in play.)

Now consider the effect if the pattern started on $\hat{4}$. At the same juncture (after note $\hat{2}$) the sense of descent is, we would argue, perceptibly stronger, and this can be attributed to the fact that $\hat{1}$ can reasonably predicted from *two* secondary zygons (Figure 5.5).

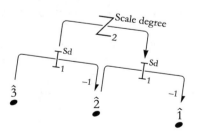

Figure 5.4 A single secondary zygonic relationship of scale degree points to a particular pitch.

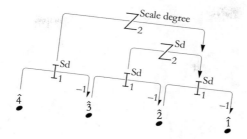

Figure 5.5 Two secondary zygonic relationships of scale degree point to a single pitch.

And so the pattern can be extended, with more and more notes yielding an ever higher number of secondary zygons through which the final pitch can reasonably be predicted to occur with increasing certainty (although, as we shall see, the impact of each additional note – and therefore of each extra secondary zygonic relationship – diminishes as the total number increases).

There is another scenario in which a single musical outcome may be projected from a plurality of zygons, and that is when the relationships concerned are *different*. Consider, for example, the following passage in which discrete sequences of imitation at the primary and secondary level converge on an individual pitch (see Figure 5.6).

Logically, how can we model the anticipatory effect of two zygonic relationships, whether the same or different, converging on a common musical event? As the example in Figure 5.6 shows, the imitative effect may be felt through relationships functioning at different levels (here, primary and secondary). And

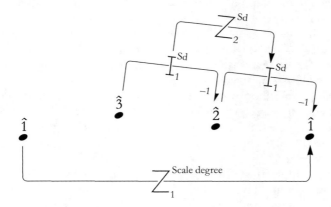

Figure 5.6 A single pitch projected from differing zygonic relationships of scale degree.

152 *Adam Ockelford and Hayley Trower*

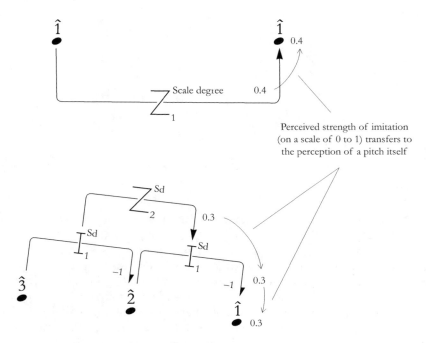

Figure 5.7 The perceived strength of imitation embodied in zygonic relationships transfers to the felt probabilities of aspects of musical events (here, their pitches) occurring.

as we have seen, each will bear a certain probabilistic 'weight' – a strength of imitative force – that will yield a particular level of expectation. It is important to appreciate that the perceived strength of imitation can be transferred down through a chain of relationships to the perceptual surface (so that it is a note itself that seems more or less likely to occur) – see Figure 5.7.

Clearly, when (at any level) probabilities converge, it cannot be a matter of simple addition, since the figures accruing could together amount to a sum that was greater than 1 – that is, to more than complete certainty – which would make neither mathematical (nor phenomenological) sense. However, treating the probabilities pertaining to events (and, as we shall see, groups and frameworks) as *sets*, with the potential for intersection, offers a more promising way forward. This means that the expectations pertaining to a given musical event arising from discrete sources of musical patterning may effectively overlap.

Take, for example, the two relationships ('X' and 'Y') shown in Figure 5.8. Let us assume that Relationship X bears the perceived probability 'x', which is equal to 0.5, and Relationship Y has an associated probability of 'y', which is equal to 0.4. In set theory, the intersection of x and y is given by their product. That is,

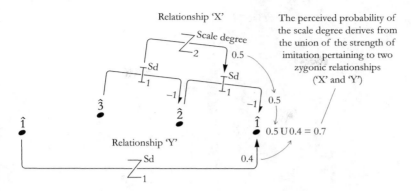

Figure 5.8 Calculating the combined effect of the strength of imitation of two zygonic relationships that point to a common outcome.

x ∩ y = xy = 0.5 ∗ 0.4 = 0.2.

The *combined* effect of the sets, or their 'union', is calculated as follows:

x ∪ y = x + y − xy = 0.5 + 0.4 − 0.2 = 0.7.

So much for the theoretical model, but does it have potential neural correlates? One approach to this issue is to express the intersection of probabilities using 'binary logic' (or 'Boolean algebra'). First, let us hypothesise that the probabilistic weight of each relationship can be expressed as nominal units of 'zygonic force'. So, for example, the perceived probability pertaining to Relationship X of x = 0.5 could be re-expressed as five units of 'zygonic force' out of a potential ten, while the perceived probability associated with Relationship Y (y = 0.4) could be re-articulated as four units, again, out of a possible ten (observe that these are *transferred* from the secondary zygonic relationship through which the imitation that generates Relationship Y occurs). This implies that Relationship X has five units of zygonic force that are not realised, while Relationship Y has six latent units (see Figure 5.9).

Now, using binary logic, let us represent the presence of a unit of zygonic force as '1', and its absence as '0'. Combining the effects of Relationships X and Y (x ∪ y, as in Figure 5.8) yields the following combinations and outcomes (see Table 5.1).

That is to say, the fusion of the probabilities associated with Relationships X and Y comprises combinations involving either $z(x)$ *or* $z(y)$, and both $z(x)$ *and* $z(y)$. In terms of binary logic, this equates to an 'OR' function (see Figure 5.10):

$z(x) \vee z(y)$.

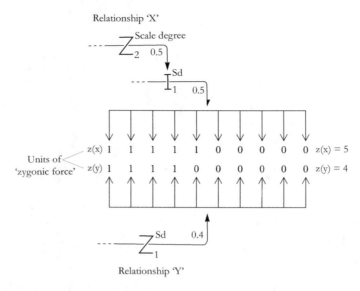

Figure 5.9 Perceived probabilities of imitation reckoned in terms of units of 'zygonic force'.

Table 5.1 Units of 'zygonic force' combined through Boolean algebra

Units of zygonic force pertaining to Relationship X: $z(x)$	1	1	1	1	1	0	0	0	0	0
Units of zygonic force pertaining to Relationship Y: $z(y)$	0	0	0	1	1	1	1	0	0	0
Combined effect of units of zygonic force	**1**	**1**	**1**	**1**	**1**	**1**	**1**	**0**	**0**	**0**

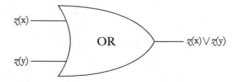

Figure 5.10 The fusion of probabilities associated with Relationships X and Y conceived as an OR function.

This way of conceptualising the issue does indeed potentially resonate at the neuronal level. If we imagine that the correlate of the probability associated with each relationship is a cluster of neuronal activity (whose extent is proportional to the number of units of zygonic force pertaining to it), then the combination of the probabilities associated with two relationships will equate to patterns of neuronal firing that use the so-called 'all-or-none' response (whereby once the threshold required for a neuron to fire has been reached, greater intensity of stimulation does not produce a stronger signal). That is to say, a neuron (or neurons) corresponding to the combined probabilistic effect of Relationships X and Y can be triggered *either* by $z(x)$ alone *or* by $z(y)$ alone *or* by both $z(x)$ *and* $z(y)$ at the same time. Clearly, this is something that future neuroscientific research may or may not verify, but here we will use the mathematical form of the zygonic model of implication and expectation in music to continue our exploration of the empirical data obtained from Trower's experiment. The important thing is that neuronal correlates of the probabilistic model can be envisaged that accord with our understanding of brain function as it currently exists.

New perspectives on Trower (2011): the function of long-term memory (frameworks)

It is not just events, processed in 'WM', to which the model applies: the same principle can help us to understand how the different weights attached to memories of relationships that are stored schematically, in LTM, arise. Consider, for example, the position of the 'interrupted' cadence in Western music (see Figure 5.1). Let us chart, hypothetically, how the impact of this cadence becomes encoded in a listener's mind. This has necessarily to be contextualised in the more common experience of perfect cadences.

So, we will begin with the notional case of listeners hearing a perfect cadence for the first time. They experience (as a harmonic percept) what music theorists would label conceptually as chord V^7, and, in that moment, intuitively seek to anticipate what may come next. However, with no previous knowledge to draw on, imagining a coherent continuation (beyond a repeat or transposition of the chord) would not be possible. Hence, uncertainty is likely to dominate, with a number of potential continuations, whose combined probabilities necessarily add up to 1 (see Figure 5.11).

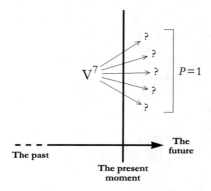

Figure 5.11 The uncertainty imagined to arise from hearing chord V^7 for the first time.

156 *Adam Ockelford and Hayley Trower*

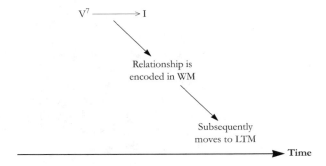

Figure 5.12 The transition from $V^7 \to I$ is assumed to move to long term memory.

Shortly afterwards, chord I is heard. The relationship between V^7 and I will be processed in WM and, let us assume, in due course, moves to LTM – see Figure 5.12.

We can assume that the representation of the relationship in LTM will have a certain perceived likelihood of reoccurrence associated with it. This will necessarily be somewhat arbitrary, since our imaginary listener will not yet have experienced alternative chordal transitions from V^7. However, he or she may also be aware (at some level) that abstract patterns of sound, in which one event is not causally linked to the next, typically have a number of options for continuation at any given point. For the sake of model building, let us assume that the perceived probability associated with the move from $V^7 \to I$ is 10% (or 0.1). The residual 90% (or 0.9) must therefore exist in the mind as a 'known unknown' – a sense of other possible chordal transitions that have not as yet been experienced. This state of affairs can be illustrated in a Venn diagram as follows (Figure 5.13).

Now let us imagine that, sometime later, the listener experiences chord V^7 again. We'll suppose that the fresh perception of the chord triggers the retrieval of its representation in LTM and rekindles the memory of the transition to chord I, with its attendant probability of 0.1. This means that, upon hearing chord V^7, the listener will anticipate that chord I will follow with only a low probability (10%), and that a *different* chord will occur from a range of unknown possibilities, with a combined likelihood of 90%. Let us further suppose that, in the event, chord vi is heard. There is no reason to think that the listener would retrospectively judge this eventuality to have been any more or less probable than the transition to I. Hence, we can assume that the $V^7 \to vi$ transition becomes encoded in LTM with an associated probability of 10% (0.1) too – see Figure 5.14.

How are the mental representations of the two transitions ($V^7 \to I$ and $V^7 \to vi$) likely to co-exist in LTM? To address this question, consider first how the probabilities of each may interact retrospectively (see Figure 5.15). The perceived retrospective probability of the transition $V^7 \to I$ followed

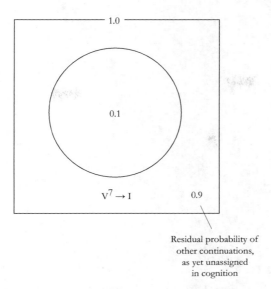

Figure 5.13 Venn diagram illustrating the perceived probabilities of chordal transitions following a single hearing of $V^7 \to I$.

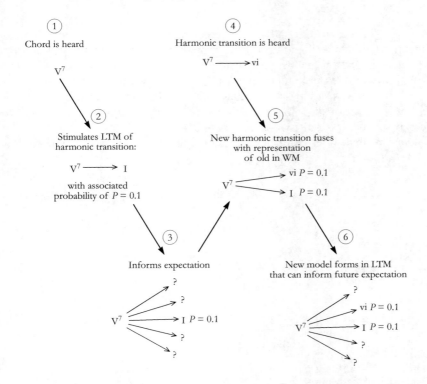

Figure 5.14 Model of the fusion of the memory of $V^7 \to I$ and the perception of $V^7 \to vi$.

158 Adam Ockelford and Hayley Trower

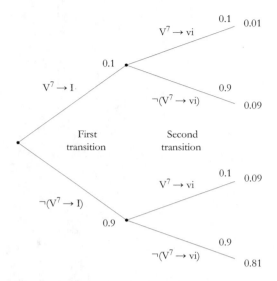

Figure 5.15 The perceived retrospective probabilities of $V^7 \to I$ and $V^7 \to vi$.

by $V^7 \to vi$ is very small (0.01). The perceived probability of *one* of the relationships being $V^7 \to I$ and the other *not* being $V^7 \to vi$, written as $\neg(V^7 \to vi)$, is somewhat greater at 0.09, and this is also true of the converse scenario: the probability of one of the relationships being $V^7 \to vi$ and the other *not* being $V^7 \to I$, written as $\neg(V^7 \to I)$, is, likewise, 0.09. Finally, the probability of *neither* of the relationships having been $V^7 \to I$ or $V^7 \to vi$ is perceived to have been by far the most likely eventuality (0.81).

These probabilities can be expressed using a Venn diagram (Figure 5.16).

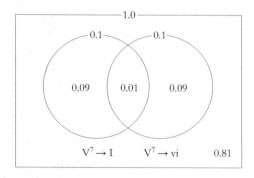

Figure 5.16 Venn diagram showing the relationship between the perceived retrospective probabilities of $V^7 \to I$ and $V^7 \to vi$.

This thinking can in turn be used to construct a neural network model, based on the following assumptions:

i   that the combination of $V^7 \to I$ and $V^7 \to vi$ has the effect of mutual negation;
ii that 'unknowns' (*not* $V^7 \to I$ or *not* $V^7 \to vi$) have no impact on other memories and
iii that a combination of unknowns merely results in further unknowns.

Together, these operations can be classed as a 'XOR' ('exclusive or') function in terms of binary logic (see Table 5.2).

Observe that this model operates differently from that proposed in relation to the combination of probabilities associated with zygonic relationships in WM. There, the probabilities pertaining to *different* relationships that pointed the listener to a common outcome were thought to combine as an 'OR' function. Here, the probabilities attributed to relationships encoded in LTM that are rooted in a common source (V^7) that have *different* outcomes are hypothesised to have a mutually nullifying effect. The principle of differing degrees of 'zygonic force' corresponding with larger networks of neurons applies in both cases, however.

The XOR function set out in Table 5.2 implies that the probabilities associated with the resultant memory traces can be conceptualised as follows (Figure 5.17). Note that the retrospective probability of the mutually negated

Table 5.2 'XOR' relationship through to connect the transitions $V^7 \to I$ and $V^7 \to vi$ in memory

Memory of relationship $V^7 \to I$	1	1	0	0
Memory of relationship $V^7 \to vi$	1	0	1	0
Resultant memory	**0**	**1** $V^7 \to I$	**1** $V^7 \to vi$	**0**

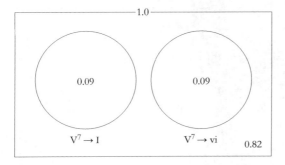

Figure 5.17 Conceptualisation of the resultant memory traces arising from hearing $V^7 \to I$ and $V^7 \to vi$.

160 *Adam Ockelford and Hayley Trower*

memories of $V^7 \to I$ and $V^7 \to vi$ returns, as it were, to the non-specified residue, whereby probabilities of 0.81 and 0.01 combine to give a probability of 0.82 associated with (as yet) unknown transitions from V^7.

In summary: hearing the second transition, $V^7 \to vi$, is likely to have a slight negative impact on the perceived probability of $V^7 \to I$ occurring again. At the same time, the perceived probability associated with $V^7 \to vi$ is slightly less than it would have been, had it not been preceded by $V^7 \to I$.

Now let us imagine a third occasion upon which the listener hears chord V^7. He or she can anticipate three potential continuations, with the probabilities set out in Figure 5.17 (see also Figure 5.18).

Let us suppose that, in the event, the transition $V^7 \to I$ is heard. As before, this experience would be processed in WM before being encoded in LTM (Figure 5.19).

How is this new input likely to interact with memories of the two transitions ($V^7 \to I$ and $V^7 \to vi$) that have already been encoded in LTM? To answer this question, we need to add a further scenario to the neural network model set out above (Table 5.2): the result of the interaction between the older memory of $V^7 \to I$ and the new one. It is suggested that this combination operates as an 'OR' function (see Figure 5.10), whereby either representation or both will generate the same single resultant memory of $V^7 \to I$. The associated probability will be a union of the values pertaining to the two 'input' relationships.

Hence, we can hypothesise that the retrospective probabilities associated with the three progressions from the chord V^7 that the listener has experienced (two of them expressing a movement to I, and one characterised by a transition to vi) will interact in LTM as follows (see Figure 5.20).

Hence, the resultant retrospective probabilities associated with the memories of the two chordal transitions will be as follows (see Figure 5.21).

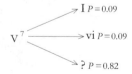

Figure 5.18 Modelling the third occasion upon which a listener hears the chord V^7.

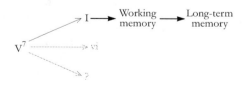

Figure 5.19 The second experience of $V^7 \to I$ will be transferred to LTM via WM.

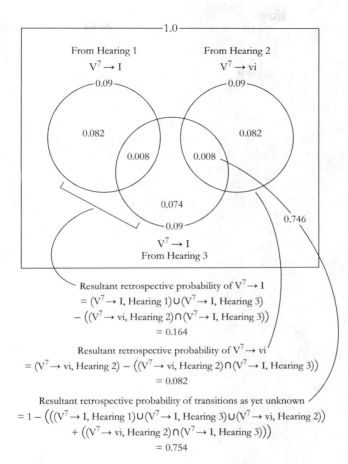

Figure 5.20 The retrospective probabilities associated with the three progressions from chord V^7 that the listener has experienced.

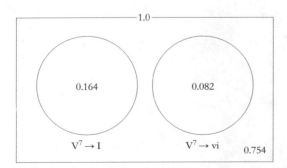

Figure 5.21 The retrospective probabilities associated with the memories of the chordal transitions $V^7 \rightarrow I$ and $V^7 \rightarrow vi$.

It is interesting to note that the ratio of the probabilities associated with the transitions $V^7 \rightarrow I$ and $V^7 \rightarrow vi$, which is 2:1, accords with their frequency of past occurrence. This is compatible with the findings of previous research that has shown that the strength of listeners' expectations in relation to given scale degrees corresponds to their distribution within a corpus of stylistically similar works (Huron, 2006, pp. 147–150). However, the thinking set out here offers two new insights: first, how the interaction of individual retrospective probabilities may function using binary logic that can be actualised in neural networks; and second, that more sophisticated estimates of expectation can be made that take into account the cumulative impact of events whose perceived probabilities of future occurrence are contingent on those that precede.

This effect can be modelled by considering a hypothetical fourth occasion upon which a transition from V^7 is heard. Let us assume once more the progression is to chord I. The interaction of the probability associated with this relationship and those heard in the past can be gauged using the same principles as before (see Figure 5.22).

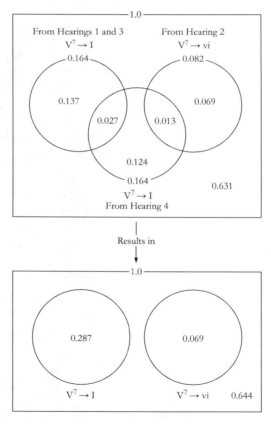

Figure 5.22 The retrospective probabilities associated with hearing of $V^7 \rightarrow I$, $V^7 \rightarrow vi$ and then two instances of $V^7 \rightarrow I$.

Table 5.3 The rise in the perceived probability of $V^7 \rightarrow I$ with repeated appearances (and the corresponding fall in the perceived probability of $V^7 \rightarrow vi$)

Following Hearing ...	Perceived probability of $V^7 \rightarrow I$	Perceived probability of $V^7 \rightarrow vi$
2	0.09	0.09
3	0.16	0.08
4	0.29	0.07
5	0.47	0.05
6	0.70	0.03
7	0.89	0.01
8	0.98	0.00
9	1	0.00

Here, the resultant ratio between the perceived retrospective probability of $V^7 \rightarrow I$, which has been heard three times, is approximately 0.29, while that pertaining to $V^7 \rightarrow vi$, heard only once, is around 0.07. The ratio between the two is about 4:1, rather higher than 3:1 suggested purely by their frequency of past occurrence. This is because the perceived probability of $V^7 \rightarrow I$ rises at an increasing rate over the first few hearings in which it occurs before falling back again as the potential maximum (1.0) is neared. Hence change is sigmoidal, as the data and graph in Table 5.3 and Figure 5.23 show.

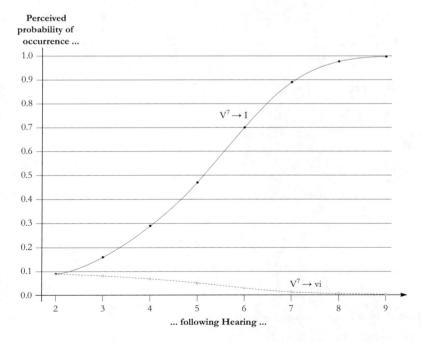

Figure 5.23 The sigmoidal changes in perceived probabilities pertaining to repeated hearings of $V^7 \rightarrow I$ in the context of a single hearing of $V^7 \rightarrow vi$.

With many repeated hearings, the outcome is very similar to that of the probability of a transition occurring that is derived only on the basis of its frequency of past occurrence, although, as the new model 'learns' from past experience, it achieves the same result more rapidly. There are also other differences between the two. For example, the new model has an order effect, whereby events that precede others in time display a certain probabilistic 'inertia', meaning that it operates asymmetrically in time. For example, if, following $V^7 \rightarrow$ I and $V^7 \rightarrow$ vi (each being heard once), the next *three* experiences that a listener has are of $V^7 \rightarrow$ I, then it would take a further *six* hearings of $V^7 \rightarrow$ vi for the probability of this transition to reach the level that $V^7 \rightarrow$ I had in Hearing 3 (see Table 5.4 and Figure 5.24).

Table 5.4 Data pertaining to the order effect of the probabilistic model that 'learns' from past experiences

Following Hearing ...	Transition	Perceived probability of V^7 to I	Perceived probability of V^7 to vi
3	$V^7 \rightarrow$ I	0.16	0.08
4	$V^7 \rightarrow$ I	0.29	0.07
5	$V^7 \rightarrow$ I	0.47	0.05
6	$V^7 \rightarrow$ vi	0.45	0.07
7	$V^7 \rightarrow$ vi	0.42	0.11
8	$V^7 \rightarrow$ vi	0.37	0.16
9	$V^7 \rightarrow$ vi	0.31	0.23
10	$V^7 \rightarrow$ vi	0.24	0.34
11	$V^7 \rightarrow$ vi	0.16	0.48

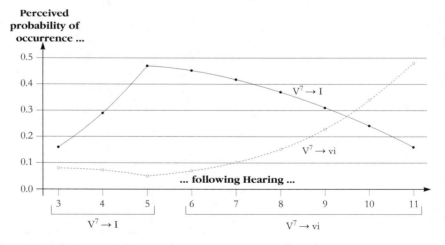

Figure 5.24 Visual representation of the order effect pertaining to three hearings of $V^7 \rightarrow$ I and six of $V^7 \rightarrow$ vi.

That is to say, once a stylistic 'norm' (such as a perfect cadence) has been established, it cannot readily be undone, and it would take many appearances of an alternative (such as an interrupted cadence) – more than would appear to be statistically justified based on the pure frequency of occurrence alone – to usurp the perceptual primacy of $V^7 \rightarrow I$. Hence, we have a mechanism to explain why, in musical terms, 'unlearning' is cognitively more demanding than learning.

Modelling the fusion of expectations deriving from events and frameworks in Hearing 1 of Trower's (2011) stimuli

We are now in a position to model how WM and LTM may have interacted to produce expectations in the first hearing of the Trower's (2011) stimuli. Let us imagine that two notes have been heard, and that a third is imminent. The first two will have been encoded in WM, and the relationship between them assessed reactively, while other connections will have been projected proactively into the future in an effort to anticipate what may occur next. Either type of relationship (reactive or proactive) may have triggered long-term memories – both of patterns of intervals and, potentially, of sequences of tonal functions (scale degrees) that may pertain to these – which, we can assume, will have been drawn into WM to exist alongside those deriving from the recent perceptual input (Figure 5.25).

The probabilities associated with relationships that point to a common outcome may combine using the 'OR' principle (see Figure 5.10). The indicative relationships shown in Figure 5.25, where $A = 0.1$, $B = 0.05$ and $C = 0.08$, point to a pitch with a net perceived probability as follows:

$$P(A \cup B \cup C) = P(A) + P(B) - P(A \cap B) + P(C) - P(A \cap B)$$
$$- P(A \cap C) + P(A \cap B \cap C)$$
$$= 0.1 + 0.05 + 0.08 - 0.005 - 0.008 - 0.004 + 0.0004$$
$$\approx 0.21$$

Other relationships stemming from the opening two notes (whether generated in WM or deriving from LTM or both) may point to alternative future options, each with their own associated probabilities. Hence, a *profile* of parallel possibilities is likely to exist in the mind before an event occurs (*cf.* Thorpe, Ockelford and Aksentijevic, 2012). As that event is perceived, one of those possibilities will become reified – and we can surmise that it is this that Trower's participants accessed in order to inform their response on the CReMA. The reified response will feed into the next cycle of anticipation, we may suppose, and so the process will continue (Figure 5.26).

166 *Adam Ockelford and Hayley Trower*

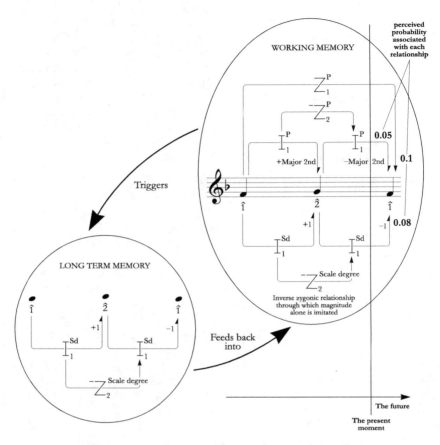

Figure 5.25 One hypothetical anticipatory outcome from two given notes, with associated probabilities.

Modelling the fusion of expectations deriving from events, frameworks and groups in Hearing 2 of Trower's (2011) stimuli

The position with regard to expectations arising in Hearing 2 is more complex, as it has the additional factor of the memory of Hearing 1. What is the nature of the storage and recall of this series of musical events? The distractor was intended to ensure that the capacity of WM was exceeded, and the conventional cognitive-psychological view is that listeners would have used long-term memory (LTM) to store the data (Goldstein, 2018, p. 153). However, there is a case for arguing that the notes are encoded in a form of 'intermediate-term' memory (ITM), as first posited by Rosenzweig *et al.* (1993). This is because the five pitches of the stimulus form a discrete group of musical events (that is encoded as a 'veridical' memory in

A zygonic approach 167

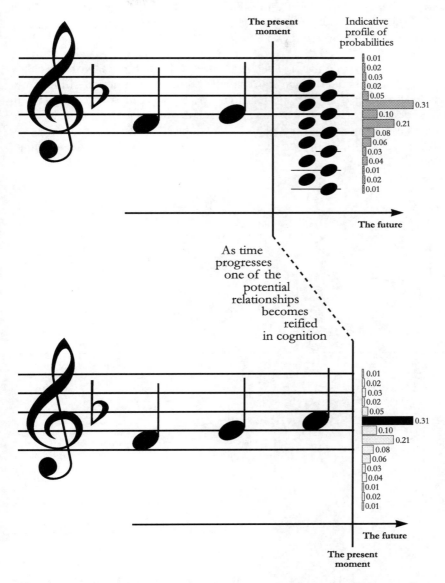

Figure 5.26 A plurality of potential continuations resolves into a single actuality.

Bharucha's terminology) but, through their recency, are too specific (yet) to contribute to a tonal schema (though that may subsequently happen in LTM). Hence, at the very least – and irrespective of terminology – there appear to be different modules in LTM that fulfil distinct functions. The line of reasoning advanced here implies that veridical musical memories can be held in both ITM and LTM, but schematic ones are present in LTM only. This additional feature can be included in the general zygonic model of implication and expectation in music (see Figure 4.6) as follows (Figure 5.27).

In formal terms, the perceived retrospective probability P with which the same note occurred in Hearing 2 (labelled 'N_{H2}') is a function of the implications arising from zygonic relationships 'z' pertaining to events (E) (in the current hearing, which we can reasonably assume are the same as or very similar to those generated by the previous hearing) and frameworks (F) (from previous hearings of stylistically congeneric pieces), and the impact

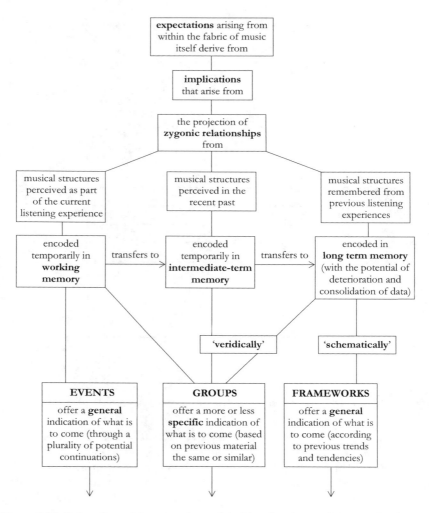

Figure 5.27 Expansion of the zygonic model of implication and expectation in music to include ITM.

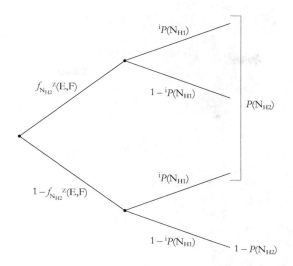

Figure 5.28 Expansion of the zygonic model of perceived retrospective probability P with which a given note heard in Hearing 1 will occur in Hearing 2.

'i' of the retrospective probability P associated with N from the first hearing, $^{i}P(N_{H1})$ (Figure 5.28).

Hence, in terms of set theory:

$$P(N_{H2}) = f_{N_{H2}}{}^{z}(E, F) \cup {}^{i}P(N_{H1})$$
$$= f_{N_{H2}}{}^{z}(E, F) + \left(1 - f_{N_{H2}}{}^{z}(E, F)\right) \cdot {}^{i}P(N_{H1})$$

where

0 (totally unexpected) $\leq P(N_{H2}) \leq 1$ (completely expected).

(Again, note the assumption that $f_{N_{H2}}{}^{z}(E, F) = f_{N_{H1}}{}^{z}(E, F)$).

Trower's data enable this fusion of different perceived probabilities to be quantified in relation to her listeners' experience of the melodic stimuli to which they were exposed. Consider, for example, the response of Trower's first participant (S_1) to the second note in the first sequence in Hearing 1 (H_{H1}), which is B in the fourth octave (B4); see Figure 5.3a. To distinguish this B4 from others, it will be labelled '$B4_{H1}$'. The expectation – that is, the perceived probability – of that musical event having the pitch B4 was, in retrospect, perceived to be 0.59.

$$S_1 : P(B4_{H1}) = f_{B4_{H1}}{}^{z}(E, F) = 0.59$$

This implies that the listener's expectation of a note *other than* B4 having occurred, of 'not B4' ('¬B4'), would have been

$$S_1 : P(\neg B4_{H1}) = 1 - f_{B4_{H1}}{}^{z}(E, F) = 1 - 0.59 = 0.41$$

170   *Adam Ockelford and Hayley Trower*

From Trower's data we also know S_1's perception of the probability pertaining retrospectively to the same note, B4, in Hearing 2:

$$S_1 : P(B4_{H2}) = f_{B4_{H2}}{}^z(E, F) + \left(\left(1 - f_{B4_{H2}}{}^z(E, F)\right) \cdot {}^iP(B4_{H1}) \right) = 0.60$$

Hence,

$$S_1 : P(\neg B4_{H2}) = 1 - \left(f_{B4_{H2}}{}^z(E, F) + \left(1 - f_{B4_{H2}}{}^z(E, F) \cdot {}^iP(B4_{H1})\right) \right) = 0.40$$

$$\Rightarrow 1 - \left(0.59 + \left(0.41 \cdot {}^iP(B4_{H1})\right)\right) = 0.40$$

$$\Rightarrow {}^iP(B4_{H1}) = 0.01/0.41 \approx 0.02$$

That is to say, around 2% of the expectation pertaining to B4 can be attributable to having heard the same group of notes previously.

In general terms, the impact of the level of expectation deriving from the first hearing of a note on that of the second – that is the *between groups* level of expectation – is

$$^iP(N_{H1}) = 1 - \frac{1 - P(N_{H2})}{1 - P(N_{H1})}$$

The binary logic of the neural network model set out above (see Table 5.1), whereby structural relationships that point to the same outcome are assumed to operate as an OR function, implies that the expectations pertaining to ${}^iP(N_{H1})$ in the second hearing of Trower's stimuli may overlap with the expectations pertaining to $f_{N_{H2}}(E, F)$. The degree of overlap, that is, $f_{N_{H2}}(E, F) \cap {}^iP(N_{H1})$, is a product of two variables:

$$f_{B4_{H2}}(E, F) \cap {}^iP(N_{H1}) = f_{B4_{H2}}(E, F) \cdot {}^iP(B4_{H1}) \approx 0.01$$

That is, in relation to B4, the expectations attributable to the effect of hearing a group of notes for a second time overlap by around 1% with those arising from events and frameworks (see Figure 5.29).

Extending the same thinking to the following two notes in Trower's Stimulus 1 (C#5 and another appearance of B4; see Figure 5.3a) yields the following results (where '$B4_{2.H1}$' refers to the *second* appearance of fourth octave B in Hearing 1):

$$S_1 : P\left(C^{\#}5_{H1}\right) = f_{C^{\#}{}_{H1}}{}^z(E, F) = 0.61$$

$$S_1 : P\left(C^{\#}5_{H2}\right) = f_{C^{\#}{}_{H2}}{}^z(E, F) + \left(\left(1 - f_{C^{\#}{}_{H2}}{}^z(E, F)\right) \cdot {}^iP\left(C^{\#}5_{H1}\right) \right) = 0.65$$

$$\Rightarrow \quad {}^iP\left(C^{\#}5_{H1}\right) \approx 0.10$$

$$f_{C^{\#}{}_{H2}}{}^z(E,F) \cap {}^iP\left(C^{\#}5_{H1}\right) = f_{C^{\#}{}_{H2}}{}^z(E, F) \cdot {}^iP\left(C^{\#}5_{H1}\right) \approx 0.06$$

A zygonic approach 171

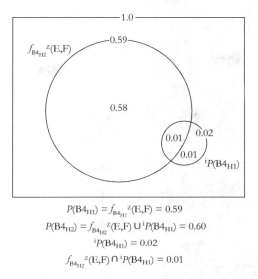

$P(B4_{H1}) = f_{B4_{H1}}{}^z(E,F) = 0.59$

$P(B4_{H2}) = f_{B4_{H2}}{}^z(E,F) \cup {}^iP(B4_{H1}) = 0.60$

${}^iP(B4_{H1}) = 0.02$

$f_{B4_{H2}}{}^z(E,F) \cap {}^iP(B4_{H1}) = 0.01$

Figure 5.29 The probabilities associated with the second hearing of the first B4 in Trower's first stimulus.

and

$$S_1 : P(B4_{2.H1}) = f_{B4_{2.H1}}{}^z(E, F) = 0.54$$

$$S_1 : P(B4_{2.H2}) = f_{B4_{2.H1}}{}^z(E, F) + \left(\left(1 - f_{B4_{2.H1}}{}^z(E, F) \cdot {}^iP(B4_{2.H1}) \right) \right) = 0.62$$

$$\Rightarrow \quad {}^iP(B4_{2.H1}) \approx 0.17$$

$$f_{B4_{2.H1}}{}^z(E, F) \cap {}^iP(B4_{2.H1}) = f_{B4_{2.H1}}{}^z(E, F) \cdot {}^iP(B4_{2.H1}) \approx 0.09$$

Visually this can be illustrated as follows (see Figure 5.30).

What do these data tell us? In accordance with the zygonic model, the expectations arising from events and frameworks continue to exert an influence in the second hearing – indeed they are main agent at work upon which the impact of the first hearing of the melody is felt as a modest force of intensification. These two effects are not additive, but overlapping. The pattern of increase and decrease in expectations relating to the first hearing is maintained in the second, although the difference between them increases with each note, which appears to be attributable to the growth in ${}^iP(N_{H1})$. It seems reasonable to speculate that this is due to a greater sense of certainty that the same group of notes will indeed be repeated as the second hearing of the series of stimuli unfolds.

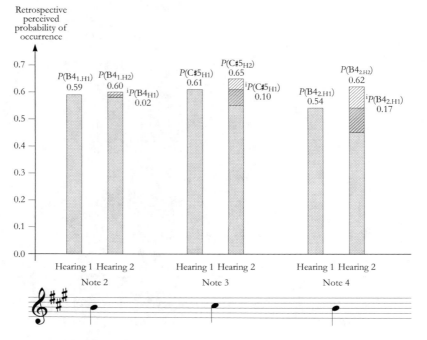

Figure 5.30 The probabilities associated with Notes 2–4 in the first and second hearings of Trower's first stimulus.

Table 5.5 The retrospective probabilities associated with Notes 2, 3 and 4 in Trower's stimuli, Hearings 1 and 2

Trial	Hearing 1			Hearing 2		
	Note 2	Note 3	Note 4	Note 2	Note 3	Note 4
1	0.59	0.61	0.54	0.60	0.65	0.62
2	0.57	0.53	0.55	0.60	0.59	0.62
3	0.60	0.61	0.64	0.57	0.57	0.62
4	0.55	0.60	0.59	0.63	0.64	0.62
5	0.58	0.62	0.66	0.64	0.65	0.67
6	0.56	0.53	0.62	0.59	0.61	0.64
7	0.56	0.57	0.59	0.58	0.59	0.65
8	0.59	0.62	0.57	0.62	0.65	0.62
9	0.60	0.63	0.65	0.60	0.65	0.64
10	0.61	0.62	0.52	0.62	0.64	0.62
11	0.56	0.55	0.56	0.61	0.63	0.59
12	0.57	0.59	0.62	0.57	0.61	0.61
13	0.60	0.59	0.60	0.65	0.62	0.65
14	0.56	0.55	0.51	0.58	0.61	0.57
15	0.55	0.53	0.56	0.60	0.61	0.66
16	0.57	0.55	0.58	0.60	0.62	0.66
Mean	**0.576**	**0.581**	**0.585**	**0.604**	**0.621**	**0.629**

These characteristics are replicated across the 16 stimuli as a whole (see Table 5.5).

In the equations that follow, means are indicated with 'bar' notation, and where a single letter represents a number of events or characteristics, it is shown in an outline font. So, for example, the first equation reads: 'Pertaining to Stimuli 1–16: the mean probability associated with all the second notes of the stimuli ("Notes 2"), Hearing 1, is the mean of the function of the structural implications of Events and Frameworks, and equals 0.576'. Observe that that the 'F' for Frameworks is not outlined, since the probabilities associated with frameworks are, for the sake of the model, deemed to be the same in each stimulus.

Note 2

$$S_{1-16}: P(\overline{\mathbb{N}_{2.H1}}) = f_{\mathbb{N}_{2.H1}}{}^z(\overline{\mathbb{E},F}) \approx 0.576$$

$$S_{1-16}: P(\overline{\mathbb{N}_{2.H2}}) = f_{\mathbb{N}_{2.H2}}{}^z(\overline{\mathbb{E},F}) + (1 - f_{\mathbb{N}_{2.H2}}{}^z(\overline{\mathbb{E},F}) \cdot {}^iP(\overline{\mathbb{N}_{2.H1}})) \approx 0.604$$

$$S_{1-16}: {}^iP(\overline{\mathbb{N}_{2.H1}}) = 1 - \frac{1 - P(\overline{\mathbb{N}_{2.H2}})}{1 - P(\overline{\mathbb{N}_{2.H1}})} \approx 0.066$$

$$S_{1-16}: f_{\mathbb{N}_{2.H2}}{}^z(\overline{\mathbb{E},F}) \cap {}^iP(\overline{\mathbb{N}_{2.H1}}) \approx 0.038$$

Note 3

$$S_{1-16}: P(\overline{\mathbb{N}_{3.H1}}) = f_{\mathbb{N}_{3.H1}}{}^z(\overline{\mathbb{E},F}) \approx 0.581$$

$$S_{1-16}: P(\overline{\mathbb{N}_{3.H2}}) = f_{\mathbb{N}_{3.H2}}{}^z(\overline{\mathbb{E},F}) + (1 - f_{\mathbb{N}_{3.H2}}{}^z(\overline{\mathbb{E},F}) \cdot {}^iP(\overline{\mathbb{N}_{3.H1}})) \approx 0.621$$

$$S_{1-16}: {}^iP(\overline{\mathbb{N}_{3.H1}}) = 1 - \frac{1 - P(\overline{\mathbb{N}_{3.H2}})}{1 - P(\overline{\mathbb{N}_{3.H1}})} \approx 0.096$$

$$S_{1-16}: f_{\mathbb{N}_{3.H2}}{}^z(\overline{\mathbb{E},F}) \cap {}^iP(\overline{\mathbb{N}_{3.H1}}) \approx 0.056$$

Note 4

$$S_{1-16}: P(\overline{\mathbb{N}_{4.H1}}) = f_{\mathbb{N}_{4.H1}}{}^z(\overline{\mathbb{E},F}) \approx 0.585$$

$$S_{1-16}: P(\overline{\mathbb{N}_{4.H2}}) = f_{\mathbb{N}_{4.H2}}{}^z(\overline{\mathbb{E},F}) + (1 - f_{\mathbb{N}_{4.H2}}{}^z(\overline{\mathbb{E},F}) \cdot {}^iP(\overline{\mathbb{N}_{4.H1}})) \approx 0.629$$

$$S_{1-16}: {}^iP(\overline{\mathbb{N}_{4.H1}}) = 1 - \frac{1 - P(\overline{\mathbb{N}_{4.H2}})}{1 - P(\overline{\mathbb{N}_{4.H1}})} \approx 0.106$$

$$S_{1-16}: f_{\mathbb{N}_{4.H2}}{}^z(\overline{\mathbb{E},F}) \cap {}^iP(\overline{\mathbb{N}_{4.H1}}) \approx 0.062$$

This analysis is represented visually in Figure 5.31. Observe that the perceived retrospective probability of notes rises as the stimulus progresses, and that the *difference* in expectation between Hearings 1 and 2 also increases with successive notes.

174　*Adam Ockelford and Hayley Trower*

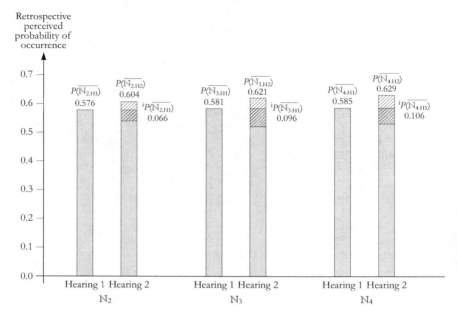

Figure 5.31 The mean changes in retrospective perceived probability associated with Notes 2–4 in Hearings 1 and 2 of Trower's stimulus.

The present study

Introduction

The present study, which constitutes part of Trower's doctoral research, seeks to test and potentially refine the zygonic model further by investigating how listeners' expectations are affected by *repeated* hearings – in the short, medium and long term. A diatonic melody of 26 notes was played to 43 individual listeners eight times (in two groups of four trials, around a week apart), and participants' responses to the question of how expected they perceived each note to have been, having just heard it, were gauged using a commercially available touch-sensitive strip, which fulfilled the same, bipolar function as the CReMA did in the previous experiment, offering listeners a continuous scale along which they could respond in real time.

What results would the model predict? From the second hearing onwards, we would expect there to be an interaction between the within-hearing expectations (deriving from events and frameworks) and those stemming from the previous hearing or hearings (arising from groups). Specifically, against a backdrop of the natural variation arising from the vagaries of human perception and cognition and the representation of thought through movement, one would

a anticipate that the 'contour' of expectations (the rise and fall of perceived probabilities arising from successive notes) would initially be maintained, but
b at a higher average level (see Figure 5.31) and
c with a tendency in subsequent hearings to move towards a 'flat line' ceiling of complete certainty ($P = 1.0$). This trend is inevitable because of the way that $f_{N_{H2}}{}^z(E, F)$ and $^iP(N_{H1})$ interact. The degree of overlap, given by $f_{N_{H2}}{}^z(E, F) \cap {}^iP(N_{H1})$, will grow as either term increases. At the same time, as $f_{N_{H2}}{}^z(E, F)$ grows, the amount of *additional* expectation, calculated by $^iP(N_{H1}) - f_{N_{H2}}{}^z(E, F) \cap {}^iP(N_{H1})$, will inevitably fall.

In addition, in the first hearing, we would anticipate a general tendency to greater certainty as the melody progressed (due to the higher number of zygonic relationships pointing to a particular outcome – *cf.* Figure 5.5).

What effect would the gap of a week have? It has long been recognised anecdotally (for a summary, see Greasley and Lamont, 2013) that overexposure to a piece can leave listeners jaded. This ties in with the prediction set out above that, as relationships between groups grow stronger, the expectations pertaining to events become less differentiated, and so eventually the music will become aesthetically monotonous. However, by refraining from excessive repetition of a piece – through leaving sufficient time between hearings – it seems that listeners can (and intuitively do) avoid the 'flat line' of expectations. What could the underlying cognitive mechanism for this be?

Logically, the one thing to have changed is the nature of the relationships between groups (that is, between hearings of the piece), in that they are subject to greater temporal separation. Could it be that this weakens the relative impact of groups compared to the greater immediacy of events and the more robust memories arising from frameworks (stemming from thousands of hours of previous exposure to stylistically congeneric material)? This issue will be explored in the analysis that follows.

Materials

The stimulus melody was the same as that used by Thorpe, Ockelford and Aksentijevic (2012) (see Figure 5.32), which was specially created and recorded digitally to fulfil the following criteria:

1 The main focus should be on pitch, and limited to notes from a major diatonic scale (a familiar framework for Western listeners).
2 Other musical elements such as rhythm, dynamics, timbre and tessitura should be kept as 'neutral' as possible.
3 The stimulus should be an unaccompanied melody to avoid the activation of expectations that may arise from harmonic relationships.
4 The stimulus should be novel so that listeners could provide a baseline response that is unaffected by previous exposure.

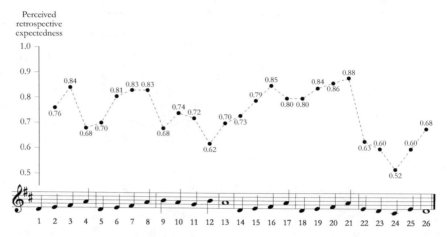

Figure 5.32 Mean levels of retrospective perceived expectedness per note pertaining to the 26-note stimulus.

The tempo was set to 40 beats per minute: slow enough to give time for participants to respond, without having a negative effect on the unfolding melodic narrative, which requires individual notes to be linked in the mind to form gestalts (Trower, 2011). Additionally, nine distractor sequences were created comprising eight randomly selected pitches within a two-octave range. They were presented at 100 beats per minute, using the same timbre as the stimulus – a Steinway grand piano.

One of the distractors was played between each presentation of the stimulus in an effort to clear any traces of it from WM, in accordance with Deutsch (1999), who found that a series of random tones of the same type of sound as the target stimulus offer an effective short-term distractor. A shorter practice melody was devised according to the criteria set out above, to acquaint participants with the rating equipment and the requirements of the task.

Participants

Forty-three adult participants, 27 males and 16 females, with a 50-year age range ($M = 33$, SD $= 12.6$), were recruited through social media and took part in the study. They had a diversity of musical backgrounds, with 0–24 years of formal musical training ($M = 4.17$). Forty participants were British (of varying ethnic legacies), with one Canadian, one Italian and one Hungarian. All participants were immersed in Western music, as listeners or performers.

Results (i): a phenomenological analysis of Hearing 1

The mean levels of expectedness per note gauged retrospectively by the 43 participants in Hearing 1 were as follows (see Figure 5.32), normalised to a scale of 0 to 1. Although it was not made explicit to participants in the study, we can assume that their judgements of expectation were made in relation to pitch, as other parameters – durations, inter-onset intervals, timbre and dynamics – were kept constant (with the exception of the longer notes at the end of each phrase), and so were very predictable. No judgement was made in relation to first note that was heard.

It is possible to interpret these results using zygonic theory by identifying the structural relationships pertaining to events, groups and frameworks that may exist in relation to each note, and tentatively assigning causal connections. Some of the interactions between different forms of structure (in particular, those involving groups) can be resolved using the probabilistic methods outlined above relating to repeated hearings. A further potential source of evidence is the expectations elicited in response to the same melody by Thorpe, Ockelford and Aksentijevic (2012), which adopted a wholly different approach to gathering data. Here, after each note, participants ($N=40$) were asked to indicate, by singing, which pitch they thought was most likely to come next. Hence, the expectations were *proactive* (and prospective) rather than *reactive* (and retrospective), and a *range* of responses was given in relation to each musical event. One may reasonably anticipate that these expressions of anticipation would be lower than those given by Tower's participants, since in effect Thorpe *et al.*'s participants were asked to respond to an open question about the future, whereas Trower's were asked to reflect on a closed outcome that was already in the past. We would further expect that the more predictable the events were (through a greater number structural relationships pointing to their existence), the closer the judgements of prospective and retrospective expectedness would become. Hence, the value of Thorpe *et al.*'s data to the current analysis is more likely to lie at points of greater ambiguity in the melody, when information may be revealed about the expectations pertaining to notes that did not actually occur, which potentially have the capacity to shed light on the perception of those that did.

The results were as follows, expressed as proportions of the research cohort ranging from 0 to 1 (Figure 5.33). Those relating to the pitches that subsequently materialised are shown in boxes. The highest proportion in each case is indicated using bold type. So, for example, following Note 1 (D4), responses ranged from G3 to D5, with the majority (48%) anticipating the second pitch of the melody correctly (E4).

Despite their differences, for these data to illuminate the results of the current study, the two need to have sufficient commonality to enable reasonable comparisons and inferences to be drawn, and the correlation between (a) the proportion of listeners anticipating a given pitch correctly in Thorpe *et al.*'s study and (b) the mean degree of expectedness assigned to the same pitch by Trower's participants is surprisingly high given the contrasting methodologies that were used. Visually, the relationship becomes apparent when Thorpe *et al.*'s figures are transposed and scaled, whereby

178   *Adam Ockelford and Hayley Trower*

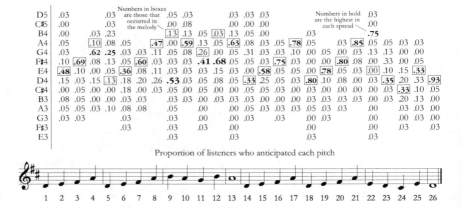

Figure 5.33 Summary of sung anticipatory responses following each note of the melody (except the last).

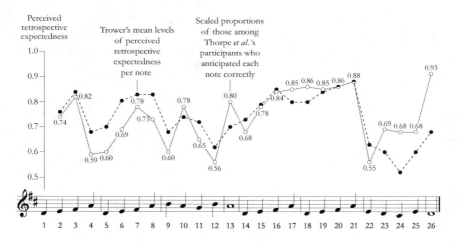

Figure 5.34 Trower's and Thorpe *et al.*'s data are highly correlated.

they have the same mean and range (Figure 5.34). The two series as a whole are strongly correlated: $R = 0.65$, $p = 0.0005$. However, there appears to be a clear point of divergence from Note 23 to the end of the melody (Note 26). Discounting these four notes (of which more later), the correlation is $R = 0.86$, $p < 0.0001$.

Hence, it is reasonable to feed these data into the zygonic phenomenological analysis of Trower's participants' responses to the first hearing of the melody (see Table 5.6). This considers the cognitive activity that we may suppose is triggered by each event, and in particular examines the implications for WM, intermediate-term memory and long-term memory.

Note	Expectation	General comments	Expectations thought to be generated from events, groups and frameworks
Before stimulus is heard	Very general (depends on the context set by experimenter)	The relationships between the three modules posited to exist in memory are held to exist as follows (see Figure 5.35). Input from the auditory processing system (APS) enters working memory (WM), which feeds into intermediate-term memory (ITM) and long-term memory (LTM), which are themselves connected. Each connection permits data flow in either direction. Expectations are generated by WM from its own representation of immediate perceptual input and using data from ITM, LTM or both. Expectations prime the auditory perceptual system. See Figure 5.35.	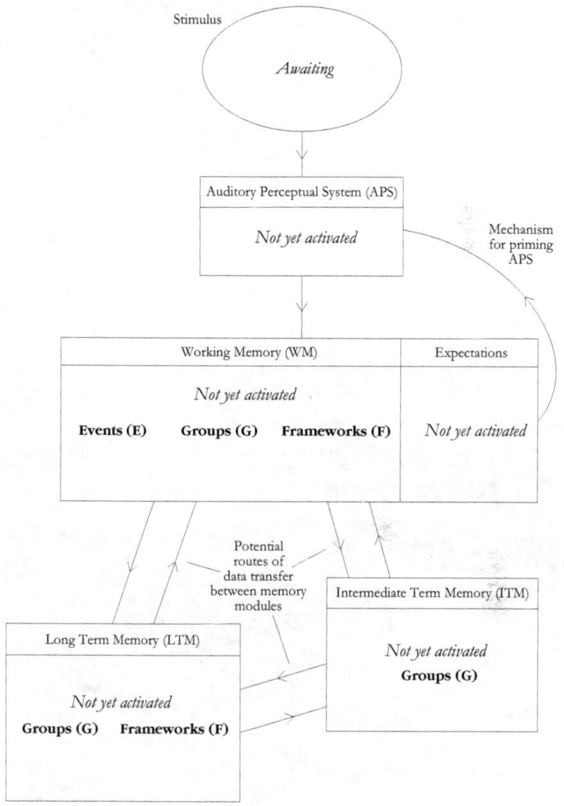

Figure 5.35 A proposed structure of the modules in musical memory.

Note	Expectation	General comments	Events, groups and frameworks
1 (D4)	Not recorded in the current study or in Thorpe et al.'s (2012)	Note 1 is encoded by the APS. This representation enters WM as $N_{1,H1}$ and stimulates frameworks (although not yet groups) in LTM. The default framework in Western listeners is the major mode. A representation of this feeds back into WM. $N_{1,H1}$ and the representation of the major mode interact to produce initial expectations. These prime the APS (see comments on Note 2 pertaining to Thorpe et al.'s participants). See Figure 5.36.	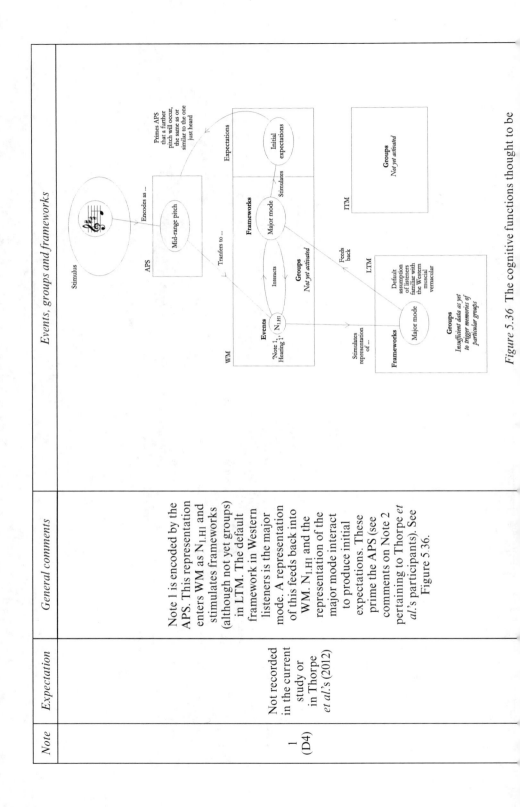

Figure 5.36 The cognitive functions thought to be

2 (E4)	0.76	Participants assigned a relatively high degree of retrospective expectedness to this note, despite it being only the second one of the melody. In Thorpe *et al.*'s (2012) study, 48% anticipated E4 correctly, showing the powerful impact of frameworks at this early stage in proceedings. Evidently, listeners strongly anticipate structure, even with few immediate data to draw on.	Accords with the principle of pitch proximity (Huron, 2006) through the imperfect primary zygonic imitation of pitch (Ockelford, 2006) – see Figure 5.37. *Figure 5.37* Expectation weakly derived from pitch proximity.	Transition from Note 1 to Note 2 comprises a major second (the most prevalent interval in the major scale, which is the most prevalent mode in Western music). It is ascending, and so conforms to the most frequent form of melodic opening (Huron, 2006) – see Figure 5.38. 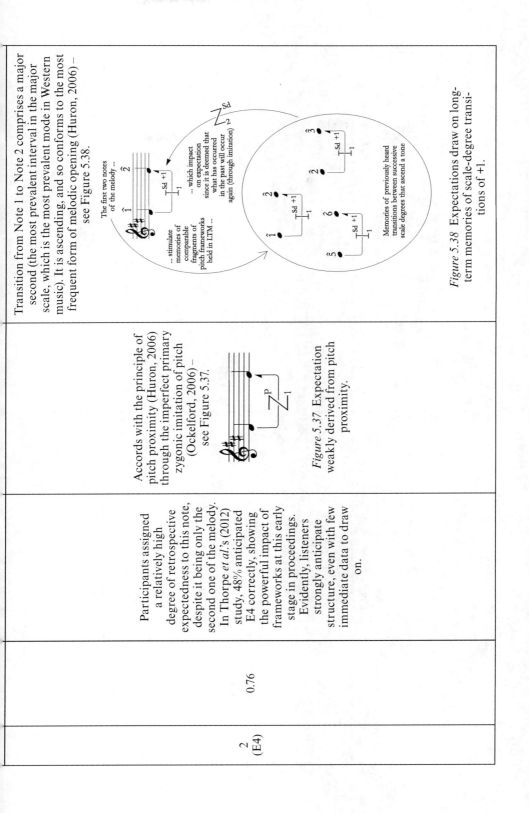 *Figure 5.38* Expectations draw on long-term memories of scale-degree transitions of +1.

Note	Expectation	General comments	Events	Frameworks
3 (F#4)	0.84	An increase in retrospective expectedness over Note 2 greater than 10% may be attributed to the first perfect zygonic relationship at the level of events. This was anticipated by around 70% of the participants in Thorpe *et al.*'s (2012) study. These data suggest just how deeply ingrained the pattern of an ascending major scale may be in stylistically attuned listeners.	Perfect imitation at the level of events lends assurance to expectation (Figure 5.39). *Figure 5.39* A solitary secondary zygonic relationship of scale degree deriving from the first interval of the melody leads to a strong prediction of Note 3.	Confirmation of the assumptions made in relation to Note 2 concerning mode and archetypal opening melodic ascent.

Note	Expectation	General comments	Events	Groups	Frameworks
4 (A4)	0.68	There is a sharp decrease (19%) in retrospective expectedness. This is well below the level attributed to Note 2, which only weakly derived from Note 1 at the level of events (more strongly at the level of frameworks). Yet now there is a perfect secondary zygonic relationship of scale degree potentially linking Notes 1, 3 and 4. So why is the perceived level of expectedness not higher? Thorpe et al.'s (2012) study indicates that 62% of listeners expected the ascending scale to continue to G4 through a further secondary zygonic relationship of scale degree, while 15% anticipated a return to D4 (possibly associated the first three notes with the opening of *Frère Jacques*). Hence, it appears to be less a case of A4 being intrinsically unexpected than other continuations being perceived as (more) probable. The cognitive processes presumed to underpin the expectations pertaining to Note 4 are shown in Figure 5.42.	The three pitches give rise to a number of coherent continuations; the logic that leads to G4 being most powerful with two zygonic connections, and to which every note contributes, with the maintenance of sequence (Figure 5.40). The stimulus melody jumps to the fifth degree of the scale to continue The most common prediction is for the ascending scale to continue *Figure 5.40* The melody's continuation is relatively unexpected as other continuations are structurally more powerful.	There is the possibility that the first three notes triggered a memory of *Frère Jacques* in LTM, which subsequently influenced expectation in some listeners (Figure 5.41). *Figure 5.41* The opening three notes of the melody may have stimulated groups in LTM.	All anticipated continuations utilise the framework of the major scale, providing the scaffolding upon which projections of pitch are hung, while constantly being reinforced by the materials that are heard.

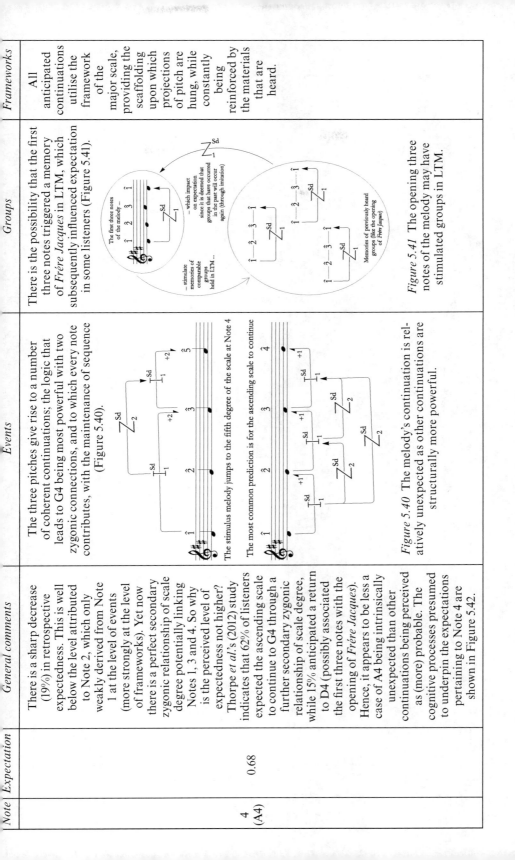

Note	Expectation	General comments	Events, groups and frameworks 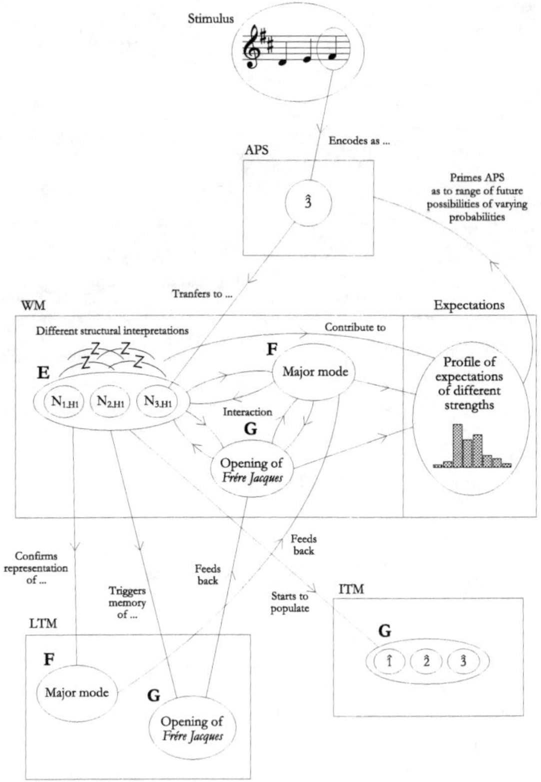

Figure 5.42 Model of the cognitive processes postulated to underpin the expectations pertaining to Note 4

Note	Expectation	General comments	Events	Frameworks
5 (D4)	0.70	Retrospective expectedness remains at a relatively low level. D4 is the first note to be repeated, but the number and spread of Thorpe *et al.*'s data (nine pitches between A3 and D5) show something of the range of logical continuations that were possible following Note 4, and listeners' open-earedness as to what may come next.	The four most frequently anticipated continuations in Thorpe *et al.*'s (2012) study are shown in Figure 5.43.	Again, the major scale provides a framework for the new material, which in turn reinforces it.

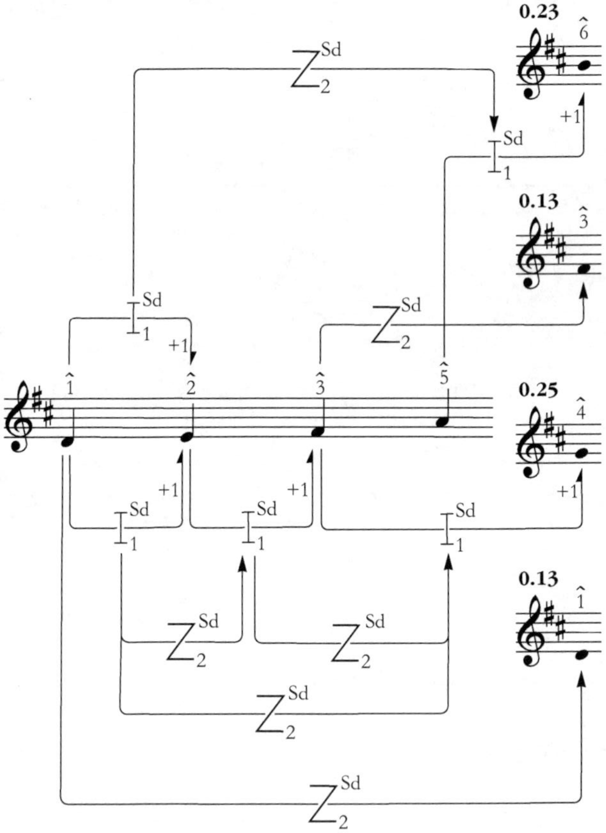

Figure 5.43 Model of the cognitive processes postulated to underpin the expectations pertaining to Note 5.

Note	Expectation	General comments	Events	Frameworks

Note	Expectation	General comments	Events	Groups	Frameworks
6 (E4)	0.81	Retrospective expectedness rises by 16% as the possibility that the first four notes will be repeated as a group gains cognitive traction. This outcome is also the one most frequently anticipated by Thorpe *et al.*'s (2012) participants, but at only 36%, the disparity between prospective and retrospective expectedness is considerable.	A repeated sequence of two events (Figure 5.44) … *Figure 5.44* The derivation of Note 6 from Note 2 parallels that of Note 5 from Note 1.	… leads to the possibility of group repetition (Figure 5.45). *Figure 5.45* Primary zygonic relationship of pitch operating at the level of groups.	The immediate repetition of motifs is a structural commonplace in the Western musical vernacular; hence, the possibility of the opening motif being repeated will be supported by previous listening experiences.
7 (F#4)	0.83	There is a further small increase in retrospective expectedness as the group repetition is confirmed. However, 60% of Thorpe *et al.*'s (2012) participants predicted the group repetition, an increase of two-thirds on the degree of expectedness pertaining to Note 6. This supports the hypothesis that retrospective and prospective expectedness will be more closely aligned when there is less structural ambiguity.	Further parallel zygonic relationships at the level of events (Figure 5.46) … *Figure 5.46* The derivation of Note 7 from Note 3 extends the imitative pattern.	… are strongly suggestive of group repetition (Figure 5.47). *Figure 5.47* The relationship between groups strengthens.	Again, the stylistic tendency to repeat motifs will add weight to the zygonic relationships functioning at the level of events and groups.

Notes	Expectation	General comments	Groups
8 (A4)	0.83	With Note 8, the repetition of the opening four-note motif is complete. To what extent are the four predictions suggested by zygonic theory (see p. 177) fulfilled? (a) Maintenance of contour (b) A generally higher level of expectedness (c) Tendency to flat line (towards 1.0) (d) Increasing expectedness through the growing impact of relationships between groups. (a) *Maintenance of contour* Contour is maintained, though the difference between the retrospective expectedness pertaining to Notes 7 and 8 is small. Why should this be the case, when, as we shall see, the fourth (and last) note of the group has more structural indicators than any of those notes that precede? It may be due to the residual feeling of surprise that the pitch A4 evoked in the first hearing of the group (g_1) being transferred to the second (g_2), following the same principle as that proposed in the re-analysis of Trower's (2011) data above (see Figure 5.48).	 *Figure 5.48* The maintenance, though weakening, of contour between Group 1('g_1') and Group 2 ('g_2') with a general increase in expectation: three potentially conflicting forces fuse in a single series of perceived probabilities.

(b) *A generally higher level of expectedness*
The mean level of expectedness pertaining to Notes 6–8 is higher than that pertaining to Notes 2–4 (0.82 as opposed to 0.76) (notwithstanding the small discrepancy in the data for Notes 2 and 5) – see Figure 5.48.

(c) *Tendency to flat line at 1.0*
The tendency towards a flat line is indicated by the average difference between successive values being 0.11 for Notes 2–4 and 0.01 for Notes 6–8 (Figure 5.48).

(d) *Increasing expectedness through the group*
The decrement between Notes 8 and 7 notwithstanding, there is a general trend of increase through the group g_2 (see Figure 5.48). Moreover, the influence of g_1 increases from 0.21 (Notes 2 and 6) to 0.47 (Notes 4 and 8). See Figure 5.49. Hence the zygonic relationships *between* groups g_1 and of g_2 override those *within* the group g_2 (Figure 5.50).

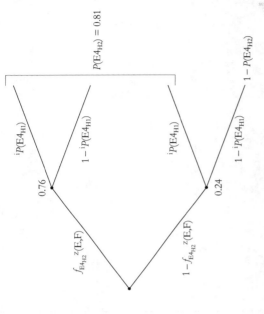

The impact of Note 2 on Note 6

$${}^{i}P(E4_{H1}) = 1 - \frac{1 - P(E4_{H2})}{1 - f_{E4_{H2}}{}^{z}(E,F)} = 1 - \frac{0.19}{0.24} \approx 0.21$$

Similarly, the impact of Note 4 on Note 8

$${}^{i}P(A4_{H1}) = 1 - \frac{1 - P(A4_{H2})}{1 - f_{A4_{H2}}{}^{z}(E,F)} = 1 - \frac{0.17}{0.32} \approx 0.47$$

Figure 5.49 The influence of notes in g1 on those that correspond in g_2 increases over the course of the group.

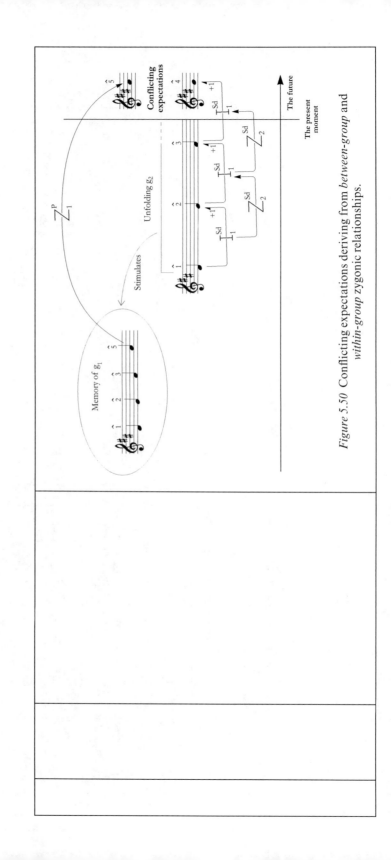

Figure 5.50 Conflicting expectations deriving from *between-group* and *within-group* zygonic relationships.

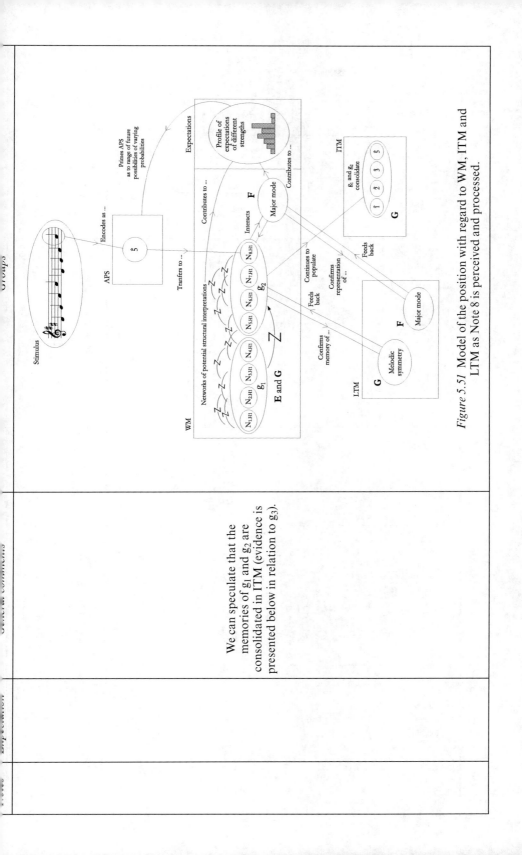

Figure 5.51 Model of the position with regard to WM, ITM and LTM as Note 8 is perceived and processed.

We can speculate that the memories of g_1 and g_2 are consolidated in ITM (evidence is presented below in relation to g_3).

Notes	Expectation	General comments	Events and groups	Frameworks
9 (B4)	0.68	Retrospective expectedness falls to its lowest level yet with the appearance of B4. This demonstrates the importance of context beyond events (particularly at the level of groups) of expectedness, since earlier instances of an ascending major second were deemed to be far more expected. Here, though, with a repeated group having just ended, it is difficult for listeners to predict what will occur next. Fifty-three per cent of Thorpe et al.'s (2012) participants predicted a further D4 – arguably the most logical choice, potentially indicative of a further repetition of g_1. However, other responses were wide-ranging, from E3 to D5, with 12 different pitches being presented as potential continuations.	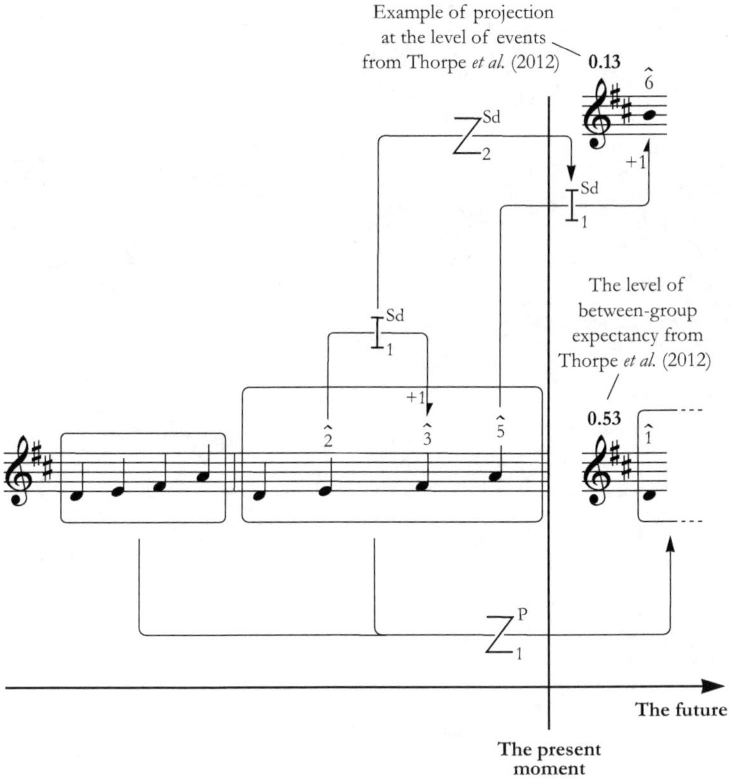 Example of projection at the level of events from Thorpe et al. (2012) 0.13 $\hat{6}$ +1 Z^{Sd}_2 The level of between-group expectancy from Thorpe et al. (2012) 0.53 $\hat{1}$ +1 $\hat{2}$ $\hat{3}$ $\hat{5}$ Z^P_1 The present moment The future	Amid the uncertainty, a further appearance of the tonic (D4) is a 'safe bet' (Krumhansl and Kessler, 1982).

Figure 5.52 In the face of uncertainty, listeners tend to opt for the relative safety of between-group projections.

Notes	Expectation	General comments	Events and groups	Frameworks
10 (A4)	0.74	A slight increase in retrospective expectedness is mirrored in 59% of Thorpe *et al.*'s participants anticipating A4 correctly. What is the source of this increase? Potentially, it could be through inversion of the opening interval of g_1 (and g_2). If so, we would anticipate G4 to be expected next. However, this expectation does not materialise (see below). Hence, it seems likely that the increase in expectedness is due to an effect of 'regression to the mean': the central pitch level of g_1 and g_2 is around $F^{\#}4$, so the further away a pitch is from that average, the more likely it is that the following pitch will be closer.	*Figure 5.53* Notes 9–11 do not tend to be heard as an inversion of Notes 5–7 (or 1–3).	Reflects the tendency of relatively high or low notes in a melody to be followed by others that are closer to the 'mean'.
11 (G4)	0.72	There are decreases in both retrospective expectedness and Thorpe *et al.*'s participants' proactive responses (with only 26% predicting G4). Hence, the interpretation of B4, A4, G4 as an inversion of D4, E4, $F^{\#}4$ is not favoured. The preferred structural interpretation is 'regression to the mean', with 41% of Thorpe *et al.*'s participants expecting $F^{\#}4$ (the approximate central pitch level of g_1 and g_2).		

Notes	Expectation	General comments	Events	Frameworks
12 (B4)	0.62	A further 14% decrease in retrospective expectedness can be attributed to the expectation expressed by 68% of Thorpe *et al.*'s participants that the descending pattern of B4, A4, G4 – now recognised as a pattern in its own right – will continue to $F^{\#}4$.	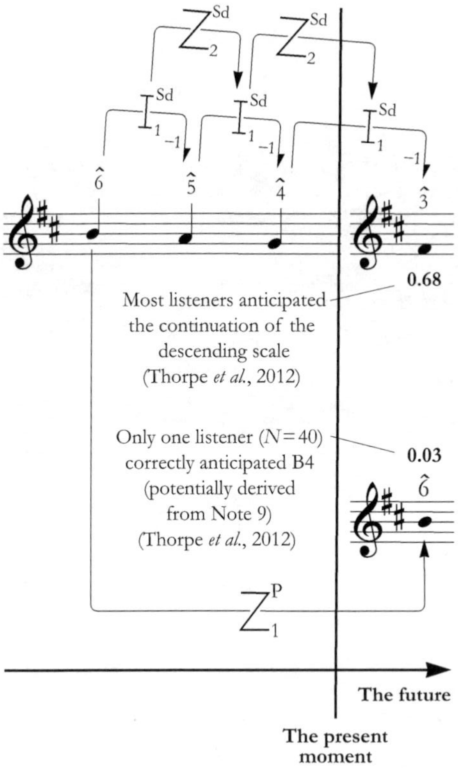Sd 2 Sd 2 Sd 1 −1 Sd 1 −1 Sd 1 −1 6̂ 5̂ 4̂ 3̂ 0.68 Most listeners anticipated the continuation of the descending scale (Thorpe et al., 2012) Only one listener (N = 40) correctly anticipated B4 (potentially derived from Note 9) (Thorpe et al., 2012) 0.03 6̂ P 1 The future The present moment *Figure 5.54* The move back up to B4 is unexpected.	Once more, the major scale provides a framework for the new material, which in turn reinforces it.

| 13 (A4) | 0.70 | Retrospective expectedness increases by 13%, a rise that can be accounted for by imitation at the level of events. Sixty-three per cent of Thorpe et al.'s participants anticipate the move to A4. There may be an added factor at work here at the level of frameworks. | 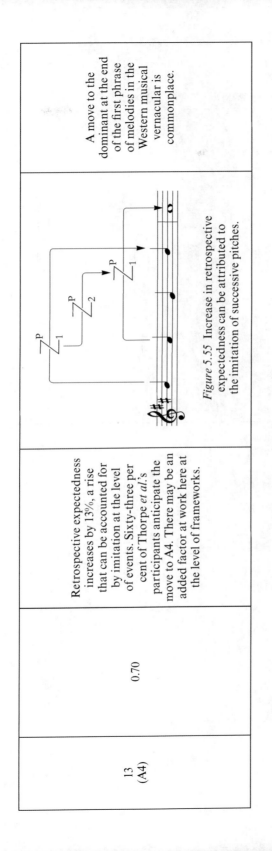 Figure 5.55 Increase in retrospective expectedness can be attributed to the imitation of successive pitches. | A move to the dominant at the end of the first phrase of melodies in the Western musical vernacular is commonplace. |

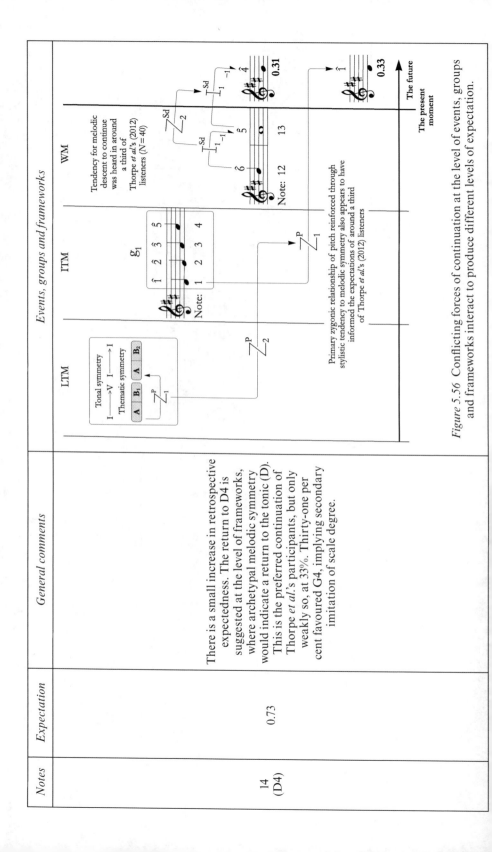

Figure 5.56 Conflicting forces of continuation at the level of events, groups and frameworks interact to produce different levels of expectation.

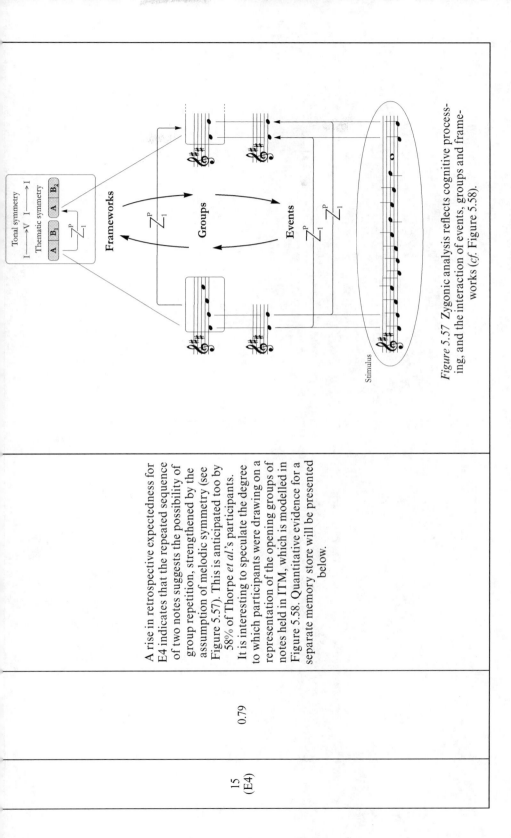

Figure 5.57 Zygonic analysis reflects cognitive processing, and the interaction of events, groups and frameworks (*cf.* Figure 5.58).

| 15 (E4) | 0.79 | A rise in retrospective expectedness for E4 indicates that the repeated sequence of two notes suggests the possibility of group repetition, strengthened by the assumption of melodic symmetry (see Figure 5.57). This is anticipated too by 58% of Thorpe *et al.*'s participants.

It is interesting to speculate the degree to which participants were drawing on a representation of the opening groups of notes held in ITM, which is modelled in Figure 5.58. Quantitative evidence for a separate memory store will be presented below. |

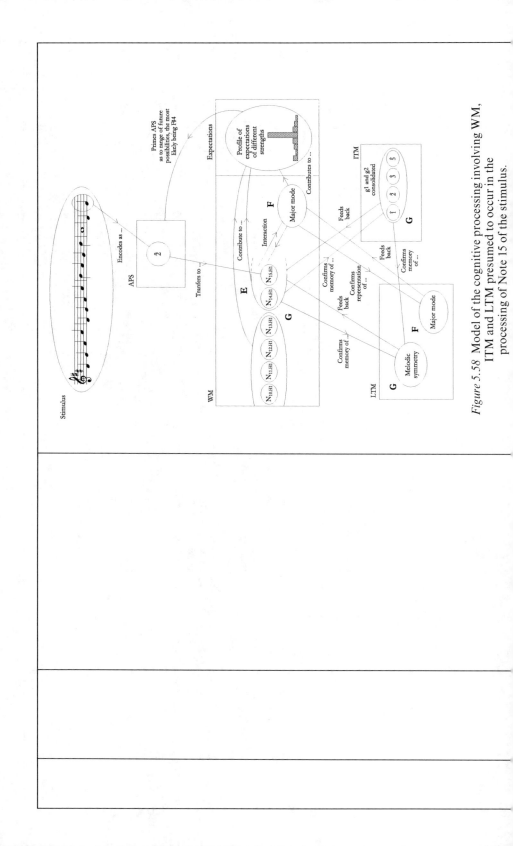

Figure 5.58 Model of the cognitive processing involving WM, ITM and LTM presumed to occur in the processing of Note 15 of the stimulus.

Notes	Expectation	General comments	Events and groups	Frameworks
16 (F#4)	0.85	Retrospective expectedness reaches its highest level yet, as imitation of g_1, supported by g_2, to produce g_3 is now unambiguous. Seventy-five per cent of Thorpe *et al.*'s participants share the same view.	*Figure 5.59* The sequence of three notes, repeated three times, is strongly suggestive of group repetition.	Archetypal melodic symmetry is now almost certain to occur.

Notes	Expectation	General comments	Groups
17 (A4)	0.80	With Note 17, g_3 ends. Again, as in g_1 and g_2, the fourth note has a dip in retrospective expectedness. It is reasonable to surmise that the expectations set up by events still play a part, despite this being the third iteration of the same series of notes. This is supported by data from Thorpe *et al.*'s study, in which 10% of participants predicted G4 (although a large majority, 78%, preferred A4). The four predictions of zygonic theory when a group is repeated (maintenance of contour, a generally higher level of expectedness, the tendency to flat line and increasing expectedness through the group) will be considered in relation to g_3 at the same time as g_4 (see below). For now, it is worth noting how the impact of g_1 and g_2 which we are assuming to have been consolidated in ITM compares with that of g_1 alone. The average impact of g_1 on g_2 is 0.25 (see Figure 5.60). The average impact of the fusion of g_1 and g_2 on g_3 is only 0.21 (see Figure 5.61). Why should this be so?	Average expectation arising internally from the second group of notes, '$g_{2.H1}$' is the same as that arising internally from the first group, '$g_{1.H1}$' $$= \frac{P(E4_{1.H1}) + P(F\sharp4_{1.H1}) + P(A4_{1.H1})}{3}$$ $$= \frac{0.76 + 0.84 + 0.68}{3} = 0.76$$ $$^{i}P(g_{1.H1}) = 1 - \frac{1 - P(g_{2.H1})}{1 - f_{g_{2.H1}}{}^{z}(E,F)} = 1 - \frac{1 - 0.82}{1 - 0.76} \approx 0.25$$ *Figure 5.60* Calculation of the impact of g_1 on g_2.

The model shown in Figure 5.58 assumes memories of $g_{1,H1}$ and $g_{2,H1}$ (and the expectations associated with them) have fused in ITM. So the data available are $f_{g_{3,H1}}{}^z(E,F)$ (which we can assume is the same as $f_{g_{1,H1}}{}^z(E,F)$) and the fusion of ${}^iP(g_{1,H1})$ and ${}^iP(g_{2,H1})$. This is represented by ${}^iP(g_{1,H1}/g_{2,H1})$. Hence the impact of $g_{1,H1}$ and $g_{2,H1}$ on $g_{3,H1}$ can be calculated as follows:

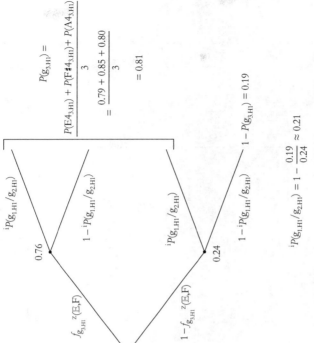

Figure 5.61 Calculation of the impact of the fused memory of g_1 and g_2 on g_3.

Consider the assumption that we have made up to this point that the memory of a note in a given context carries with it its perceived retrospective expectedness in that context. When the memory of a note is combined with the memory of its repetition, we can assume that the values of retrospective expectedness fuse too. The potential neurological mechanisms through which this process may occur are discussed below (see pp. 254–255). For now, it is worth noting that the reduction in impact between g_1 on g_2, and the fusion of g_1 and g_2 on g_3, though small, is not what the model to be presented would predict (rather, a small rise). Further research would be needed to clarify the position.

Notes	Expectation	General comments	Events and groups	Frameworks
18 (D4)	0.80	Following Note 17, two potential continuations are indicated in the preceding material at the level of groups: repeat the four-note motif, or move up to B4. It is suggested that the melodic symmetry offered by repetition of the motif is likely to be preferred at the level of frameworks. This supposition is reinforced by the high level of retrospective expectedness pertaining to Note 17 being maintained; without it the possibility of the move to B4 may have had a greater negative impact.	 *Figure 5.62* Imitation of groups influences the way the brain is likely to interpret the repetition of intervals.	Archetypal melodic symmetry is preferred.

| --- | --- | --- | --- |
| 19 (E4) | 0.84 | Following the repeat of D4 and E4, the level of retrospective expectedness increases as a further repetition of group is anticipated. Three sources of memory (WM, ITM and LTM) converge in a common expectation. | *Figure 5.63* The three modules in memory (WM, ITM and LTM) each contribute to the strengthening sense of expectation as g_4 starts to unfold. |
| 20 ($F^{\#}4$) | 0.86 | There is a further increase in retrospective expectedness as g_4 further unfolds. | The interactions between the different forms of memory shown in Figure 5.63 continue and strengthen expectedness further. |

Notes	Expectation	General comments	Groups
21 (A4)	0.88	As the fourth appearance of the four-note motif (g_4) concludes, we can once again examine the extent to which the four predictions indicated by zygonic theory are realised: (a) Maintenance of contour (b) A generally higher level of expectedness (c) Tendency to flat line (towards 1.0) (d) Increasing expectedness through the growing impact of relationships between groups. We will consider first (b): whether mean levels of retrospective expectedness of each of the four groups do indeed rise. The figures are as follows (see Figure 5.64). As predicted, there is an upward trend in values, with a disruption between g_2 and g_3, which is attributable to the interpolation of material between the two groups, and the fusion of the memories of g_1 and g_2 in ITM.	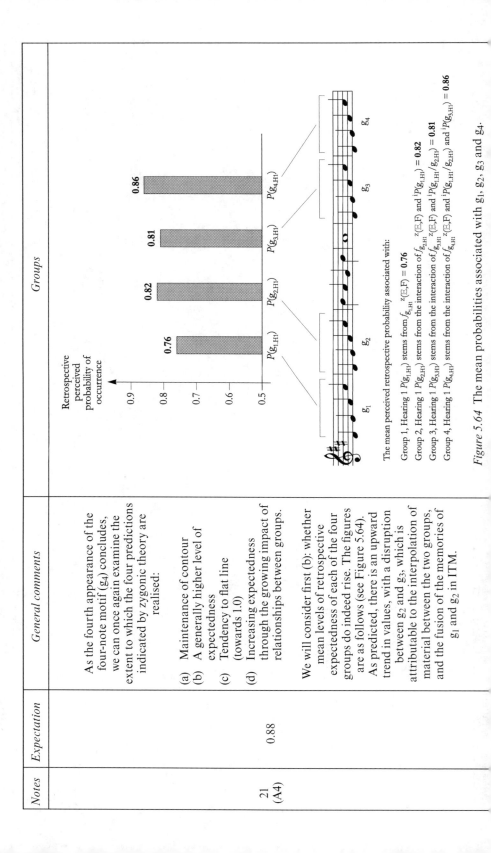 Figure 5.64 The mean probabilities associated with g_1, g_2, g_3 and g_4.

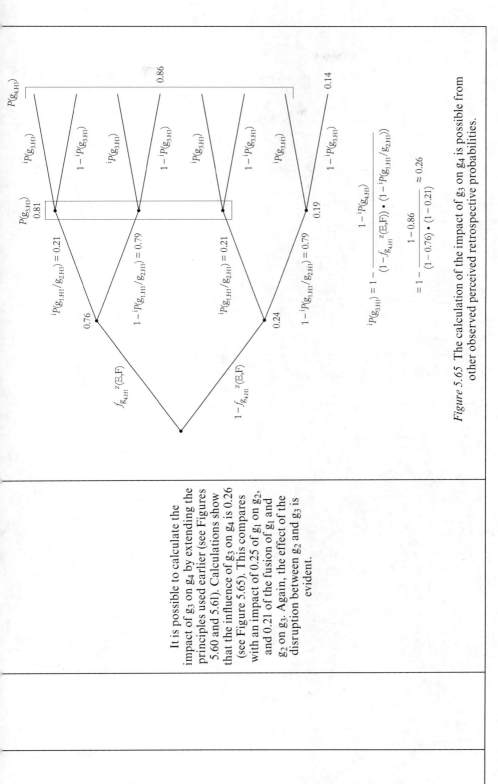

Figure 5.65 The calculation of the impact of g_3 on g_4 is possible from other observed perceived retrospective probabilities.

It is possible to calculate the impact of g_3 on g_4 by extending the principles used earlier (see Figures 5.60 and 5.61). Calculations show that the influence of g_3 on g_4 is 0.26 (see Figure 5.65). This compares with an impact of 0.25 of g_1 on g_2, and 0.21 of the fusion of g_1 and g_2 on g_3. Again, the effect of the disruption between g_2 and g_3 is evident.

With regard to (a), (c) and (d), which pertain, in one way or another, to contour, it is interesting to note how potentially conflicting tendencies interact. The contours of retrospective expectedness associated with Notes 2 to 4 of each group are shown in Figure 5.66. Since g_1's contour shows a fall between Notes 3 and 4, one issue is the extent to which this drop will be maintained in the contours pertaining to subsequent hearings (g_2, g_3 and g_4), given the purported tendency of retrospective expectedness to rise through each of the groups as it is repeated. In g_2 the fall is all but eliminated (Note 4 actually has a very slightly lower value of retrospective expectedness than Note 3), but there appears to be something of a 're-set' with g_3 (which, as we have noted, follows after the interposition of different materials). With g_4, the fall in expectedness is replaced with a small rise.

In summary, we can say that the maintenance of contour and the tendency for retrospective expectedness to rise in the course of a repeated group may conflict, and, on the evidence presented here, it is the latter that is likely to dominate as more repetitions of the group are heard.

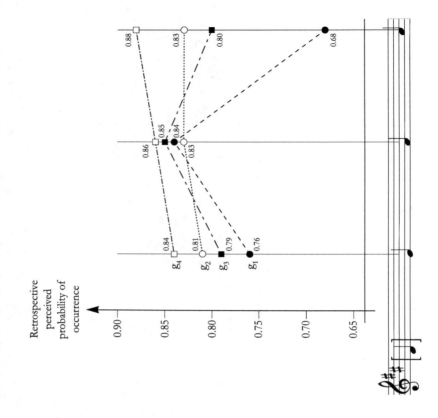

Figure 5.66 The changing contour of expectations across g_1, g_2, g_3 and g_4.

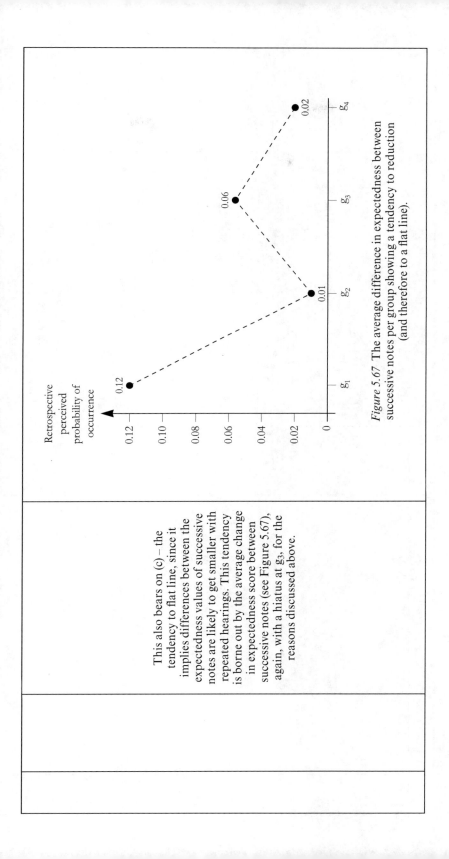

Figure 5.67 The average difference in expectedness between successive notes per group showing a tendency to reduction (and therefore to a flat line).

This also bears on (c) – the tendency to flat line, since it implies differences between the expectedness values of successive notes are likely to get smaller with repeated hearings. This tendency is borne out by the average change in expectedness score between successive notes (see Figure 5.67), again, with a hiatus at g_3, for the reasons discussed above.

Notes	Expectation	General comments	Events and groups
22 (E4)	0.63	The descent to E4 produces the lowest level of retrospective expectedness thus far. Although E4 can be understood as a rational continuation of the melody at this point, none of Thorpe *et al.*'s participants predicted it, while 75% anticipated a further B4 (which occurred in the first half of the melody). See Figure 5.68.	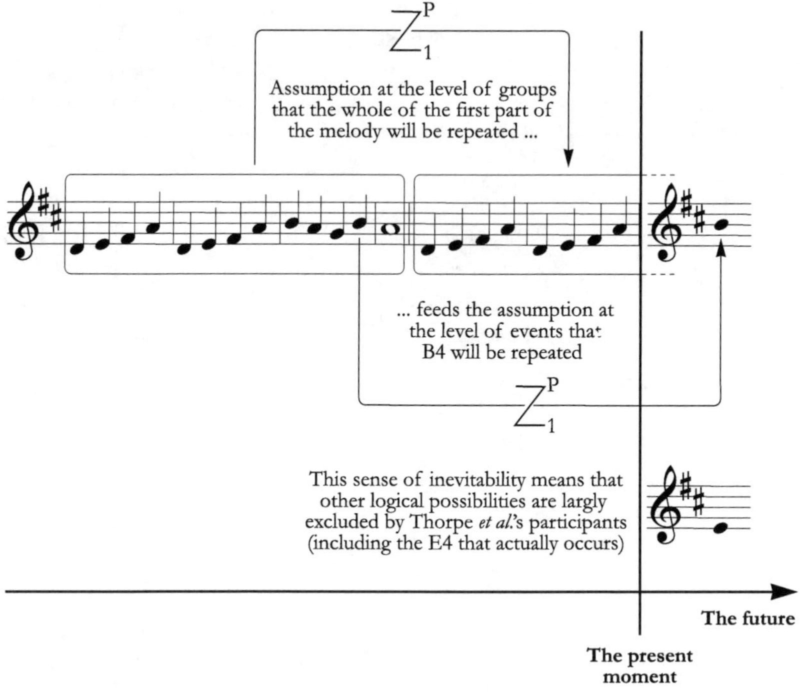

Figure 5.68 The expectation of group repetition has an impact on expectation at the level of events.

Notes	Expectation	General comments	Events
23 (D4)	0.60	The move to D4 evokes an even lower expectedness response, which runs counter to the research undertaken by Thorpe *et al.*, who found that D4 was predicted by the highest number of participants (although this was only 35%). It is difficult to explain theoretically too, since the move to D4 is logical, in terms of both events and groups. See Figure 5.69.	*Figure 5.69* Potential sources of derivation of Note 23 (D4), which were apparently utilised by Thorpe *et al.*'s participants, but not by Trower's.

Notes	Expectation	General comments	Events
24 (C#4)	0.52	Note 24 sees a dramatic fall in expectedness response of 13% – the lowest value in the experiment. Again, it is difficult to explain in terms of Thorpe *et al.*'s results (33% of participants predicted the C#4) or in terms of theory, since C#4 was predictable at the level of events, groups and frameworks (see Figure 5.70).	
25 (E4)	0.60	The level of retrospective expectedness recovers to that associated with Note 23, suggesting that the transposition of the cadential melodic group from the first half of the melody is now recognised (Figure 20).	
26 (D4)	0.68	The level of retrospective expectedness increases again – further evidence that the transposition of the cadential group is recognised. However, the level is well below that of Thorpe *et al.*'s participants, 93% of whom correctly predicted the final tonic. It could be that the expectedness value in the current study is strongly influenced by the preceding values (whereby the *relative* component of the measure – that is, the relationship of a given assessment of expectancy to those that immediately precede – negatively influences the absolute; see Figure 5.34).	*Figure 5.70* As the melodic stimulus draws to a close, the increasing sense of certainty that listeners experience derives from structure at the level of events (utilising WM), groups (drawing on ITM) and frameworks (with data taken from LTM).

Table 5.6 The data from Hearings 1 and 2 of the stimulus

Note number	Hearing 1: Perceived retrospective probability note by note	Difference between successive values	Hearing 2: Perceived retrospective probability note by note	Difference between successive values
2	0.76	–	0.83	–
3	0.84	0.08	0.89	0.06
4	0.68	0.16	0.82	0.07
5	0.70	0.02	0.84	0.02
6	0.81	0.10	0.88	0.04
7	0.83	0.03	0.92	0.03
8	0.83	0.00	0.87	0.04
9	0.68	0.15	0.74	0.14
10	0.74	0.06	0.79	0.05
11	0.72	0.02	0.79	0.00
12	0.62	0.10	0.66	0.13
13	0.70	0.09	0.75	0.09
14	0.73	0.03	0.82	0.08
15	0.79	0.07	0.84	0.02
16	0.85	0.06	0.87	0.02
17	0.80	0.05	0.85	0.02
18	0.80	0.00	0.85	0.00
19	0.84	0.04	0.88	0.03
20	0.86	0.03	0.89	0.01
21	0.88	0.02	0.88	0.00
22	0.63	0.25	0.69	0.19
23	0.60	0.03	0.71	0.03
24	0.52	0.08	0.65	0.06
25	0.60	0.08	0.62	0.03
26		0.08	0.71	0.09
Mean	**0.74**	**0.07**	**0.80**	**0.05**

Following Hearing 1, we can assume that cognitive activity pertaining to the perception of the stimulus continues. We may suppose that some representation of the melody remains in WM (about to be overwritten by the distractor sequence of tones), while in ITM, we can presume that the process of abstraction that initially involved fusing repeated motifs proceeds further, whereby information about the melody is compressed to facilitate storage. Perceptual ('absolute') memories are, we can assume, gradually replaced with generative rules, anchored in the relativities of tonal system. So the opening three notes can be coded as an ascending scale, for example, and the repeated and transposed motifs stored as units of musical information and tagged as to their positions in the melody for the purposes of potential recall (Ockelford, 2004). We may suppose that a listener's representation of the melody as a whole acquires the status of a self-contained conceptual entity in its own right (that could potentially be given a verbal label to facilitate later access). And it may be that some or all of the encoded materials start to be embedded in LTM (see Figure 5.71). This is the position (following the distractor sequence) when Hearing 2 begins.

212 *Adam Ockelford and Hayley Trower*

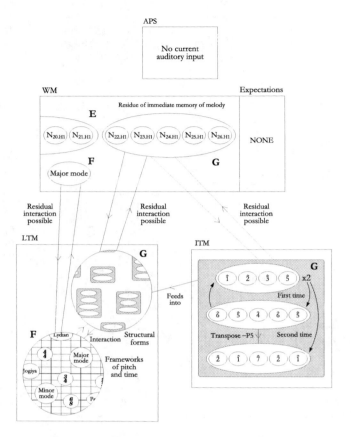

Figure 5.71 Model of the modules in memory and their interaction following the first complete hearing of the stimulus.

Hearing 2

The predictions stemming from zygonic theory in relation to the second hearing of the stimulus are essentially the same as those between groups *within* a hearing. The melody is now regarded as one large group ('G'), and accordingly, in Hearing 2, we would anticipate listeners' retrospective expectedness values to show:

a   the maintenance of contour,
b   a generally higher level of expectedness and
c   a tendency to flat line (towards 1.0).

Note, however, that the theory does not predict, in the context of the second (and subsequent) hearings, an increasing expectedness through the growing

A zygonic approach 213

impact of relationships between groups (as was the case in Hearing 1). This is because listeners would soon become aware that the melodies were going to be the same. Hence, the uncertainty that characterises hearing motifs in a tune for the first time, when it is not initially apparent whether repetition of the group of notes will occur or not, does not apply when a melody itself is repeated.

The values of retrospective expectedness from Hearing 2 (set alongside those of Hearing 1) are as follows (see Table 5.6).

The three predictions from zygonic theory are met, each with high degrees of statistical significance:

a   The maintenance of contour
    The contour of the retrospective expectedness values of Hearing 2 is highly correlated with that of Hearing 1: $R=0.93$, $p < 0.0001$ (see Figure 5.72).
b   A generally higher level of expectedness
    The average level of retrospective expectation in Hearing 2 ($M=0.80$) is significantly higher than in Hearing 1: ($M=0.74$), $t(24)=8.41$, $p < 0.0001$ (see Table 5.6)
c   A tendency to flat line (towards 1.0)
    There is tendency towards a reduction in the magnitude of the differences between successive values of retrospective expectedness between Hearing 2 and Hearing 1. The difference is significant: $t(23)=2.39$, $p <0.025$ (see Table 5.6).

It is possible to interrogate these data using the techniques employed in relation to the first hearing of the melody – in particular to consider the impact of the first hearing on the second both in general terms and in detail, note by note.

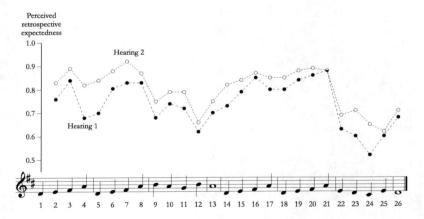

Figure 5.72 Visual representation of the levels of perceived retrospective expectedness in Hearings 1 and 2.

214 *Adam Ockelford and Hayley Trower*

In Hearing 1 ('H1'), the retrospective expectedness associated with any given note ('N') is a function of events ('E'), frameworks ('F') and, on some occasions, groups ('g'). That is:

$$P(N_{H1}) = f_{N_{H1}}{}^z(E, F, (g))$$

(The parentheses around 'g' show that their impact is only sometimes present.)

Hence, the mean expectedness across all the notes in Hearing 1 can be expressed as follows:

$$P(\overline{N_{H1}}) = f_{\overline{N_{H1}}}{}^z(\overline{E, F, g})$$

The impact of the expectations pertaining to the first hearing of the melody $^iP(G_{H1})$ on those of the second $P(G_{H2})$ can be calculated as shown in Figure 5.73.

Here, in Hearing 2, the 'internal' forces are assumed to be the same as they were in Hearing 1, so

$$f_{\overline{N_{H1}}}{}^z(\overline{E, F, g}) = f_{\overline{N_{H2}}}{}^z(\overline{E, F, g})$$

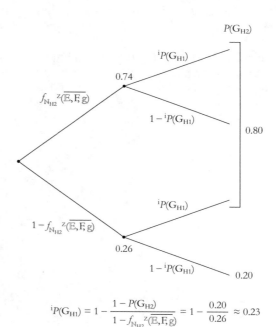

$$^iP(G_{H1}) = 1 - \frac{1 - P(G_{H2})}{1 - f_{\overline{N_{H2}}}{}^z(\overline{E, F, g})} = 1 - \frac{0.20}{0.26} \approx 0.23$$

Figure 5.73 The calculation of $^iP(G_{H1})$.

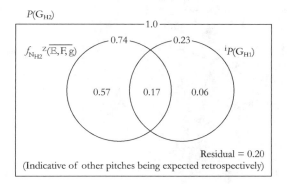

Figure 5.74 The factors making up $P(G_{H2})$.

The additional element, $^{i}P(G_{H1})$, is the impact that the memory of expectations pertaining to the first hearing have on the second. The degree of retrospective expectedness in Hearing 2 is deemed to be the union of two factors (in which *either* or *both* may play a part) – see Figure 5.29. The mean degree of overlap between the factors is calculated as their intersection (see Figure 5.74).

This means that the part of the influence of $^{i}P(G_{H1})$ that is additional to $f_{N_{H2}}{}^{z}(\overline{E,F},g)$ is 0.06, and the part of $f_{N_{H2}}{}^{z}(\overline{E,F},g)$ that is unaffected by $^{i}P(G_{H1})$ is 0.57. Note by note, these patterns of influence are as follows (see Table 5.7).

The breakdown of sources of retrospective perceived expectation in Hearing 2 can be illustrated as follows (see Figure 5.75).

This analysis has explanatory power in relation to the predictions made by zygonic theory that pertain to Hearing 2. For example, the maintenance of the contour of the series of values is almost inevitable given the domination of $f_{N_{H2}}{}^{z}(\overline{E,F},g)$ in proceedings, which accounts for 92% of the retrospective expectedness that is perceived. So the impact of Hearing 1, $^{i}P(G_{H1})$, results in only a modest average increase of 8%; over twice this figure is absorbed in the intersection with $f_{N_{H2}}{}^{z}(\overline{E,F},g)$. It seems that the perceptual immediacy of the stimulus was a more powerful force acting on retrospective expectedness than the recall of notes and their associated perceived probabilities from ITM. This characteristic of music cognition must surely play a key role in listeners' sustained pleasure in a piece when they hear it more than once.

The tendency of the contour to move to a higher, flatter line can be accounted for by the very strong negative correlation between the values of $f_{N_{H2}}{}^{z}(\overline{E,F},g) - {}^{i}P(G_{H1}) \cap f_{N_{H2}}{}^{z}(\overline{E,F},g)$ and $^{i}P(G_{H1}) - {}^{i}P(G_{H1}) \cap f_{N_{H2}}{}^{z}(\overline{E,F},g)$ (found in the rightmost columns of Table 5.7); $R = -0.90$, $p < 0.0001$ that is, the internal forces of retrospective expectedness (based on E, F and g) within Hearing 2 *without* those that overlap with memories of Hearing 1, and the impact

216 *Adam Ockelford and Hayley Trower*

Table 5.7 Patterns of influence on of $P(G_{H2})$, note by note

$f_{N_{H2}}{}^z(\overline{E,F,g})$	$P(G_{H2})$	$^iP(G_{H1})$	$^iP(G_{H1}) \cap f_{N_{H2}}{}^z(\overline{E,F,g})$	$f_{N_{H2}}{}^z(\overline{E,F,g}) - {}^iP(G_{H1}) \cap f_{N_{H2}}{}^z(\overline{E,F,g})$	$^iP(G_{H1}) - {}^iP(G_{H1}) \cap f_{N_{H2}}{}^z(\overline{E,F,g})$
0.76	0.83	0.30	0.22	0.53	0.07
0.84	0.89	0.32	0.27	0.57	0.05
0.68	0.82	0.43	0.29	0.39	0.14
0.70	0.84	0.45	0.32	0.39	0.13
0.81	0.88	0.39	0.31	0.49	0.08
0.83	0.92	0.50	0.41	0.42	0.08
0.83	0.87	0.25	0.21	0.62	0.04
0.68	0.74	0.18	0.12	0.56	0.06
0.74	0.79	0.20	0.14	0.59	0.05
0.72	0.79	0.25	0.18	0.54	0.07
0.62	0.66	0.11	0.07	0.55	0.04
0.70	0.75	0.16	0.11	0.59	0.05
0.73	0.82	0.35	0.26	0.47	0.10
0.79	0.84	0.25	0.20	0.60	0.05
0.85	0.87	0.12	0.10	0.75	0.02
0.80	0.85	0.26	0.21	0.59	0.05
0.80	0.85	0.24	0.19	0.61	0.05
0.84	0.88	0.23	0.19	0.64	0.04
0.86	0.89	0.16	0.14	0.73	0.02
0.88	0.88	0.01	0.01	0.88	0.00
0.63	0.69	0.15	0.10	0.53	0.06
0.60	0.71	0.29	0.17	0.43	0.12
0.52	0.65	0.28	0.14	0.37	0.13
0.60	0.62	0.04	0.03	0.57	0.02
0.68	0.71	0.10	0.07	0.61	0.03
Mean 0.74	**0.80**	**0.24**	**0.18**	**0.56**	**0.06**

of the perceived probabilities associated with Hearing 1 *without* those that overlap with incoming data from Hearing 2. In other words, the impact of Hearing 1 is felt differentially: the lower the expectations generated purely within Hearing 2, the greater the effect of the memory of Hearing 1 (see Figure 5.76). Clearly, then, to the extent that changing levels of expectedness play a part in the appeal of a musical narrative, this mechanism may explain why listeners will eventually become jaded if they listen to the same piece of music – even a favourite song – over and over again.

There is an intriguing connection too between the expectedness pertaining to notes that function as part of groups g *within* Hearing 2, and the levels of expectedness deriving from the larger group ('G') that constitutes Hearing 1. Those pitches that are predictable through their membership of smaller groups g, tend to be influenced less by $^iP(G_{H1})$, although there are insufficient data for the difference to be statistically significant (see Figure 5.77). It seems as though the zygonic relationships operating within a more local timeframe are more potent than those relying solely on data in ITM.

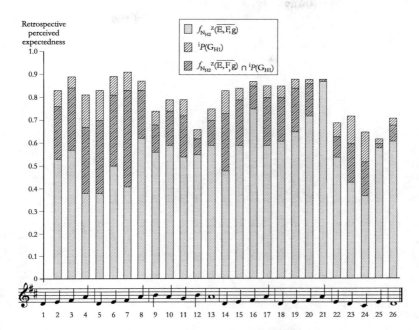

Figure 5.75 Visual representation of the sources of retrospective perceptation operating in Hearing 2.

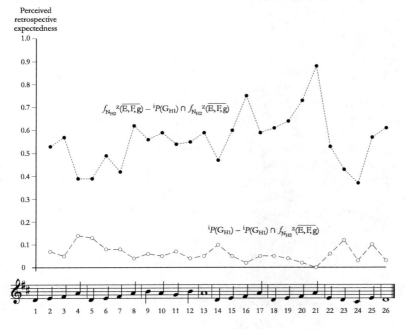

Figure 5.76 Visual representation of the negative correlation between $f_{N_{H2}}{}^{z}(\overline{E,F,g}) - {}^{i}P(G_{H1}) \cap f_{N_{H2}}{}^{z}(\overline{E,F,g})$ and ${}^{i}P(G_{H1}) - {}^{i}P(G_{H1}) \cap f_{N_{H2}}{}^{z}(\overline{E,F,g})$.

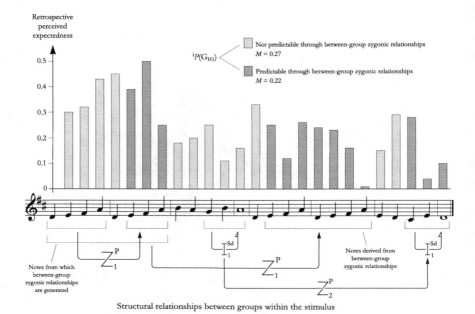

Figure 5.77 The interaction of between-group relationships within the stimulus and between trials.

Hearing 3

Following Hearing 2, we can again presume (as was the case after Hearing 1) that the brain continues to process the data pertaining to the stimulus. Once more, it seems probable that elements of the melody are retained in WM (although some of these may be erased by the distractor pitches), while in ITM, we can assume that memories G_{H1} and G_{H2} are fused (*cf.*, for example, Figure 5.51, which shows the assumed merger of the memories of g_1 and g_2). There may be movement of data to LTM. So the position as Hearing 3 begins can be modelled as follows (see Figure 5.78).

Taking Hearing 3 as a whole, retrospective expectedness is on average 5% higher than that pertaining to Hearing 2 (rather less than the 8% increase that differentiated Hearing 2 from Hearing 1), and the contour of expectedness values is maintained once more, with a close correlation between this and the contour of Hearing 2: $R = 0.95$, $p < 0.0001$. (The relationship with the contour of Hearing 1 will be discussed in due course.) See Figure 5.79 and Table 5.8.

There is an apparent anomaly in the data at Note 19, whose associated retrospective expectedness diminishes slightly between Hearings 2 and 3. There are a number of potential reasons for this irregularity. First, in any

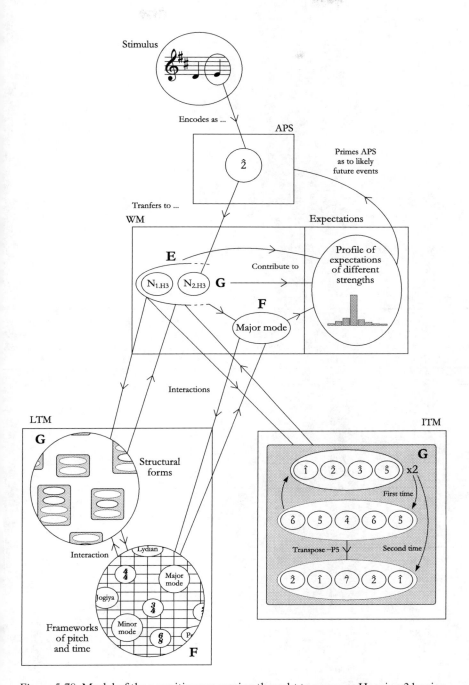

Figure 5.78 Model of the cognitive processing thought to occur as Hearing 3 begins.

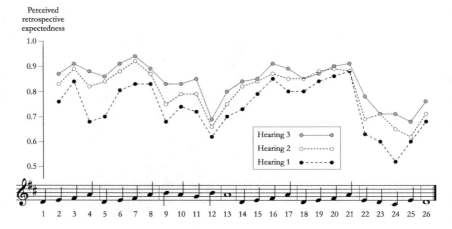

Figure 5.79 Visual representation of the levels of perceived retrospective expectedness in Hearings 1–3.

Table 5.8 The data from Hearings 1–3 of the stimulus

	Hearing 1: Perceived retrospective probability note by note	Difference between successive values	Hearing 2: Perceived retrospective probability note by note	Difference between successive values	Hearing 3: Perceived retrospective probability note by note	Difference between successive values
	0.76	–	0.83	–	0.87	–
	0.84	0.08	0.89	0.06	0.91	0.05
	0.68	0.16	0.82	0.07	0.88	0.03
	0.70	0.02	0.84	0.02	0.86	0.03
	0.81	0.10	0.88	0.04	0.91	0.05
	0.83	0.03	0.92	0.03	0.94	0.03
	0.83	0.00	0.87	0.04	0.89	0.05
	0.68	0.15	0.74	0.14	0.83	0.06
	0.74	0.06	0.79	0.05	0.83	0.01
	0.72	0.02	0.79	0.00	0.86	0.04
	0.62	0.10	0.66	0.13	0.69	0.17
	0.70	0.09	0.75	0.09	0.80	0.11
	0.73	0.03	0.82	0.08	0.84	0.04
	0.79	0.07	0.84	0.02	0.85	0.01
	0.85	0.06	0.87	0.02	0.91	0.06
	0.80	0.05	0.85	0.02	0.89	0.02
	0.80	0.00	0.85	0.00	0.85	0.04
	0.84	0.04	0.88	0.03	0.87	0.02
	0.86	0.03	0.89	0.01	0.90	0.03
	0.88	0.02	0.88	0.00	0.91	0.00
	0.63	0.25	0.69	0.19	0.78	0.13
	0.60	0.03	0.71	0.03	0.71	0.06
	0.52	0.08	0.65	0.06	0.71	0.00
	0.60	0.08	0.62	0.03	0.68	0.03
	0.68	0.08	0.71	0.09	0.76	0.07
Mean	**0.74**	**0.067**	**0.80**	**0.053**	**0.84**	**0.048**

A zygonic approach 221

task involving human judgement, there is bound to be a certain amount of 'natural variation', which means that the models that have been developed in this chapter, constructed on the basis of errorless learning and recall, will only ever approximate to the data that research participants generate. To some extent, discrepancies are mitigated since the judgements made by participants are averaged across a cohort, thereby minimising the effect of individual perturbations in the data. The sources of variation may arise in the course of the perceptual and cognitive processing demanded by the intuitive calculation of expectedness, through storage or retrieval errors, that may be caused, for example, by a momentary lack of attention. Then there are the added complications that listeners are asked to engage in an unfamiliar act of metacognition (reflecting on their intuition), and, in short order, to reify the result in physical terms on the touch-sensitive strip. Here, there are other challenges: for instance, the difference in expectedness pertaining to Hearings 2 and 3 of Note 19 is around 0.15%, which equates to a difference of less than a millimetre.

In most cases, the errors that we can assume exist are insufficient to challenge the integrity of the model and are likely to remain undetected. On other occasions, the variation in responses lies beyond permitted the tolerances that are theoretically permitted – for example, when expectedness is reported to *decrease* in successive trials (as is the case with Note 19, Hearings 2 and 3). What are the options for analysis? Data such as this could be treated in the usual way (ignoring anomalies, particularly when the impact of these is minimal), rejected (as an error) or transformed (to permit its assimilation), or the model could be modified to accommodate outliers. There are precedents for each in psychological research. The decision of which analytical strategy to adopt will be informed by the judgement of which of the data can reasonably be regarded as errors, and, conversely, how secure the model is believed to be. This in turn will be determined by proportion of data that conforms to the model, and the proportion that is exceptional. As at this stage (following Hearing 3), 74 out of 75 data points (around 98.5%) accord with the model, it is reasonable to assume that Note 19, Hearing 3, is indeed an error – albeit a very small one. In subsequent hearings, we should expect errors to increase as the average difference between equivalent values in successive trials diminishes.

The differences between successive values of retrospective expectedness in Hearing 3 are on average less than those in Hearing 2 (as the tendency to move to a flat line would predict), though the difference between the means is not on this occasion statistically significant. A more detailed analysis using the techniques developed above enables us to interrogate what is going on in more depth. The impact of the fusion of G_{H1} and G_{H2} can be calculated as follows (see Figure 5.80).

The interaction of the two sources of expectedness of the pitches in G_{H3}, which are $f_{N_{H3}}{}^{z}(\overline{E,F},g)$ and $^{i}P(G_{H1}/G_{H2})$, is shown in Figure 5.81.

This shows that the part of the influence of $^{i}P(G_{H1}/G_{H2})$ that is additional to $f_{N_{H3}}{}^{z}(\overline{E,F},g)$ is 0.10, and the part of $f_{N_{H3}}{}^{z}(\overline{E,F},g)$ that is unaffected by

222 *Adam Ockelford and Hayley Trower*

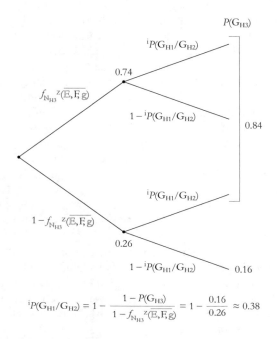

Figure 5.80 The calculation of $^iP(G_{H1}/G_{H2})$.

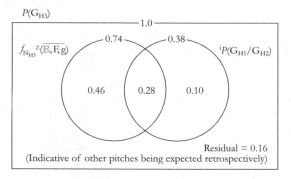

Figure 5.81 The factors making up $P(G_{H3})$.

$^iP(G_{H1}/G_{H2})$ is 0.46. The equivalent figures for Hearing 2 are 0.06 and 0.57 respectively. Hence, there is an *increase* in the influence of previous hearings on expectedness, and a *decrease* in the impact of internal structures. This can be attributed to the fact that there are now two longer-term memories to draw on. This will have the effect of further dampening the variation in listeners' expectations as the stimulus unfolds. Note by note, the impact is as follows (see Table 5.9 and Figures 5.81 and 5.82).

Table 5.9 Patterns of influence on of $P(G_{H3})$, note by note

$f_{N_{H3}}^{z}(\overline{E,F,g})$	$P(G_{H3})$	$^{i}P(G_{H1}/G_{H2})$	$\dfrac{^{i}P(G_{H1}/G_{H2})\ \cap\ f_{N_{H3}}^{z}(\overline{E,F,g})}{f_{N_{H3}}^{z}(\overline{E,F,g})}$	$\dfrac{f_{N_{H3}}^{z}(\overline{E,F,g})\ -\ ^{i}P(G_{H1}/G_{H2})\ \cap\ f_{N_{H3}}^{z}(\overline{E,F,g})}{f_{N_{H3}}^{z}(\overline{E,F,g})}$	$\dfrac{^{i}P(G_{H1}/G_{H2})\ -\ f_{N_{H3}}^{z}(\overline{E,F,g})\ \cap\ ^{i}P(G_{H1}/G_{H2})}{^{i}P(G_{H1}/G_{H2})}$
0.76	0.87	0.45	0.34	0.41	0.11
0.84	0.91	0.48	0.40	0.44	0.08
0.68	0.88	0.63	0.43	0.25	0.20
0.70	0.86	0.51	0.36	0.34	0.15
0.81	0.91	0.53	0.43	0.38	0.10
0.83	0.94	0.64	0.53	0.30	0.11
0.83	0.89	0.36	0.30	0.53	0.06
0.68	0.83	0.49	0.33	0.35	0.16
0.74	0.83	0.34	0.25	0.48	0.09
0.72	0.86	0.52	0.37	0.35	0.15
0.62	0.69	0.20	0.12	0.49	0.08
0.70	0.80	0.33	0.23	0.47	0.10
0.73	0.84	0.40	0.29	0.43	0.11
0.79	0.85	0.28	0.22	0.57	0.06
0.85	0.91	0.41	0.35	0.50	0.06
0.80	0.89	0.44	0.35	0.44	0.09
0.80	0.85	0.26	0.21	0.59	0.05
0.84	0.87	0.23	0.19	0.65	0.04
0.86	0.90	0.29	0.25	0.61	0.04
0.88	0.91	0.22	0.19	0.69	0.03
0.63	0.78	0.40	0.25	0.38	0.15
0.60	0.71	0.29	0.17	0.42	0.12
0.52	0.71	0.40	0.21	0.31	0.19
0.60	0.68	0.21	0.13	0.47	0.08
0.68	0.76	0.25	0.17	0.51	0.08
Mean 0.74	**0.84**	**0.38**	**0.28**	**0.46**	**0.10**

The combined impact of Hearings 1 and 2 operates differentially: the lower the expectations generated only within Hearing 3, the greater the effect of the memory of Hearings 1 and 2. The strong negative correlation between them, $R = -0.91$, $p < 0.0001$, mirrors that found in Hearing 2, contributing further to the greater uniformity of expectation with repeated exposure to the stimulus melody (*cf.* Figures 5.76 and 5.83).

Hearing 4

The retrospective expectedness data for Hearing 4, in comparison to those pertaining to Hearings 1–3, are shown in Table 5.10.

The means and standard deviations of each hearing are as follows (see Table 5.10 and Figure 5.85).

Taking the four hearings as a whole, the differences between them are significant: $F(1.65,\ 39.6) = 104$, $p < 0.0001$. A Tukey multiple comparisons test shows that the differences between each hearing are all significant too, $p < 0.001$.

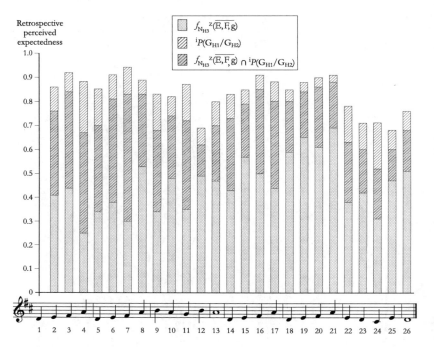

Figure 5.82 Visual representation of the sources of retrospective perceptation operating in Hearing 3.

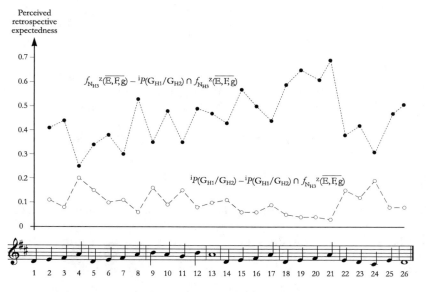

Figure 5.83 Visual representation of the negative correlation between $f_{N_{H3}}{}^z(\overline{E,F,g}) - {}^iP(G_{H1}/G_{H2}) \cap f_{N_{H3}}{}^z(\overline{E,F,g})$ and ${}^iP(G_{H1}/G_{H2}) - {}^iP(G_{H1}/G_{H2}) \cap f_{N_{H3}}{}^z(\overline{E,F,g})$.

Table 5.10 The data from Hearings 1–4 of the stimulus

Hearing 1: Perceived retrospective probability note by note	Difference between successive values	Hearing 2: Perceived retrospective probability note by note	Difference between successive values	Hearing 3: Perceived retrospective probability note by note	Difference between successive values	Hearing 4: Perceived retrospective probability note by note	Difference between successive values
0.76	–	0.83	–	0.87	–	0.89	–
0.84	0.08	0.89	0.06	0.91	0.05	0.91	0.02
0.68	0.16	0.82	0.07	0.88	0.03	0.88	0.03
0.70	0.02	0.84	0.02	0.86	0.03	0.90	0.03
0.81	0.10	0.88	0.04	0.91	0.05	0.91	0.01
0.83	0.03	0.92	0.03	0.94	0.03	0.92	0.01
0.83	0.00	0.87	0.04	0.89	0.05	0.91	0.01
0.68	0.15	0.74	0.14	0.83	0.06	0.82	0.09
0.74	0.06	0.79	0.05	0.83	0.01	0.85	0.03
0.72	0.02	0.79	0.00	0.86	0.04	0.87	0.02
0.62	0.10	0.66	0.13	0.69	0.17	0.69	0.17
0.70	0.09	0.75	0.09	0.80	0.11	0.82	0.13
0.73	0.03	0.82	0.08	0.84	0.04	0.88	0.06
0.79	0.07	0.84	0.02	0.85	0.01	0.90	0.02
0.85	0.06	0.87	0.02	0.91	0.06	0.91	0.02
0.80	0.05	0.85	0.02	0.89	0.02	0.90	0.01
0.80	0.00	0.85	0.00	0.85	0.04	0.89	0.01
0.84	0.04	0.88	0.03	0.87	0.02	0.90	0.01
0.86	0.03	0.89	0.01	0.90	0.03	0.92	0.01
0.88	0.02	0.88	0.00	0.91	0.00	0.92	0.01
0.63	0.25	0.69	0.19	0.78	0.13	0.79	0.13
0.60	0.03	0.71	0.03	0.71	0.06	0.78	0.01
0.52	0.08	0.65	0.06	0.71	0.00	0.73	0.04
0.60	0.08	0.62	0.03	0.68	0.03	0.71	0.02
0.68	0.08	0.71	0.09	0.76	0.07	0.78	0.07
Mean **0.74**	**0.067**	**0.80**	**0.053**	**0.84**	**0.048**	**0.86**	**0.040**

226 *Adam Ockelford and Hayley Trower*

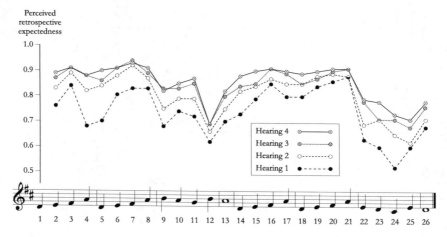

Figure 5.84 Visual representation of the levels of perceived retrospective expectedness in Hearings 1–4.

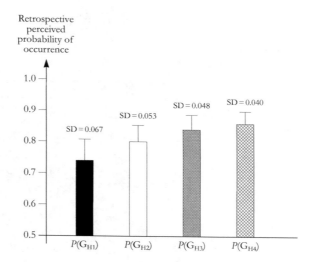

Figure 5.85 The means and standard deviations of the retrospective perceived probability of occurrence of the pitches in Hearings 1–4 of the stimulus.

The pattern is one of decreasing change, which potentially sheds light on the way that memories of the melody are subject to fusion in ITM. As a starting point, $^{i}P(G_{H1}/G_{H2}/G_{H3})$, which can be written as $^{i}P(G_{H1-H3})$, can be calculated as follows (see Figure 5.86).

Setting this finding against those pertaining to Hearings 2 and 3, where $^{i}P(G_{H1}) = 0.23$ and $^{i}P(G_{H1}/G_{H2}) = 0.38$ (see Figure 5.80), a line of reasoning

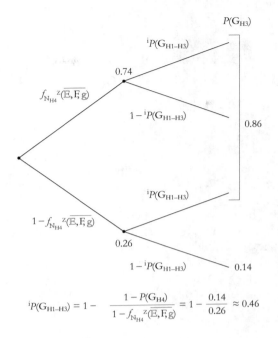

Figure 5.86 The calculation of $^iP(G_{H1-H3})$.

can be developed that enables the way that $^iP(G_{H1})$, $^iP(G_{H2})$ and $^iP(G_{H3})$ interact in ITM to be quantified. If we assume that the fusion works as a union of two sets of probabilities (implying an 'OR' function at the neuronal level – see Figure 5.10), then in relation to Hearing 3 we have

Hearing 3: $^iP(G_{H1}) \cup {}^iP(G_{H2}) = 0.38$

Let us presume that $^iP(G_{H2})$ functions at the same level as $^iP(G_{H1})$ did in relation to Hearing 2 (that is, 0.23). However, it is conceivable that, by the time of Hearing 3, the impact of G_{H1} may have declined somewhat, as it is further in the past and has been subject to the interference of other material. So we have

Hearing 3: $^iP(G_{H1}) \cup 0.23 = 0.38$
$\Rightarrow$ Hearing 3: $\left(^iP(G_{H1}) + 0.23\right) - \left(^iP(G_{H1}) \cdot 0.23\right) = 0.38$
$\Rightarrow$ Hearing 3: $^iP(G_{H1}) = 0.19$

Similarly, in Hearing 4, we can assume that $^iP(G_{H3})$ functions at the same level as $^iP(G_{H1})$ did in relation to Hearing 2 (that is, 0.23), and that $^iP(G_{H2})$

228 *Adam Ockelford and Hayley Trower*

functions at the same level as ${}^{i}P(\mathrm{G}_{\mathrm{H1}})$ did in relation to Hearing 3 (that is, 0.19). With regard to ${}^{i}P(\mathrm{G}_{\mathrm{H1}})$:

Hearing 4: ${}^{i}P(\mathrm{G}_{\mathrm{H1}}) \cup 0.38 = 0.46$

$\Rightarrow$ Hearing 4: $\left({}^{i}P(\mathrm{G}_{\mathrm{H1}}) + 0.38\right) - \left({}^{i}P(\mathrm{G}_{\mathrm{H1}}) \cdot 0.38\right) = 0.46$

Hearing 4: ${}^{i}P(\mathrm{G}_{\mathrm{H1}}) = 0.13$

This suggests that the union of the probabilities associated with musical events may well be an effective way of modelling their fusion in ITM, indicating that the impact of successive events declines with time and the interpolation of other material (through the decay or displacement of neuronal connections).

The increasing impact of previous hearings, and the ever greater degree of overlap between these and internal structural forces, through which expectations are in part generated, are summarised in Figure 5.87.

In Hearing 4, the contour of retrospective expectedness values is maintained once more, with very high correlations between this and the contour pertaining to Hearings 1–3. It is of interest to note that the correlations between the contours of successive hearings increase in strength (between Hearings 1 and 2, $R = 0.93$; between Hearings 2 and 3, $R = 0.96$ and between Hearings 3 and 4, $R = 0.97$), attributable in terms of the model set out above to the fact that each hearing draws on memories from all those that precede, locking expectations together ever more closely. See Table 5.11.

The differences between successive values of retrospective expectedness in Hearing 4 are on average less than those in Hearing 3 (as the tendency to move to a flat line would suggest), though the difference between the means (see Table 5.10) is not statistically significant. This can be seen as part of a more general tendency to a reduction in the differences between successive values of expectedness with each new hearing, reflected in the diminishing standard deviations of the data sets (see Table 5.12).

These data offer insights into the aesthetic impact of the repeated hearings. The pattern of retrospective unexpectedness derived from *events*, *frameworks* and *groups* that exists within each hearing is maintained – and, we can assume, the associated changes in affective response, but these are gradually evened out by the dampening effect of the between-group relationships that exist between hearings. More generally (and with due regard to the findings of the detailed phenomenological account of Hearing 1), it appears that the *unexpectedness* of musical elements derives from events and frameworks, setting up the 'affective kick' that listeners experience, and that the *expectedness* that subsequently regulates these stems from relationships between groups, differentially softening the affective kicks associated with each event. It seems that the optimal listening experience

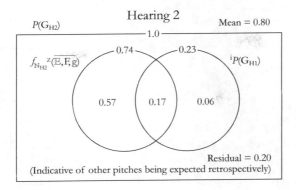

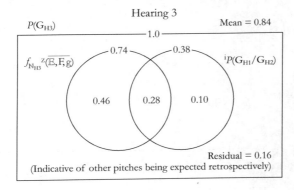

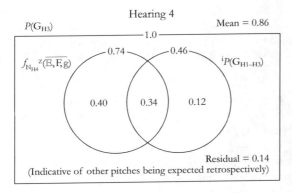

Figure 5.87 The changing balance of factors making up $P(G_{H2})$, $P(G_{H3})$ and $P(G_{H2})$.

combines both of these opposing forces, offering a balance between expectedness and unexpectedness that listeners can control individually by choosing to experience a piece repeatedly, but only up to a certain point (see Figure 5.88).

Table 5.11 The increasing strength of correlations between patterns of expectations pertaining to successive hearings

Correlations between	G_{H2}	G_{H3}	G_{H4}
G_{H1}	0.93	0.88	0.88
G_{H2}	–	0.96	0.97
G_{H3}	–	–	0.97

$p < 0.0001$ in all cases.

Table 5.12 Decreasing mean standard deviations are indicative of the trend to flat line over the four hearings of the melodic stimulus

Set of differences between successive values of expectedness	Hearing 1	Hearing 2	Hearing 3	Hearing 4
Mean standard deviation	0.098	0.086	0.075	0.070

Figure 5.88 The continuum of expectedness and unexpectedness as derives from frameworks, events and groups, and its relationship to aesthetic experience.

The competing sources of retrospective expectedness (those arising within Hearing 4, those stemming from previous hearings and those deriving from both) vary on a note-by-note basis as shown in Table 5.13 and Figure 5.89.

The impacts of Hearings 1–3 combine and operate differentially: the lower the expectations generated solely within Hearing 4, the greater the effect of the memory of Hearings 1–3.

The impacts of Hearings 1–3 operate differentially: the lower the expectations generated only within Hearing 4, the greater the effect of the memory of Hearings 1–3. The very strong negative correlation between them, $R = -0.93$, $p < 0.0001$, follows that found in Hearings 2 and 3, making a further contribution to the greater uniformity of expectation that repeated exposure to the stimulus produces (Figure 5.90).

Table 5.13 Patterns of influence on of $P(G_{H4})$, note by note

$f_{N_{H4}}{}^z(\overline{E,F,g})$	$P(G_{H4})$	$^iP(G_{H1-H3})$	$^iP(G_{H1-H3}) \cap f_{N_{H4}}{}^z(\overline{E,F,g})$	$f_{N_{H4}}{}^z(\overline{E,F,g}) - {}^iP(G_{H1-H3}) \cap f_{N_{H4}}{}^z(\overline{E,F,g})$	$^iP(G_{H1-H3}) - f_{N_{H4}}{}^z(\overline{E,F,g}) \cap {}^iP(G_{H1-H3})$
0.76	0.89	0.54	0.41	0.35	0.13
0.84	0.91	0.43	0.36	0.48	0.07
0.68	0.88	0.62	0.42	0.26	0.20
0.70	0.90	0.68	0.48	0.23	0.20
0.81	0.91	0.56	0.45	0.36	0.11
0.83	0.92	0.54	0.45	0.38	0.09
0.83	0.91	0.46	0.38	0.45	0.08
0.68	0.82	0.44	0.30	0.38	0.14
0.74	0.85	0.43	0.32	0.42	0.11
0.72	0.87	0.53	0.38	0.34	0.15
0.62	0.69	0.20	0.12	0.49	0.08
0.70	0.82	0.40	0.28	0.42	0.12
0.73	0.88	0.56	0.41	0.32	0.15
0.79	0.90	0.50	0.40	0.39	0.10
0.85	0.91	0.42	0.36	0.49	0.06
0.80	0.90	0.50	0.40	0.40	0.10
0.80	0.89	0.46	0.37	0.42	0.09
0.84	0.90	0.41	0.34	0.50	0.07
0.86	0.92	0.38	0.33	0.53	0.05
0.88	0.92	0.36	0.32	0.56	0.04
0.63	0.79	0.43	0.27	0.36	0.16
0.60	0.78	0.45	0.27	0.33	0.18
0.52	0.73	0.45	0.23	0.29	0.22
0.60	0.71	0.28	0.17	0.43	0.11
0.68	0.78	0.31	0.21	0.46	0.10
Mean **0.74**	**0.86**	**0.45**	**0.34**	**0.40**	**0.12**

Hearing 5

Hearings 5–8 were separated by a week from Hearings 1–4. Early on during this period, we can assume that the fused memories of the stimulus migrated from ITM to LTM. In this process, the perceptual qualities of the melody, such as its absolute pitch, would have been lost – or, at least, become more fuzzy – leaving (within broad parameters) a residue of abstract values (such as melodic intervals) and rules (such as 'repeat the opening motif'). We can assume that these would be informed by the more general abstractions held in LTM: the framework of the major scale, for example, and its probabilistic patterns of usage. Moreover, the fresh materials would theoretically have reinforced these deeper memories, though their impact would actually have been insignificant, given the conventional nature of their design and the fact that they would have made up only a vanishingly small proportion of the total musical experiences of each listener. Hence, the position just before Hearing 5 begins can be modelled as shown in Figure 5.91.

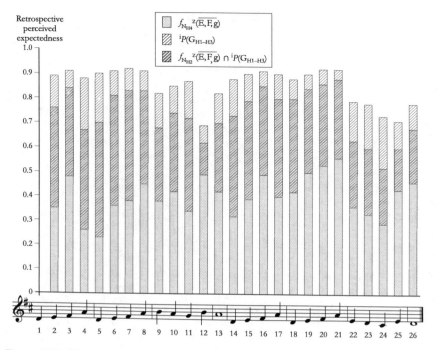

Figure 5.89 Visual representation of the sources of retrospective perceived expectation operating in Hearing 4.

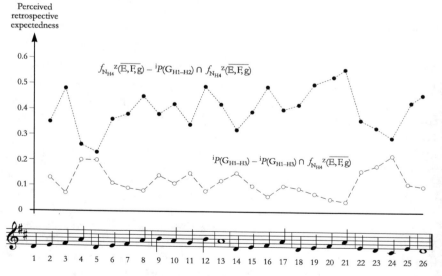

Figure 5.90 Visual representation of the negative correlation between $f_{N_{H4}}{}^z(\overline{E,F,g}) - {}^iP(G_{H1-H3}) \cap f_{N_{H4}}{}^z(\overline{E,F,g})$ and ${}^iP(G_{H1-H3}) - {}^iP(G_{H1-H3}) \cap f_{N_{H4}}{}^z(\overline{E,F,g})$.

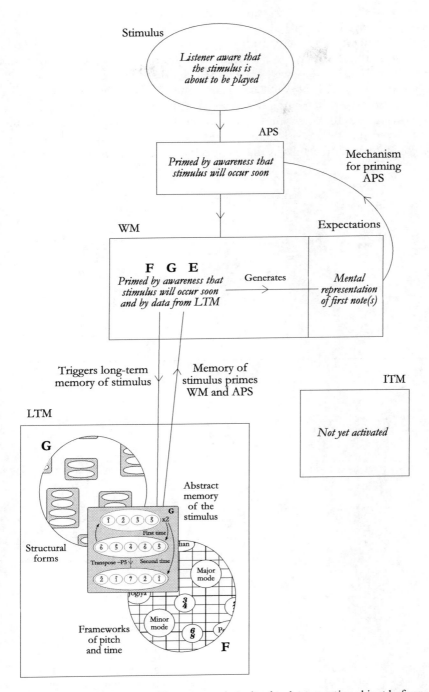

Figure 5.91 Model of the cognitive systems imagined to be operational just before a listener hears the stimulus for the fifth time.

What would we predict in terms of retrospective expectedness, as Hearing 5 gets underway? There will be two components. First, through the recognition of internal structures (stemming from events, frameworks and groups): $f_{N_{H5}}{}^{z}(E,F,g)$. We can assume that these factors will generate the same level of expectedness as they did in Hearings 1–4, which is 0.74. Second, there will be expectations arising from the fused memory of Hearings 1–4 in LTM, which will be activated by anticipating and then hearing the stimulus again (*cf.* Figure 5.91).

However, because the memory of Hearings 1–4 exists only as an abstraction of the perceptual data originally processed in WM and held in ITM, there will be fewer relationships available through which projections can be made

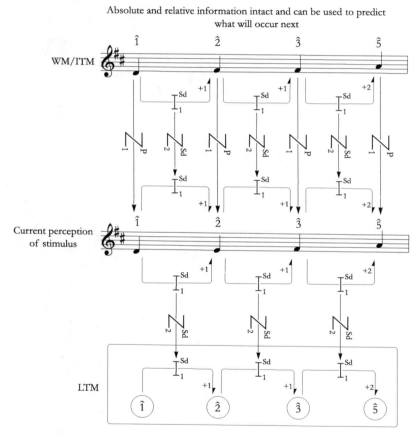

Figure 5.92 Immediate memories of the stimulus hold more information than those in LTM; hence, there are potentially more zygonic relationships from which to make predictions, which in consequence are likely to be firmer.

than was the case in Hearings 2–4. Take, for example, the opening phrase. In the domain of pitch, in Hearings 2–4, retrospective expectedness can derive both from the memories of the pitches themselves, and from the intervals between them. However, in Hearing 5, only the intervals that are present in LTM can be used as a springboard for expectations. See Figure 5.92.[1]

Hence, we would anticipate $^{i}P(G_{H1-H4})$ to be less than $^{i}P(G_{H1-H3})$, and the expectations pertaining to Hearing 5 to be lower than those arising from Hearing 4. Similarly, while we would anticipate that the contour of responses would be maintained, we would also predict that the relative differences between values would increase (hence the data series as a whole would show a tendency *away* from a 'flat line'). These conjectures do indeed transpire, as shown in Table 5.14 and Figure 5.93.

The mean level of retrospective expectation pertaining to Hearing 5 is 0.80: that is, 0.06 lower than that arising from Hearing 4. Contour is maintained ($R = 0.88$, $p < 0.0001$) though with twice the relative differences between successive values ($M = 0.80$ as opposed to $M = 0.40$).

Table 5.14 The data from Hearings 4 and 5 of the stimulus

	Hearing 4: Perceived retrospective probability note by note	*Difference between successive values*	*Hearing 5: Perceived retrospective probability note by note*	*Difference between successive values*
	0.89	–	0.76	–
	0.91	0.02	0.86	0.10
	0.88	0.03	0.78	0.08
	0.90	0.03	0.76	0.02
	0.91	0.01	0.87	0.11
	0.92	0.01	0.92	0.05
	0.91	0.01	0.87	0.05
	0.82	0.09	0.72	0.15
	0.85	0.03	0.83	0.11
	0.87	0.02	0.85	0.02
	0.69	0.17	0.58	0.27
	0.82	0.13	0.80	0.22
	0.88	0.06	0.82	0.02
	0.90	0.02	0.88	0.06
	0.91	0.02	0.90	0.02
	0.90	0.01	0.85	0.05
	0.89	0.01	0.87	0.02
	0.90	0.01	0.91	0.05
	0.92	0.01	0.94	0.03
	0.92	0.01	0.86	0.07
	0.79	0.13	0.71	0.16
	0.78	0.01	0.67	0.03
	0.73	0.04	0.69	0.02
	0.71	0.02	0.63	0.06
	0.78	0.07	0.81	0.17
Mean	**0.86**	**0.040**	**0.80**	**0.080**

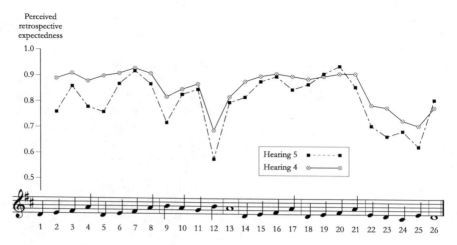

Figure 5.93 Visual representation of the levels of perceived retrospective expectedness in Hearings 4 and 5.

Hearing 6

Hearing 6 offers the first example of WM, ITM and memories of the stimulus held in LTM working together to produce expectations (*cf.* Figure 5.96). We would anticipate the relationship between Hearing 6 and Hearing 5 to be similar to that between Hearing 2 and Hearing 1, with a general increase in retrospective expectedness and the contour of successive values maintained, though with the differences between them reduced (producing a move to more of a 'flat line' of expectation). This is what occurs (Figure 5.94) with a strong correlation between the two sets of data of $R = 0.85$, $p < 0.0001$, an average increase in retrospective expectation of 0.06, which is statistically significant, $t(24) = 4.99$, $p < 0.0001$, and a mean reduction in differences between successive values of 0.23, which is statistically significant too: $t(23) = 2.76$, $p = 0.01$. See Table 5.15 and Figure 5.94.

It is possible to disaggregate the expectation pertaining to Hearing 6 using the probabilistic approach adopted earlier (see Figure 5.65), this time distinguishing between data derived from LTM and those taken from ITM (indicated using the appropriate suffix in each case) – see Figure 5.95.

It is of interest to note that the influence of ITM is stronger in Hearing 6 than in Hearing 2 (0.30 as opposed to 0.23). Why should this be the case? One intriguing possibility is that there could be feedback from LTM into ITM, meaning that it is fed from two sources (the other being WM). (See Figure 5.96).

Table 5.15 The data from Hearings 5 and 6 of the stimulus

	Hearing 5: Perceived retrospective probability note by note	Difference between successive values	Hearing 6: Perceived retrospective probability note by note	Difference between successive values
	0.76	–	0.88	–
	0.86	0.10	0.92	0.03
	0.78	0.08	0.87	0.04
	0.76	0.02	0.89	0.01
	0.87	0.11	0.88	0.00
	0.92	0.05	0.93	0.04
	0.87	0.05	0.93	0.00
	0.72	0.15	0.76	0.17
	0.83	0.11	0.83	0.07
	0.85	0.02	0.85	0.02
	0.58	0.27	0.68	0.17
	0.80	0.22	0.81	0.13
	0.82	0.02	0.78	0.03
	0.88	0.06	0.89	0.12
	0.90	0.02	0.92	0.03
	0.85	0.05	0.90	0.02
	0.87	0.02	0.90	0.00
	0.91	0.05	0.93	0.02
	0.94	0.03	0.93	0.01
	0.86	0.07	0.94	0.00
	0.71	0.16	0.76	0.18
	0.67	0.03	0.83	0.07
	0.69	0.02	0.80	0.02
	0.63	0.06	0.74	0.06
	0.81	0.17	0.85	0.11
Mean	**0.80**	**0.080**	**0.86**	**0.057**

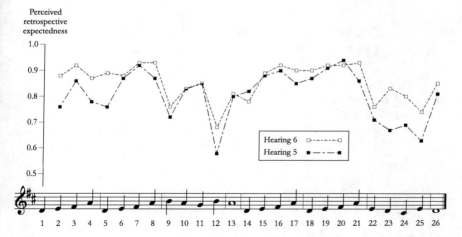

Figure 5.94 Visual representation of the levels of perceived retrospective expectedness in Hearings 5 and 6.

238　*Adam Ockelford and Hayley Trower*

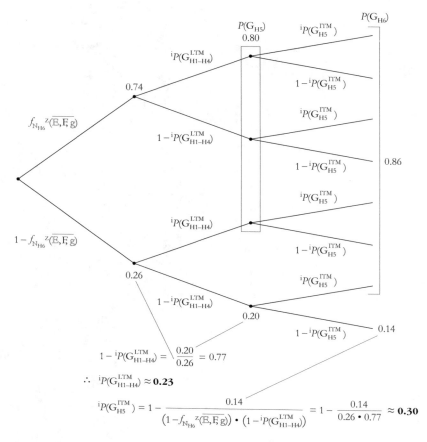

Figure 5.95 The calculation of $1 - {}^iP\left(G_{H1-H4}^{LTM}\right)$ and ${}^iP\left(G_{H5}^{ITM}\right)$.

Hearing 7

The retrospective expectedness data for Hearing 7, in comparison to those pertaining to Hearing 6, are as follows (see Table 5.16 and Figure 5.97).

The retrospective judgements of expectedness in Hearing 7 ($M = 0.88$) are on average higher than those in Hearing 6 ($M = 0.86$), and significantly so in statistical terms, $t(24) = 3.15$, $p < 0.01$, despite individual values being lower on five occasions. As discussed above, these divergences from the predicted pattern of increase between hearings may arise from a number of perceptual, cognitive or physical reasons (the latter on account of the challenge of recording responses on the short, touch-sensitive strip). And, as noted, we should expect such discrepancies to increase in number as the average difference in expectedness between hearings diminishes, and there

A zygonic approach 239

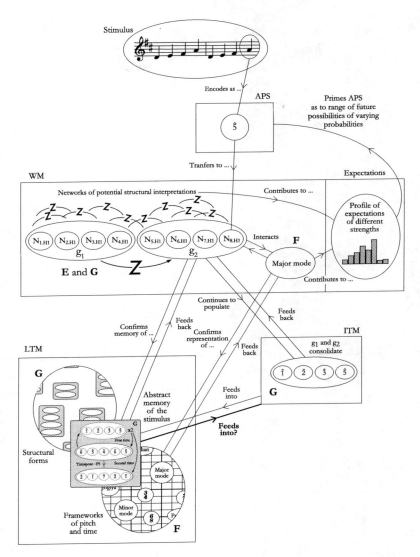

Figure 5.96 Possible feedback from LTM into ITM in Hearing 6.

is a tendency towards a 'flat line' (shown both by the reduction in differences between successive values in each hearing (Hearing 6, $M = 0.033$ as opposed to Hearing 7, $M = 0.057$) and the standard deviations (Hearing 6, SD = 0.071 compared to Hearing 7, SD = 0.052)). Once again, the two series of values are very highly correlated ($R = 0.915$, $p < 0.0001$).

The average contributions of WM, ITM and LTM to expectedness across Hearing 7 are shown in Figure 5.98.

Table 5.16 The data from Hearings 6 and 7 of the stimulus

	Hearing 6: Perceived retrospective probability note by note	Difference between successive values	Hearing 7: Perceived retrospective probability note by note	Difference between successive values
	0.88	–	0.92	–
	0.92	0.03	0.92	0.00
	0.87	0.04	0.91	0.01
	0.89	0.01	0.90	0.01
	0.88	0.00	0.92	0.02
	0.93	0.04	0.93	0.01
	0.93	0.00	0.91	0.03
	0.76	0.17	0.82	0.09
	0.83	0.07	0.86	0.04
	0.85	0.02	0.84	0.02
	0.68	0.17	0.78	0.05
	0.81	0.13	0.82	0.03
	0.78	0.03	0.87	0.06
	0.89	0.12	0.91	0.03
	0.92	0.03	0.92	0.01
	0.90	0.02	0.89	0.03
	0.90	0.00	0.91	0.02
	0.93	0.02	0.93	0.01
	0.93	0.01	0.93	0.01
	0.94	0.00	0.92	0.02
	0.76	0.18	0.81	0.11
	0.83	0.07	0.82	0.01
	0.80	0.02	0.82	0.00
	0.74	0.06	0.76	0.07
	0.85	0.11	0.87	0.11
Mean	**0.86**	**0.057**	**0.88**	**0.033**

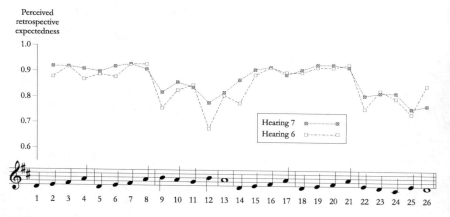

Figure 5.97 Visual representation of the levels of perceived retrospective expectedness in Hearings 6 and 7.

A zygonic approach 241

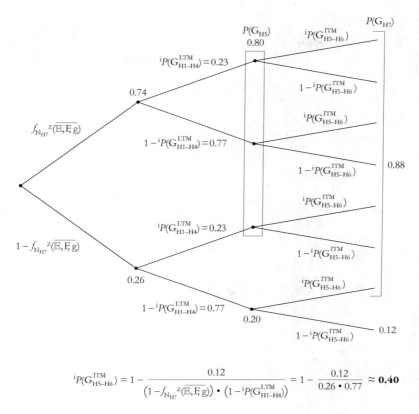

Figure 5.98 The calculation of $^iP\left(G_{H5-H6}^{ITM}\right)$.

Hearing 8

Finally, the retrospective expectedness data for Hearing 8, in comparison to those pertaining to Hearing 5–7, are as follows (see Table 5.16 and Figures 5.97 and 5.99).

The means and standard deviations of each hearing are as follows (see Table 5.16 and Figure 5.100).

Taking the four hearings as a whole, the differences between them are significant: $F(1.70, 34.5) = 34.5$, $p < 0.0001$. A Tukey multiple comparisons test shows that the differences between each hearing are all significant too at the level of $p < 0.001$, with the exception of the differences between Hearings 6 and 7, and between 7 and 8, which are significant at the level of $p < 0.05$.

In Hearing 8, the contour of retrospective expectedness values is again maintained, with very high correlations between this and the contours of Hearings 5–7, with a general increase in strength. See Table 5.17.

Table 5.17 The data from Hearings 5–8 of the stimulus

Hearing 5: Perceived retrospective probability note by note	Difference between successive values	Hearing 6: Perceived retrospective probability note by note	Difference between successive values	Hearing 7: Perceived retrospective probability note by note	Difference between successive values	Hearing 8: Perceived retrospective probability note by note	Difference between successive values
0.76	–	0.88	–	0.92	–	0.90	–
0.86	0.10	0.92	0.03	0.92	0.00	0.93	0.02
0.78	0.08	0.87	0.04	0.91	0.01	0.88	0.05
0.76	0.02	0.89	0.01	0.90	0.01	0.91	0.03
0.87	0.11	0.88	0.00	0.92	0.02	0.94	0.03
0.92	0.05	0.93	0.04	0.93	0.01	0.94	0.00
0.87	0.05	0.93	0.00	0.91	0.03	0.94	0.00
0.72	0.15	0.76	0.17	0.82	0.09	0.81	0.13
0.83	0.11	0.83	0.07	0.86	0.04	0.90	0.09
0.85	0.02	0.85	0.02	0.84	0.02	0.89	0.01
0.58	0.27	0.68	0.17	0.78	0.05	0.78	0.11
0.80	0.22	0.81	0.13	0.82	0.03	0.86	0.08
0.82	0.02	0.78	0.03	0.87	0.06	0.87	0.00
0.88	0.06	0.89	0.12	0.91	0.03	0.90	0.04
0.90	0.02	0.92	0.03	0.92	0.01	0.92	0.02
0.85	0.05	0.90	0.02	0.89	0.03	0.91	0.01
0.87	0.02	0.90	0.00	0.91	0.02	0.93	0.02
0.91	0.05	0.93	0.02	0.93	0.01	0.93	0.00
0.94	0.03	0.93	0.01	0.93	0.01	0.94	0.01
0.86	0.07	0.94	0.00	0.92	0.02	0.91	0.03
0.71	0.16	0.76	0.18	0.81	0.11	0.82	0.09
0.67	0.03	0.83	0.07	0.82	0.01	0.85	0.03
0.69	0.02	0.80	0.02	0.82	0.00	0.84	0.02
0.63	0.06	0.74	0.06	0.76	0.07	0.82	0.02
0.81	0.17	0.85	0.11	0.87	0.11	0.89	0.07
Mean **0.80**	**0.080**	**0.86**	**0.057**	**0.88**	**0.033**	**0.89**	**0.038**

A zygonic approach 243

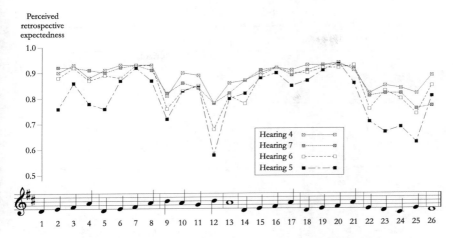

Figure 5.99 Visual representation of the levels of perceived retrospective expectedness in Hearings 5–8.

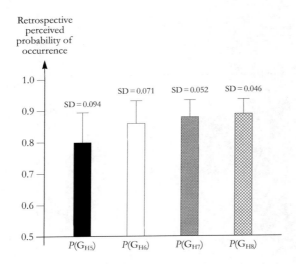

Figure 5.100 The means and standard deviations of the retrospective perceived probability of occurrence of the pitches in Hearings 5–8 of the stimulus.

Once more, there is a general tendency to a reduction in the differences between successive values of expectedness with each new hearing, reflected in the diminishing standard deviations of the data sets (see Tables 5.18 and 5.19).

The average contributions of WM, ITM and LTM to expectedness across Hearing 8 are shown in Figure 5.101.

Using the data available from all hearings, it is possible to track the changing contributions of WM, ITM and LTM across Hearings 6–8. See Figure 5.102.

Table 5.18 The correlations between patterns of expectations pertaining to Hearings 5–8

Correlations between	G_{H6}	G_{H7}	G_{H8}
G_{H5}	0.85	0.85	0.90
G_{H6}	–	0.92	0.94
G_{H7}	–	–	0.91

Table 5.19 Decreasing mean standard deviations are indicative of the trend to flat line over the four hearings of the melodic stimulus

Set of differences between successive values of expectedness	Hearing 5	Hearing 6	Hearing 7	Hearing 8
Mean standard deviation	0.094	0.071	0.052	0.046

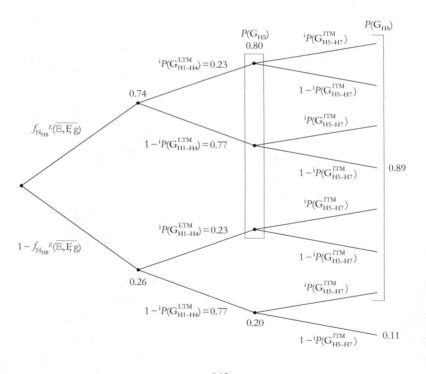

$$^{i}P(G^{ITM}_{H5-H7}) = 1 - \frac{0.12}{\left(1-f_{N_{H8}}{}^{z}(\overline{E,F,g})\right)\cdot\left(1-{}^{i}P(G^{LTM}_{H1-H4})\right)} = 1 - \frac{0.11}{0.26\cdot 0.77} \approx \mathbf{0.45}$$

Figure 5.101 The calculation of $^{i}P\left(G^{ITM}_{H5-H7}\right)$.

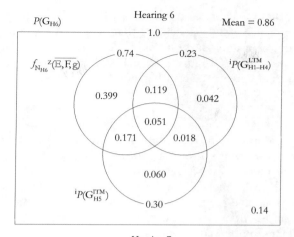
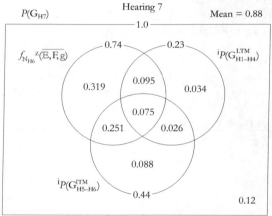
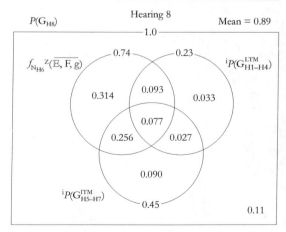

Figure 5.102 The changing contributions of WM, ITM and LTM across Hearings 6–8.

246 *Adam Ockelford and Hayley Trower*

It is evident that the changes are driven by ITM, which comes to exert an ever greater influence with each hearing that occurs. We would expect these to be consolidated in due course in LTM (*cf.* Figure 5.22), though with the loss of absolute values (*cf.* Figure 5.92), expectancy would fall back again if further hearings to occur after another significant break.

Conclusion

The analysis undertaken in this chapter shows the power of categorising musical structure as events, groups or frameworks, and linking these to different forms of memory (WM, ITM and LTM). It enables relatively simple data, derived from listeners' intuitive reflections as to how expected they perceived notes to have been, to be used to build sophisticated theories as to the changing nature of our aesthetic response to a piece as it is heard repeatedly. Overall, the mathematical models constructed in this chapter show that our cognition of music is dominated by relationships that we perceive between events, frameworks and groups *within* a given performance, and that the veridical memories deriving from earlier hearings of a piece have relatively little impact when it comes to the expectancies generated by patterns of notes. That is why 'interrupted' cadences continue to sound surprising, long after we would have expected them to lost their effect, and why we can listen (and, indeed, enjoy listening), time and again, to favourite pieces of music without them becoming jaded.

Note

1 It also sheds light on the issue of absolute pitch possessors tending to find memorising and recalling music easier than those with relative pitch alone (see Ockelford, 2016).

6 Conclusion

Graham Welch and Adam Ockelford

To conclude, we will reflect where the interdisciplinary field of applied musicology, set out here extensively for only the second time (following Ockelford, 2012a), sits in relation to other modes of thinking used in music education and music psychology research, and sketch out some potential future areas of work.

A central question for music psychologists in particular is how a certain person (or a given group of people) perceives, processes, responds to and recalls music. The approach that has been adopted by researchers most frequently over the years has been to elicit retrospective verbal responses from those participating in the research. Investigators have then interpreted these responses using further language to conceptualise, analyse and report on what they have found. Hence, much of the academic discourse about the experience of music

> is what may be termed a 'second-level metanarrative': it is *about* what people think *about* music, rather than being directed at our perception of the sounds themselves. Of course, this is perfectly appropriate: in epistemological hybrids of the arts and social sciences ... one would expect people's accounts of what of they perceive, of their feelings and preferences, and of how they learn, acquire and share expertise, to be presented as headline acts on the main stage of intellectual action. But the human activity in which we are interested is ultimately engagement with *music* – and all too often there appears to be a reluctance to get to grips with the world of organised sound that lies at the heart of things.
>
> (Ockelford, 2012a, p. 3)

Adapting the model developed in Chapter 5, this process can be illustrated as follows (see Figure 6.1). In terms of zygonic theory, listeners are responding at the level of whole pieces, or *Sounds of Intent* Level 5 (see Chapter 2, this volume).

The chief advantage of this approach, which can be conceptualised as a 'retrospective verbal response' strategy, is that it enables thoughts and feelings about music to be accessed that could only be captured in words. However, it may also be the case that, traditionally, many researchers working in

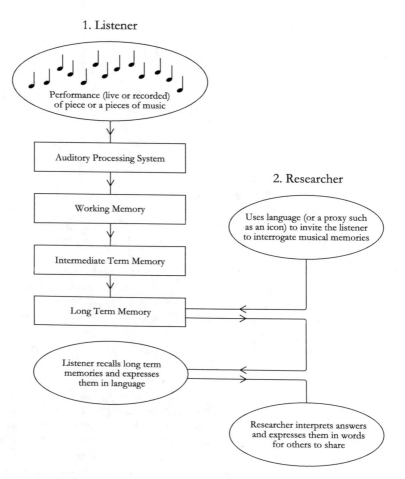

Figure 6.1 Model of one of the traditional approaches adopted in music psychology and music education research, functioning at *Sounds of Intent* Level 5, which produces a 'second-level metanarrative'.

the fields of music psychology have lacked the necessary music-theoretical expertise to do anything except adopt an 'other-than-musical' approach to their work. And, conversely, most music analysts and musicologists have, until recently, refused to countenance considering how most people make sense of music most of the time, preferring rather to adopt the stance of an 'elite listener'.

Around the turn of the century, though, a new wave of thinking crystallised in what Eric Clarke and Nicholas Cook (2004) termed 'empirical musicology', which exhorted those working in the field of music theory to take on board data sets beyond their immediate intuitions as sophisticated

Conclusion 249

listeners. Around the same time, Richard Parncutt was advancing the cause of 'systematic musicology', which, again, is primarily empirical and data-oriented (Parncutt, 2007). It was in this epistemological context that the notion of 'applied musicology' was born (Ockelford, 2012a), drawing on a scientific approach to music analysis to inform music education, music psychology and music therapy research.

To function, applied musicology needs data that derive from identifiable features in the fabric of musical design. The type of retrospective verbal responses modelled in Figure 6.1, which are drawn from listeners' long-term memories music, and involve cognitive processing *at Sounds of Intent* Level 5, are too general in nature to provide sufficient traction for applied musicological analysis to get underway. But what of other approaches to music-psychological research that have asked listeners to make more immediate responses to identified *chunks* of music, thus operating at *Sounds of Intent* Level 4? For sure, verbal descriptions produced in this way are specific enough for researchers to gain some insight into the manner in which elements of musical structure and content are processed. Examples are to be found throughout the relatively short history of music-psychological research, from the early work on music and emotion undertaken by Kate Hevner (for instance, 1936), to the seminal paper by John Sloboda in the early 1990s, which sought to connect affect to specific features of music.

> Eighty-three music listeners completed a questionnaire in which they provided information about the occurrence of a range of physical reactions while listening to music. Shivers down the spine, laughter, tears and lump in the throat were reported by over 80% of respondents. Respondents were asked to locate specific musical passages that reliably evoked such responses. Structural analysis of these passages showed that tears were most reliably evoked by passages containing sequences and appoggiaturas, while shivers were most reliably evoked by passages containing new or unexpected harmonies.
>
> (Sloboda, 1991, p. 110)

In order to undertake this metacognitive activity, listeners would 'often take the trouble to find musical scores and find precise bars numbers' (Sloboda, *op. cit.*, p. 112), and would therefore have had to re-hear performances in their imaginations, or re-play the music physically so that the required passages could be located. Hence, Sloboda's research participants appear to have been drawing principally on intermediate-term memory (ITM) (informed by long-term memory (LTM), and populated by working memory (WM)) to make their responses. See Figure 6.2.

While the results of Sloboda's study and others similar offer a more nuanced picture of how we hear music, by requiring listeners to respond retrospectively to *groups* of musical sounds, the data still do not reveal precisely how listeners are processing music, event by event, in real time – that is, at *Sounds of Intent*

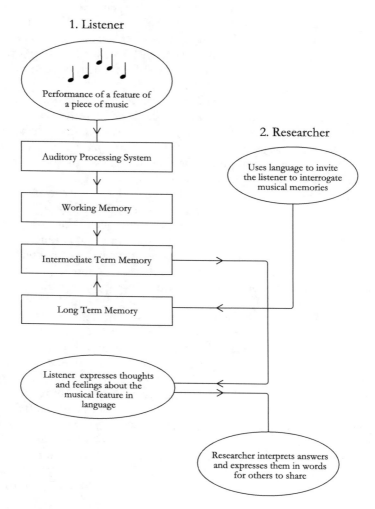

Figure 6.2 Model of listeners responding to more specific features of music, at *Sounds of Intent* Level 4.

Level 3. A number of different approaches have been adopted that address this issue. One has been to obtain direct physical correlates of changes in pitch and rhythm that are heard. These may be produced through participants being asked to recognise or produce visual representations of sound, in the form of drawings (for example, Bamberger, 1995; Bonetti and Costa, 2019) or, in the case of blind children, raised diagrams (Welch, 1991; Ockelford, 2008).

Jeanne Bamberger (2013, p. 10) set children the task of putting down on paper whatever they thought would help them remember a rhythm the following day, or to help someone else to play it. And her strategy worked:

Conclusion 251

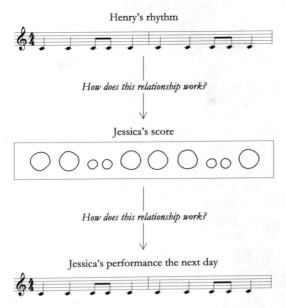

Figure 6.3 Jessica's transcription of Henry's rhythm using circles of different sizes to represent long and short notes.

a rhythm improvised by Henry was notated by seven-year-old Jessica, who was able to reproduce it, assisted – at least in part – by her invented notation, 24 hours later (see Figure 6.3).

What logical and cognitive processes can we assume are in play here? Bamberger herself describes Jessica's approach to rhythmic representation as 'formal', in that she attempts to show the relative distances in time between the events by matching them with circles of two different sizes (Bamberger, *op. cit.*, p. 12). This interpretation implies a consistent and coherent connection between duration and diameter, which, in terms of zygonic theory, equates to regular cross-modal mapping (Figure 6.4; see also Chapter 3, this volume).

In terms of cognitive processing, what does this imply? It would seem reasonable to assume that the 'episodic buffer', as conceived by Alan Baddeley in his model of WM, which is said to link the visuospatial sketchpad with the phonological loop, thereby connecting information from the visual and auditory domains (Baddeley, 2012), has a role to play in the necessary cross-domain mapping. Hence in making the transcription, we can postulate the following. Jessica initially perceived Henry's sounds through her auditory processing system (APS), before they entered a music module in her WM – this being a refinement of Baddeley's 'phonological loop' that was proposed by Berz (1995) and Ockelford (2007). The data were transferred to the episodic buffer, where non-domain-specific information was abstracted

252 *Graham Welch and Adam Ockelford*

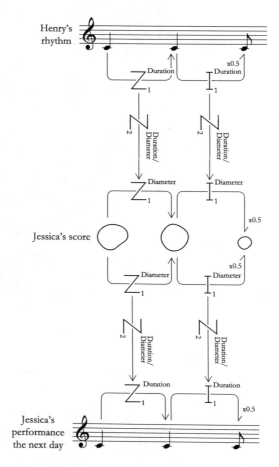

Figure 6.4 The cross-modal mapping implied in Jessica's transcription of Henry's rhythm using circles of different sizes to represent long and short notes.

(in the form of relationships of ratio or identity – that is, zygonic relationships), which could be used supramodally (see Thorpe, 2015). This resulting pattern was sent to the visuospatial sketchpad, which provided Jessica with the necessary information to create her score. At the same time, the auditory and visual information was directed to ITM and LTM. Bamberger, who heard Henry's improvisation and saw Jessica's score, was able to use these two sources of information to surmise how Jessica modelled the simple rhythmic pattern in cognition (see Figure 6.5).

When Jessica performed the improvisation the following day, the process was reversed, confirming for Bamberger the efficacy of Jessica's method of notation and her internal representation of rhythm (Figure 6.6).

Conclusion 253

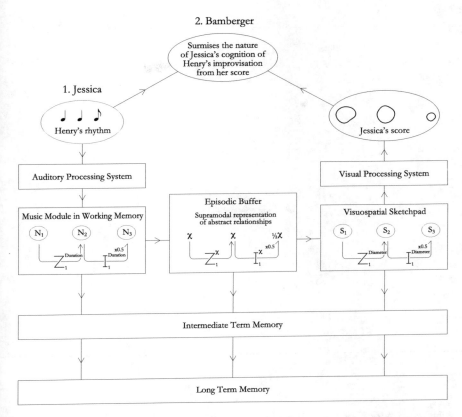

Figure 6.5 Model of Jessica's cognitive processing in relation to the creation of a graphic score from Henry's improvisation.

Another method of seeking to understand how listeners process music that can be used in applied musicological analysis is to elicit movement from them in response to sequences of notes (see, for instance, Himonides, 2011; Goodchild, Wild and McAdams, 2019), and this is the approach that was adopted by Hayley Trower in her research reported in Chapter 5 of this book. To understand the logic behind the supposition that the position of a listener's finger on a touch-sensitive strip can offer an analogy of their feelings of musical expectation, we will again draw on the thinking set out in Chapter 3, which used the *Sounds of Intent* model to investigate creative activities in other-than-musical domains.

As we saw in Chapter 5, the occurrence of a particular musical event is retrospectively felt to have been more or less probable according to its relationship with previous notes and groups of notes, and its position within tonal and metrical frameworks. Expectation is perceived to exist on a

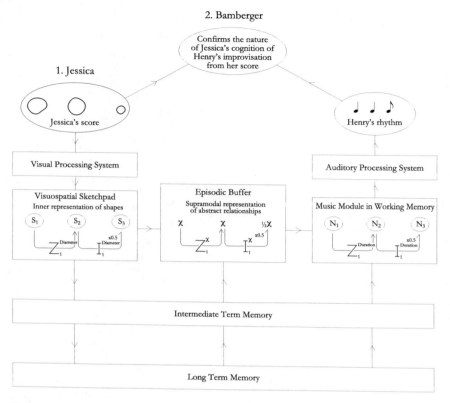

Figure 6.6 Model of Jessica's cognitive processing in relation to the re-creation of Henry's improvisation from her graphic score.

continuum, which can be thought of as a linear scale. Hence, through crossmodal mapping – which occurs at *Sounds of Intent* Level 3 – it is possible to represent varying degrees of expectation (retrospective or prospective) as different positions along a line (the touch-sensitive strip). The situation pertaining to the listener and the researcher can be modelled as shown in Figure 6.7.

Listeners' responses to music may be observed even more directly through taking measurements of physiological change (for example, Rickard, 2004; Kim and André, 2009) or neurological activity, through EEG (for instance, Baumgartner, Esslen and Jänke, 2006) or fMRI (for example, Mitterschiffthaler *et al.*, 2007), and, again, the data produced may be susceptible to applied musicological analysis.

Finally, it is possible to gauge how people process music by having them respond to what they hear (or have heard) by producing musical sounds themselves (see Figure 6.8). Notwithstanding the approaches illustrated

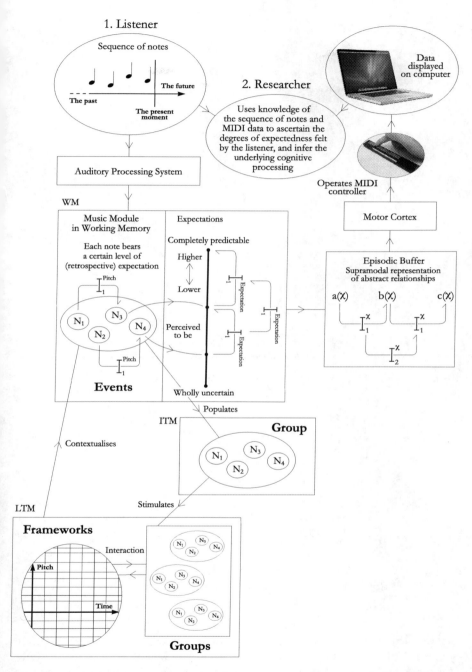

Figure 6.7 Model of the neurological and technological processes underlying the use of a touch-sensitive MIDI strip to gauge musical expectation.

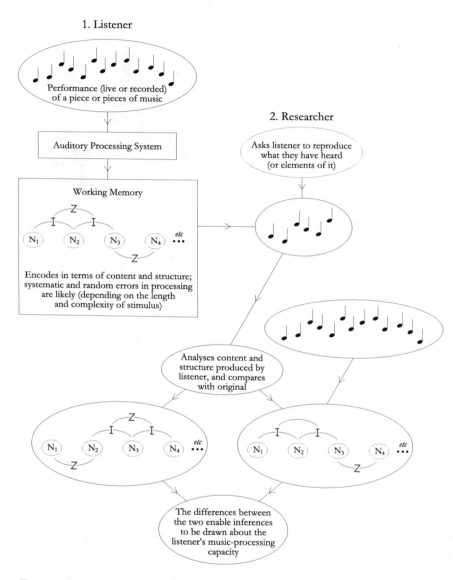

Figure 6.8 Model of the core approach of applied musicology: producing a musical response to a musical stimulus.

above, this strategy is the one that is core to applied musicological research (Ockelford, 2012a). Of course, such an approach has its limitations. Listeners tend to be incapable of reproducing much of what they can evidently hear in their heads: they may be able to recognise a melody without being able to sing it, for example, or be capable of distinguishing between several different interpretations of a piano sonata without being able to play a note of it themselves. Nonetheless, people tend to underestimate their capacity for making music, and can often produce fragments (by humming or tapping a rhythm, for instance) much more effectively than they believe. And there are particular groups of people – some children on the autism spectrum, for example – whose capacity to interact musically may offer a unique window onto their thinking, given a paucity or even a complete absence of language. Indeed, in certain circumstances, gauging intentionality and influence in musical interaction may offer proxy measures of communicative intent. Hence, the familiar scenario of words being used to describe musical engagement may be reversed, and music may itself be employed to explicate and share thoughts and feelings that would usually be captured and conveyed by language.

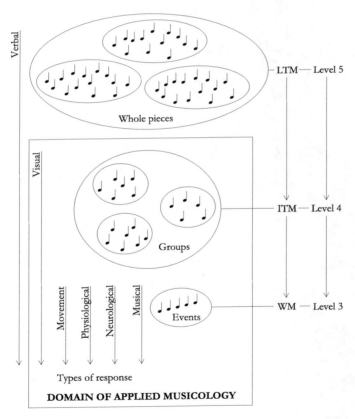

Figure 6.9 The domain of applied musicology functions principally at *Sounds of Intent* Levels 3 and 4, utilising WM and ITM.

258   *Graham Welch and Adam Ockelford*

To summarise: research in music psychology and music education has used a variety of methodologies that can helpfully be conceptualised in terms of the *Sounds of Intent* framework – as pertaining to Level 3, 4 or 5. Each has different implications for the nature of the cognitive processing involved, particularly in terms of memory: WM, ITM or LTM. And different strategies for eliciting information about listeners' or performers' engagement with music are variously effective at different levels. 'Applied musicology' forms a distinct subset of such approaches, which uses data pertaining to the fabric of music itself to interrogate our understanding and appreciation of music, and to gauge intentionality and patterns of interaction in improvisation. See Figure 6.9.

References

Aarden, B. J. (2003) Dynamic melodic expectancy, PhD dissertation, School of Music, Ohio State University.

Adams, H., Kwon, J., Marshall, F., de Blieck, E., Pearce, D. and Mink, J. (2007) 'Neuropsychological symptoms of juvenile-onset Batten disease: experiences from two studies', *Journal of Child Neurology*, **22**(5), 621–627.

Amoore, J. (1970) *Molecular Basis of Odor*, Springfield, Illinois: Thomas.

Arnheim, R. (1974) *Art and Visual Perception: A Psychology of the Creative Eye*, Berkeley and Los Angeles: University of California Press.

Aslin, R. and Newport, E. (2012) 'Statistical learning: from acquiring specific items to forming general rules', *Current Directions in Psychological Science*, **21**(3), 170–176.

Baddeley, A. (2012) 'Working memory: theories, models and controversies', *Annual Review of Psychology*, **63**(1), 1–29.

Bahrick, L. and Lickliter, R. (2012) 'The role of intersensory redundancy in early perceptual, cognitive, and social development', in A. Bremner, D. Lewkowicz and C. Spence (eds), *Multisensory Development*, Oxford: Oxford University Press, pp. 183–205.

Balkwill, L. and Thompson, W. (1999) 'A cross-cultural investigation of the perception of emotion in music: psychophysical and cultural cues', *Music Perception*, **17**(1), 43–64.

Bamberger, J. (1995) *The Mind behind the Musical Ear: How Children Develop Musical Intelligence*, Cambridge, Massachusetts: Harvard University Press.

Bamberger, J. (2013) *Discovering the Musical Mind: A View of Creativity as Learning*, New York: Oxford University Press.

Barnard, P. and deLahunta, S. (2017) 'Intersecting shapes in music and dance', in D. Leech-Wilkinson and H. Prior (eds), *Music and Shape*, New York: Oxford University Press, pp. 328–350.

Baron-Cohen, S., Burt, L., Smith-Laittan, F., Harrison, J. and Bolton, P. (1996) 'Synaesthesia: prevalence and familiarity', *Perception*, **25**(9), 1073–1079.

Baron-Cohen, S., Johnson, D., Asher, J., Wheelwright, S., Fisher, A., Gregersen, P. and Allison, C. (2013) 'Is synaesthesia more common in autism?', *Molecular Autism*, **4**: 40.

Baumgartner, T., Esslen, M. and Jänke, L. (2006) 'From emotion perception to emotion experience: emotions evoked by pictures and classical music', *International Journal of Psychophysiology*, **60**(1), 34–43.

260 *References*

Berz, W. (1995) 'Working memory in music: a theoretical model', *Music Perception*, **12**(3), 353–364.

Bharucha, J. (1987) 'Music cognition and perceptual facilitation: a connectionist framework', *Music Perception*, **5**(1), 1–30.

Bigand, E., Filipic, S. and Lalitte, P. (2005) 'The time course of emotional responses to music', *Annals of the New York Academy of Sciences*, **1060**(1), 429–437.

Bills, W., Johnston, L., Robert, W. and Graham, L. (1998) *Teach and Be Taught: A Guide to Teaching Students with Batten Disease*, Columbus, Ohio: Batten Disease Support and Research Association.

Birnholtz, J. and Benacerraf, B. (1983) 'The development of human fetal hearing', *Science*, **222**(4623), 516–518.

Bonetti, L. and Costa, M. (2019) 'Musical mode and visual-spatial cross-modal associations in infants and adults', *Musicae Scientiae*, **23**(1), 50–68.

de Bot, K., Lowie, W. and Verspoor, M. (2007) 'A dynamic systems theory approach to second language acquisition', *Bilingualism: Language and Cognition*, **10**(1), 7–21.

Burt, C. (1922) *Mental and Scholastic Tests*, London: P.S. King and Son, Ltd.

Buss, E., Hall, J. and Grose, J. (2012) 'Development of auditory coding as reflected in psychophysical performance', in L. Werner, R. Fay and A. Popper (eds), *Human Auditory Development*, New York: Springer, pp. 107–136.

Caldwell, P. and Horwood, J. (2008) *Using Intensive Interaction and Sensory Integration*, London: Jessica Kingsley Publishers.

Cheng, E. (2010) Musical behaviours and development of children and young people with complex needs: three longitudinal case studies, unpublished PhD dissertation, Institute of Education, University of London.

Cheng, E., Ockelford, A. and Welch, G. (2009) 'Researching and developing music provision in special schools in England for children and young people with complex needs', *Australian Journal of Music Education*, **2**, 27–48.

Clarke, E. and Cook, N. (eds) (2004) *Empirical Musicology: Aims, Methods, Prospects*, New York: Oxford University Press.

Cooper, J. (2016) The Village School 'Marks of Intent' project: an exploratory study into the possibilities of developing and using the 'Sounds of Intent' model as an assessment and curriculum framework for art with PMLD children, unpublished Master's essay, University of Roehampton.

Cooper, J. (2017) Exploring the potential development of the Sounds of Intent model as a curricular framework and assessment tool for dance with children who have profound and multiple disabilities, unpublished Master's dissertation, University of Roehampton.

Cox, M. and Cotgreave, S. (1996) 'The human figure drawings of normal children and those with mild learning difficulties', *Educational Psychology*, **16**(4), 433–438.

Cox, M. and Howarth, C. (1989) 'The human figure drawings of normal children and those with severe learning difficulties', *British Journal of Developmental Psychology*, **7**(4), 333–339.

Crowder, R. (1985) 'Perception of the major/minor distinction: III. Hedonic, musical, and affective discriminations', *Bulletin of the Psychonomic Society*, **23**(4), 314–316.

Cytowic, R. and Eagleman, D. (2011) *Wednesday Is Indigo Blue: Discovering the Brain of Synesthia*, Cambridge, Massachusetts: MIT Press.

Dassa, A. and Amir, D. (2014) 'The role of singing familiar songs in encouraging conversation among people with middle to late stage Alzheimer's disease', *Journal of Music Therapy*, **51**(2), 131–153.

References 261

Davidoff, J., Fonteneau, E. and Fagot, J. (2008) Local and global processing: observations from a remote culture, *Cognition*, **108**(3), 702–709.

Davies, C. (2012) *Creating Multisensory Environments*, Abingdon: Routledge.

Davis, S. (2000) *Color Perception*, New York: Oxford University Press.

Department for Education (2018) *Early Years Foundation Stage Profile Results in England, 2018*, London: DfE.

Deutsch, D. (1999) 'Grouping mechanisms in music', in D. Deutsch (ed.), *The Psychology of Music* (Second Edition), San Diego, California: Academic Press, pp. 299–348.

Dickinson, J. (1976) *Proprioceptive Control of Human Movement*, Princeton, New Jersey: Princeton Book Co.

Dowling, J. (1982) 'Melodic information processing and its development', in D. Deutsch (ed.), *The Psychology of Music*, New York: Academic Press, pp. 413–429.

Dowling, J. and Harwood, D. (1986) *Music Cognition*, London: Academic Press.

Eckstein, S. (1999) 'A dynamic model of cognitive growth in a population: spatial tasks and conservation', *Journal of Mathematical Psychology*, **43**(1), 34–70.

Eckstein, S. (2000) 'Growth of cognitive abilities: dynamic models and scaling', *Developmental Review*, **20**(1), 1–28.

Eliot, T.S. (1933) *The Use of Poetry and the Use of Criticism*, Cambridge, Massachusetts: Harvard University Press.

Eliot, T.S. (1960) *The Sacred Wood*, London: Methuen.

Fandel, J. (2006) *Beethoven's 5th Symphony*, Mankato, Minnesota: Creative Co.

Fowler, S. (2008) *Multisensory Rooms and Environments*, London: Jessica Kingsley Publishers.

Engelen, L. (2012) 'Oral receptors', in J. Chen and L. Engelen (eds), *Food Oral Processing*, Chichester: Wiley Blackwell, pp. 15–44.

Fox, S., Levitt, P. and Nelson, C. (2010) 'How the timing and quality of early experiences influence the development of brain architecture', *Child Development*, **81**(1), 28–40.

Gabrielsson, A. (2011) *Strong Experiences with Music: Music is Much More than Just Music*, Oxford: Oxford University Press.

Gabrielsson, A. and Lindström, S. (2000) 'The influence of musical structure on emotional expression', in P. Juslin and J. Sloboda (eds), *Music and Emotion: Theory and Research*, New York: Oxford University Press, pp. 223–248.

Gaser, C. and Schlaug, G. (2003) 'Brain structures differ between musicians and non-musicians', *The Journal of Neuroscience*, **23**(27), 9240–9245.

van Geert, P. (1991) 'A dynamic systems model of cognitive and language growth', *Psychological Review*, **98**(1), 3–53.

van Geert, P. and Steenbeek, H. (2005) 'Explaining after by before: basic aspects of a dynamic systems approach to the study of development', *Developmental Review*, **25**(3–4), 408–442.

Goldberg, J. (2012) *The Vestibular System*, Oxford: Oxford University Press.

Goldstein, E.B. (2018) *Cognitive Psychology: Connecting Mind, Research, and Everyday Experience* (Fifth Edition), Belmont, California: Wadsworth Publishing Company, Inc.

Goodchild, M., Wild, J. and McAdams, S. (2019) 'Exploring emotional responses to orchestral gestures', *Musicae Scientiae*, **23**(1), 25–49.

Greasley, A. and Lamont, A. (2013) 'Keeping it fresh: how listeners regulate their own exposure to familiar music', in E. King and H. Prior (eds), *Music and Familiarity: Listening, Musicology and Performance*, Farnham: Ashgate, pp. 13–31.

262 References

Grundy, R. and Ockelford, A. (2014) 'Expectations evoked on hearing a piece of music for the first time: evidence from a musical savant', *Empirical Musicology Review*, **9**(2), 47–97.

Grunwald, M. (2008) *Human Haptic Perception*, Basel: Birkhäuser.

Gundlach, R. (1935) 'Factors determining the characterization of musical phrases', *The American Journal of Psychology*, **47**(4), 624.

Happé, F. and Frith, U. (eds) (2010) *Autism and Talent*, Oxford: Oxford University Press.

Haltia, M., Elleder, M., Goebel, H., Lake, B. and Mole, S. (2011) 'The NCLs: evolution of the concept and classification', in S. Mole, R. Williams and H. Goebel (eds), *The Neuronal Ceroid Lipofuscinoses (Batten Disease)*, Contemporary Neurology Series (Second Edition), Oxford: Oxford University Press, pp. 1–19.

Hamilton, R., Pascual-Leone, A. and Schlaug, G. (2004) 'Absolute pitch in blind musicians', *Neuroreport*, **15**(5), 803–806.

Hannon, E. and Trainor, L. (2007) 'Music acquisition: effects of enculturation and formal training on development', *Trends in Cognitive Sciences*, **11**(11), 466–472.

Hargreaves, D. (1986) *The Developmental Psychology of Music*, Cambridge: Cambridge University Press.

Harrison, J. (2001) *Synaesthesia: The Strangest Thing*, Oxford: Oxford University Press.

Hevner, K. (1936) 'Experimental studies of the elements of expression in music', *The American Journal of Psychology*, **48**(2), 246–268.

Himonides, E. (2011) 'Mapping a beautiful voice: the continuous response measurement apparatus (CReMA)', *Journal of Music, Technology and Education*, **4**(1), 5–25.

Himonides, E., Ockelford, A. and Voyajolu, A. (2017) 'Technology, SEN and EY', in A. King, E. Himonides and S. Ruthmann (eds), *The Routledge Companion to Music, Technology and Education*, New York: Routledge, pp. 79–89.

von Hippel, P. and Huron, D. (2000) 'Why do skips precede reversals? The effect of tessitura on melodic structure', *Music Perception*, **18**(1), 59–85.

Hogg, J., Cavet, J., Lambe, L. and Smeddle, M. (2001) 'The use of 'Snoezelen' as multisensory stimulation with people with intellectual disabilities: a review of the research', *Research in Developmental Disabilities*, **22**(5), 353–372.

Hollins, M., Bensmaïa, S., Karlof, K. and Young, F. (2000) 'Individual differences in perceptual space for tactile textures: evidence from multidimensional scaling', *Perception & Psychophysics*, **62**(8), 1534–1544.

Hollins, M., Faldowski, R., Rao, S. and Young, F. (1993) 'Perceptual dimensions of tactile surface texture: a multidimensional scaling analysis', *Perception & Psychophysics*, **54**(6), 697–705.

Hope, K. (1998) 'The effects of multisensory environments on older people with dementia', *Journal of Psychiatric and Mental Health Nursing*, **5**(5), 377–385.

Howe, M., Davidson, J. and Sloboda, J. (1998) 'Innate talents: reality or myth?', *Behavioral and Brain Sciences*, **21**(3), 399–442.

Hunter, P., Schellenberg, G. and Stalinski, S. (2011) 'Liking and identifying emotionally expressive music: age and gender differences', *Journal of Experimental Child Psychology*, **110**(1), 80–93.

Huron, D. (2006) *Sweet Anticipation: Music and the Psychology of Expectation*, Cambridge, Massachusetts: MIT Press.

References 263

Iarocci, G. and McDonald, J. (2006) 'Sensory integration and the perceptual experience of persons with autism', *Journal of Autism and Developmental Disorders*, **36**(1), 77–90.

Jackendoff, R. (1991) 'Musical parsing and musical affect', *Music Perception*, **9**(2), 199–230.

Jairazbhoy, N. and Khan, V. (1971) *The Rags of North Indian Music*, Middletown, Connecticut: Wesleyan University Press.

Johnson-Laird, P. and Oatley, K. (1992) 'Basic emotions, rationality, and folk theory', *Cognition and Emotion*, **6**(3), 201–223.

Jolley, R. (2010) *Children and Pictures: Drawing and Understanding*, Chichester: John Wiley & Sons Ltd.

Juslin, P. (1997) 'Perceived emotional expression in synthesized performances of a short melody: capturing the listener's judgement policy', *Musicae Scientiae*, **1**(1), 225–256.

Juslin, P., Friberg, A. and Bresin, R. (2001) 'Toward a computational model of expression in music performance: the GERM model', *Musicae Scientiae*, **5**(1 suppl.), 63–122.

Kellogg, R. (1969) *Analyzing Children's Art*, Palo Alto, California: National Press Books.

Kessen, W., Levine, J. and Wendrich, K. (1979) 'The imitation of pitch in infants', *Infant Behavior and Development*, **2**, 93–99.

Kim, J. and André, E. (2009) 'Emotion recognition based on physiological changes in music listening', *IEEE Transactions on Pattern Analysis and Machine Intelligence*, **30**(12), 2067–2083.

Koelsch, S., Maess, B., Grossmann, T. and Friederici, A. (2003) 'Electric brain responses reveal gender differences in music processing', *NeuroReport*, **14**(5), 709–713.

Krumhansl, C. (1997) 'An exploratory study of musical emotions and psychophysiology', *Canadian Journal of Experimental Psychology/Revue Canadienne de Psychologie Expérimentale*, **51**(4), 336–353.

Krumhansl, C. and Kessler, E. (1982) 'Tracing the dynamic changes in perceived tonal organization in a spatial representation of musical keys', *Psychological Review*, **89**(4), 334–368.

Kuhl, P. (2004) 'Early language acquisition: cracking the speech code', *Nature Reviews Neuroscience*, **5**(11), 831–843.

Kuhl, P. and Meltzoff, A. (1982) 'The bimodal perception of speech in infancy', *Science*, **218**(4577), 1138–1141.

Lacher, K. and Mizerski, R. (1994) 'An exploratory study of the response and relationships involved in the evaluation of, and in the intention to purchase new rock music', *Journal of Consumer Research*, **21**(2), 366–380.

Lamont, A. (2008) 'Young children's musical worlds: musical engagement in 3.5-year-olds', *Journal of Early Childhood Research*, **6**(3), 247–261.

Lasky, R. and Williams, A. (2005) 'The development of the auditory system from conception to term', *Neuroreviews*, **6**(3), 141–152.

Legerstee, M. (1990) 'Infants use multimodal information to imitate speech sounds', *Infant Behavior and Development*, **13**(3), 343–354.

Lerdahl, F. (2001) *Tonal Pitch Space*, New York: Oxford University Press.

Lotan, M. and Gold, C. (2009) 'Meta-analysis of the effectiveness of individual intervention in the controlled multisensory environment (Snoezelen®) for individuals

264   References

with intellectual disability', *Journal of Intellectual and Developmental Disabilities*, **34**(3), 207–215.

Lou, H. and Kristensen, K. (1973) 'A clinical and psychological investigation into juvenile amaurotic idiocy in Denmark', *Developmental Medicine and Child Neurology*, **15**(3), 313–323.

Lowenfeld, V. (1947) *Creative and Mental Growth: A Textbook on Art Education*, New York: Macmillan Co.

Machón, J. (2009/2013) *Children's Drawings: The Genesis and Nature of Graphic Representation: A Developmental Study*, Madrid: Fibulus Publishers.

Malchiodi, C. (1998) *Understanding Children's Drawings*. New York: Guilford Press.

Malloch, S. (1999) 'Mothers and infants and communicative musicality', *Musicae Scientiae*, **3**(1 suppl.), 29–57.

Malloch, S. and Trevarthen, C. (2008) *Communicative Musicality: Exploring the Basis of Human Companionship*, Oxford: Oxford University Press.

Mang, E. (2005) 'The referent of children's early songs', *Music Education Research*, **7**(1), 3–20.

Margulis, E. (2003) Melodic expectation: a discussion and model, PhD dissertation, Columbia University.

Margulis, E. (2005) 'A model of melodic expectation', *Music Perception*, **22**(4), 663–713.

Margulis, E. (2014) *On Repeat: How Music Plays the Mind*, New York: Oxford University Press.

Markou, K. (2010) The relationship between music therapy and music education in special school settings: the practitioners' views, unpublished PhD dissertation, University of Roehampton.

Mazzeschi, A. (2015) Exploring perception, learning and memory in a prodigious musical savant through comparison with other savants and 'neurotypical' musicians with absolute pitch, unpublished PhD dissertation, University College London, Institute of Education.

McEvoy, R., Loveland, K. and Landry, S. (1988) 'The functions of immediate echolalia in autistic children: a developmental perspective', *Journal of Autism and Developmental Disorders*, **18**(4) 657–668.

Meltzoff, A. and Prinz, W. (2002) *The Imitative Mind: Development, Evolution and Brain Bases*, Cambridge: Cambridge University Press.

Meyer, L. (1956) *Emotion and Meaning in Music*, Chicago, Illinois: University of Chicago Press.

Meyer, L. (1967) *Music, the Arts, and Ideas: Patterns and Predictions in Twentieth-Century Culture*, Chicago, Illinois: University of Chicago Press.

Meyer, L. (1989) *Style and Music*, Philadelphia, Pennsylvania: University of Pennsylvania Press.

Meyer, L. (2001) 'Music and emotion: distinctions and uncertainties', in P. Juslin and J. Sloboda (eds), *Music and Emotion: Theory and Research*, New York: Oxford University Press, pp. 341–360.

Mills, A. (1993) 'Visual handicap', in D. Bishop and K. Mogford (eds), *Language Development in Exceptional Circumstances*, Hillsdale, New Jersey: Lawrence Erlbaum Associates, pp. 150–164.

Mitterschiffthaler, M., Fu, C., Dalton, J. Andrew, C. and Williams, S. (2007) 'Functional MRI study of happy and sad – affective states induced by classical music', *Human Brain Mapping*, **28**(11), 1150–1162.

References   265

Miyamoto, Y., Nisbett, R. and Masuda, T. (2006) 'Culture and the physical environment: holistic versus analytic perceptual affordances. *Psychological Science*, 17(2), 113–119.

Mole, S., Williams, R. and Goebel, H. (eds) (2011) *The Neuronal Ceroid Lipofuscinoses (Batten Disease)*, Contemporary Neurology Series (Second Edition), Oxford: Oxford University Press.

Moog, H. (1968/1976) *The Musical Experiences of the Pre-School Child* (trans. C. Clarke), London: Schott.

Mount, H. and Cavet, J. (1995) 'Multi-sensory environments: an exploration of their potential for young people with profound and multiple learning difficulties', *British Journal of Special Education*, 22(2), 52–55.

Narmour, E. (1977) *Beyond Schenkerism: The Need for Alternatives in Music Analysis*, Chicago, Illinois: University of Chicago Press.

Narmour, E. (1990) *The Analysis and Cognition of Basic Melodic Structures*, Chicago, Illinois: University of Chicago Press.

Narmour, E. (1992) *The Analysis and Cognition of Melodic Complexity*, Chicago, Illinois: University of Chicago Press.

Narmour, E. (1996) 'Analyzing form and measuring perceptual content in Mozart's Sonata K.282: a new theory of parametric analogues', *Music Perception*, 13(3), 265–318.

Nemoto, I., Fujimaki, T. and Wang, L. (2010) 'fMRI measurement of brain activities to major and minor chords and cadence sequences', *2010 Annual International Conference of the IEEE Engineering in Medicine and Biology*, 5640–5643.

Newlove, J. and Dalby, J. (2004) *Laban for All*, London: Nick Hern Books.

Nielzén, S. and Cesarec, Z. (1982) 'Emotional experience of music as a function of musical structure', *Psychology of Music*, 10(2), 7–17.

Nisbett, R. and Miyamoto, Y. (2005) 'The influence of culture: holistic versus analytic perception', *Trends in Cognitive Sciences*, 9(10), 467–473.

North, A. and Hargreaves, D. (1997) 'Music and consumer behaviour', in A. North, A. and D. Hargreaves (eds), *The Social Psychology of Music*, Oxford: Oxford University Press, pp. 268–289.

Norton, A., Winner, E., Cronin, K., Overy, K., Lee, D. and Schlaug, G., 'Are there pre-existing neural, cognitive, or motoric markers for musical ability?', *Brain and Cognition*, 59(2), 124–134.

Ockelford, A. (1988) 'Some observations concerning the musical education of blind children and those with additional handicaps', paper presented at the 32nd Conference of the *Society for Research in Psychology of Music and Music Education* (now *'SEMPRE'*) at the University of Reading.

Ockelford, A. (1991) 'The role of repetition in perceived musical structures', in P. Howell, R. West and I. Cross (eds), *Representing Musical Structure*, London: Academic Press, pp. 129–160.

Ockelford, A. (1993) A theory concerning the cognition of order in music, unpublished PhD dissertation, University of London.

Ockelford, A. (1999) *The Cognition of Order in Music: A Metacognitive Study*, London: Roehampton Institute.

Ockelford, A. (2000) 'Music in the education of children with severe or profound learning difficulties: issues in current UK provision, a new conceptual framework, and proposals for research', *Psychology of Music*, 28(2), 197–217.

266 References

Ockelford, A. (2001) *Objects of Reference* (Third Edition), London: Royal National Institute for the Blind.

Ockelford, A. (2002) 'The magical number two, plus or minus one: some limitations on our capacity for processing musical information', *Musicae Scientiae*, 6(2), 185–219.

Ockelford, A. (2004) 'On similarity, derivation, and the cognition of musical structure', *Psychology of Music*, 32(1), 23–74.

Ockelford, A. (2005) *Repetition in Music: Theoretical and Metatheoretical Perspectives*, Farnham: Ashgate.

Ockelford, A. (2006) 'Implication and expectation in music: a zygonic model', *Psychology of Music*, 34(1), 81–142.

Ockelford, A. (2007) 'A music module in working memory? Evidence from the performance of a prodigious musical savant', *Musicae Scientiae*, Special Issue on Performance, 5–36.

Ockelford, A. (2008) *Music for Children and Young People with Complex Needs*, Oxford: Oxford University Press.

Ockelford, A. (2009) 'Zygonic theory: introduction, scope, and prospects', *Zeitschrift der Gesellschaft für Musiktheorie*, 6(1), 91–172.

Ockelford, A. (2011) 'Another exceptional musical memory: evidence from a savant of how atonal music is processed in cognition', in I. Deliège and J. Davidson (eds), *Festschrift for John Sloboda*, Oxford: Oxford University Press, pp. 237–288.

Ockelford, A. (2012a) *Applied Musicology: Using Zygonic Theory to Inform Music Education, Therapy, and Psychology Research*, New York: Oxford University Press.

Ockelford, A. (2012b) 'Songs without words: exploring how music can serve as a proxy language in social interaction with autistic children', in R. MacDonald, G. Kreutz, and L. Mitchell (eds), *Music, Health, and Wellbeing*, New York: Oxford University Press, pp. 289–323.

Ockelford, A. (2013) *Music, Language and Autism: Exceptional Strategies for Exceptional Minds*, London: Jessica Kingsley.

Ockelford, A. (2015) *Sounds of Intent in the Early Years*, Oxford: Soundabout.

Ockelford, A. (2017) *Comparing Notes: How We Make Sense of Music*, London: Profile.

Ockelford, A. (2019) *Sounds of Intent in the Early Years: Research and Dissemination Project 2015–2018*. Oxford: Soundabout.

Ockelford, A. and Matawa, C. (2009) *Focus on Music 2: Exploring the Musical Interests and Abilities of Blind and Partially-Sighted Children with Retinopathy of Prematurity*, London: Institute of Education.

Ockelford, A. and Pring, L. (2005) 'Learning and creativity in a prodigious musical savant', *Elsevier International Congress Series*, 1282, 903–907.

Ockelford, A. and Sergeant, D. (2012) 'Musical expectancy in atonal contexts: musicians' perception of "antistructure"', *Psychology of Music*, 41(2), 139–174.

Thorpe, M. and Ockelford, A. and Aksentijevic, A. (2012) 'An empirical exploration of the zygonic model of expectation in music', *Psychology of Music*, 40(4), 429–470.

Ockelford, A. and Welch, G. (2012) 'Mapping musical development in learners with the most complex needs: the *Sounds of Intent* project', in G. McPherson and G. Welch (eds), *Oxford Handbook of Music Education*, Vol. 2, Oxford: Oxford University Press, pp. 11–30.

References 267

Ockelford, A., Welch, G., Cheng, E., Vogiatzoglou, A., Jewell-Gore, L. and Himonides, E. (2011) 'Sounds of Intent, Phase 2: gauging the music development of children with complex needs', *European Journal of Special Needs Education*, **26**(2), 177–199.

Ockelford, A., Welch, G., Jewell-Gore, L., Cheng, E., Vogiatzoglou, A. and Himonides, E. (2011) *'Sounds of Intent*, Phase 2: approaches to the quantification of music-developmental data pertaining to children with complex needs', *European Journal of Special Needs Education*, **26**(2), 177–199.

Ockelford, A., Welch, G. and Zimmermann, S. (2002) 'Focus of practice: music education for pupils with severe or profound and multiple difficulties – current provision and future need', *British Journal of Special Education*, **29**(4), 178–182.

Ockelford, A., Welch, G., Zimmermann, S. and Himonides, E. (2005) '"Sounds of intent": mapping, assessing and promoting the musical development of children with profound and multiple learning difficulties', *International Congress Series*, **1282**, 898–902.

Pagliano, P. (1999) *Multisensory Environments*, London: David Fulton.

Papoušek, M. (1996) 'Intuitive parenting: a hidden source of musical stimulation in infancy', in I. Deliège and J. Sloboda (eds), *Musical Beginnings*, Oxford: Oxford University Press, pp. 88–112.

Parncutt, R. (2007) 'Systematic musicology and the history and future of Western musical scholarship', *Journal of Interdisicplinary Music Studies*, **1**(1), 1–32.

Peretz, I. (1998) 'Music and emotion: perceptual determinants, immediacy, and isolation after brain damage', *Cognition*, **68**(2), 111–141.

Plumb, C. and Meigs, W. (1961) 'Human vibration perception, Part I: vibration perception at different ages (normal ranges)', *Archives of General Psychiatry*, **4**(6), 611–614.

Qualifications and Currirulum Authority (2001) *Planning, Teaching and Assessing the Curriculum for Pupils with Learning Difficulties: Music*, London: QCA.

Read, H. (1945) *Education through Art*, London: Faber and Faber.

Reybrouck, M. and Podlipniak, P. (2019) 'Preconceptual spectral and temporal cues as a source of meaning in speech and music', *Brain Sciences*, **9**(3), 53.

Rickard, N. (2004) 'Intense emotional responses to music: a test of the physiological arousal hypothesis', *Psychology of Music*, **32**(4), 371–388.

Robinson, B. and Mervis, C. (1998) 'Disentangling early language development: modeling lexical and grammatical acquisition using and extension of case-study methodology', *Developmental Psychology*, **34**(2), 363–375.

Rosenzweig, M., Bennett, E., Colombo, P., Lee, D. and Serrano, P. (1993) 'Short-term, intermediate-term, and long-term memories', *Behavioural Brain Research*, **57**(2), 193–198.

Roskies, A. (1999) 'The binding problem', *Neuron*, **24**(1), 7–9.

Saffran, J. (2003) 'Statistical language learning: mechanisms and constraints', *Current Directions in Psychological Science*, **12**(4), 110–114.

Schellenberg, E. G. (1996) 'Expectancy in melody: tests of the implication-realization model'. *Cognition*, **58**(1), 75–125.

Schellenberg, E. (1997) 'Simplifying the implication-realization model of melodic expectancy', *Music Perception*, **14**(3), 295–318.

Scherer, K. (1991) 'Emotion expression in speech and music', in J. Sundberg, L. Nord and R. Carlson (eds), *Music, Language, Speech and Brain*, London: MacMillan, pp. 146–156.

268   References

Scherer, K., Banse, R. and Wallbott, H. (2001) 'Emotion inferences from vocal expression correlate across languages and cultures', *Journal of Cross-Cultural Psychology*, **32**(1), 76–92.

Scherer, K. and Oshinsky, J. (1977) 'Cue utilization in emotion attribution from auditory stimuli', *Motivation and Emotion*, **1**(4), 331–346.

Schmuckler, M. and Boltz, M. (1994) 'Harmonic and rhythmic influences on musical expectancy', *Attention, Perception, and Psychophysics*, **56**(3), 313–325.

Selfe, L. (1977) *Nadia*, London: Academic Press.

Selfe, L. (2011) *Nadia Revisited*, Abingdon: Psychology Press.

Selincourt, B. de (1920) 'Music and duration', *Music and Letters*, **1**(4), 286–293.

Shalom, D. (2005) 'Autism and the experience of a perceptual object', *Consciousness and Cognition*, **14**(3), 641–644.

Sherborne, V. (1993/2001) *Developmental Movement for Children*, London: Worth Publishing.

Shibazaki, K., Ockelford, A. and Marshall, N. (2013) 'Extending zygonic theory to analyse patterns of musical influence between children creating pieces of music in groups, in England and Japan', *Musicae Scientiae*, **17**(4), 429–471.

Siegel, J. and Siegel, W. (1977) 'Categorical perception of tonal intervals: musicians can't tell *sharp* from *flat*', *Perception and Psychophysics*, **21**(3), 399–407.

Siegler, R. (2006) 'Microgenetic analyses of learning', in R. Siegler and D. Kuhn (eds), *Handbook of Child Psychology* (Sixth Edition), Vol. 2, *Cognition, Perception and Language,* New York: John Wiley & Sons, Inc., pp. 464–510.

Simner, J., Mulvenna, C. Sagiv, N., Tsakanikos, E., Witherby, S., Fraser, C., Scott, K. and Ward, J. (2006) 'Synaesthesia: the prevalence of atypical cross-modal experiences', *Perception*, **35**(8), 1024–1033.

Slevin, E. and McClelland, A. (1999) 'Multisensory environments: are they therapeutic? A single-subject evaluation of the clinical effectiveness of a multisensory environment', *Journal of Clinical Nursing*, **8**(1), 48–56.

Sloboda, J. (1991) 'Music structure and emotional response: some empirical findings', *Psychology of Music*, **19**(2), 110–120.

Sparshott, F. (1994) 'Music and feeling', *Journal of Aesthetics and Art Criticism*, **52**(1), 23–35.

Staal, J., Pinkney, L. and Roane, D. (2003) 'Assessment of stimulus preferences in multisensory environment therapy for older people with dementia', *The British Journal of Occupational Therapy*, **66**(12), 542–550.

Stephenson, J. (2002) 'Characterization of multisensory environments: why do teachers use them?', *Journal of Applied Research in Intellectual Disabilities*, **15**(1), 73–90.

Stephenson, J. and Carter, M. (2011) 'The use of multisensory environments in schools for students with severe disabilities: perceptions from teachers', *Journal of Developmental and Physical Disabilities*, **23**(4), 339–357.

Sterponi, L. and Shankey, J. (2014) 'Rethinking echolalia: repetition as interactional resource in the communication of a child with autism', *Journal of Child Language*, **41**(2), 275–304.

Suzuki, M., Okamura, N., Kawachi, Y., Tashiro, M., Arao, H., Hoshishiba, T., Gyoba, J. and Yanai, K. (2008) 'Discrete cortical regions associated with the musical beauty of major and minor chords', *Cognitive, Affective, & Behavioral Neuroscience*, **8**(2), 126–131.

Tafuri, J. (2008) *Infant Musicality: New Research for Educators and Parents*, Farnham: Ashgate.

References 269

Takeuchi, A. and Hulse, S. (1993) 'Absolute pitch', *Psychological Bulletin*, **113**(2), 345–361.

von Tetzchner, S., Fosse, P. and Elmerskog, B. (2013) 'Juvenile neuronal ceroid lipofuscinosis and education', *Biochimica et Biophysica Acta*, **1832**(11), 1894–1905.

Thompson, W. and Robitaille, B. (1992) 'Can composers express emotions through music?', *Empirical Studies of the Arts*, **10**(1), 79–89.

Thompson, W. and Stainton, M. (1996) 'Expectancy in Bohemian folk song melodies: evaluation of implicative principles for implicative and closural intervals', *Music Perception*, **15**(3), 231–252.

Thorpe, M. (2015) 'The recognition of transformed auditory and visual patterns: investigating a supramodal structural processing mechanism', unpublished PhD dissertation, University of Roehampton.

Thorpe, M, Ockelford, A. and Aksentijevic, A. (2012) 'An empirical exploration of the zygonic model of expectation in music', *Psychology of Music*, **40**(4), 429–470.

Trehub, S. and Nakata, T. (2001/2002) 'Emotion and music in infancy', *Musicae Scientiae*, **5**(1 suppl.), 37–61.

Trower, H. (2011) An investigation into the effect of tonality on memory for melodies, unpublished Master's dissertation, University of Roehampton.

Vogiatzoglou, A., Ockelford, A., Welch, G. and Himonides, E. (2011) 'Sounds of intent: interactive software to assess the musical development of children and young people with complex needs', *Music and Medicine*, **3**(3), 189–195.

Vygotsky, L. (1978) 'Interaction between learning and development', in L. Vygotsky (ed.), *Mind and Society: Development of Higher Psychological Processes*, Cambridge, Massachusetts: Harvard University Press, pp. 79–91.

Warren, R. (2008) *Auditory Perception*, Cambridge: Cambridge University Press.

Watson, K. (1942) 'The nature and measurement of musical meanings', *Psychological Monographs*, **54**(2), i–43.

Welch, G. (1988) 'Observations on the incidence of absolute pitch (AP) in the early blind', *Psychology of Music*, **16**(1), 77–80.

Welch, G. (1991) 'Visual metaphors for sound: a study of mental imagery, language and pitch perception in the congenitally blind', *Canadian Journal of Research in Music Education*, **33** (Special ISME Research Edition), 215–222.

Welch, G. (2006) 'The musical development and education of young children', in B. Spodek and O. Saracho (eds), *Handbook of Research on the Education of Young Children*, Mahwah, New Jersey: Lawrence Erlbaum Associates, pp. 251–267.

Welch, G., Ockelford, A., Carter, F.-C., Zimmermann, S. and Himonides, E. (2009) 'Sounds of Intent: mapping musical behaviour and development in children and young people with complex needs,' *Psychology of Music*, **37**(3), 348–370.

Welch, G., Ockelford, A. and Zimmermann, S. (2001) *PROMISE (The Provision of Music in Special Education)*, London: Institute of Education.

Welch, G., Ockelford, A., Zimmermann, S., Himonides, E. and Wilde, E. (2016) 'The provision of music in special education (PROMISE) 2015', paper presented at the *26th International Seminar of the ISME Commission on Research*, London 18–22 July 2016 (available at http://imerc.org).

Welch, G. and Preti, C. (2018) 'Singing as inter- and intra-personal communication', in G. Welch, D. Howard and J. Nix (eds) *The Oxford Handbook of Singing*, New York: Oxford University Press, doi:10.1093/oxfordhb/9780199660773.013.73

Welch, G., Saunders, J., Papageorgi, I. and Himonides, E. (2012) 'Sex, gender and singing development: making a positive difference to boys' singing through a

270 References

national programme in England', in S. Harrison, G. Welch and A. Adler (eds), *Perspectives on Males and Singing*, London: Springer, pp. 37–54.

Wiltshire, S. (1989) *Cities*, London: Dent.

Wiltshire, S. (1991) *Floating Cities*, New York: Summit Books.

Wiltshire, S. and Casson, H. (1987) *Drawings*, London: Dent.

Winner, E. (2000) 'The origins and ends of giftedness', *American Psychologist*, **55**(1), 159–169.

Wood, D., Bruner, J. and Ross, G. (1976) 'The role of tutoring in problem solving', *Journal of Child Psychology and Psychiatry*, **17**(2), 89–100.

Wu, Y.-T. (2017) Musical development of young children of the Chinese diaspora in London, unpublished PhD dissertation, University College London, Institute of Education.

Zajonc, R. (1968). Attitudinal effects of mere exposure. *Journal of Personality and Social Psychology*, **9**(2), 1–27.

Zbikowski, L. (2002) *Conceptualizing Music: Cognitive Structure, Theory, and Analysis*, New York: Oxford University Press.

Zbikowski, L. (2017) *Foundations of Musical Grammar*, New York: Oxford University Press.

Index

Note: **Bold** page numbers refer to tables; *italic* page numbers refer to figures and page numbers followed by 'n' denote endnotes.

Aarden, Bret 115
absolute music 3, *3*
absolute pitch ('AP') 57, 146, 231, 246
activity representation 41, *41*
adjacency ('Z1') 115
adjacency and recency ('Z2') 115
adjacency, recency and between-group projections ('Z3') 115
adults: artistic programmes for 68; led activity 23, *23*, 53; musical development 53; recreational and artistic programmes 68; *Sounds of Intent* domains 53
adult songs 21
aesthetic predilections 69
aesthetic response, melody 2, 4, 11, 141, 246
affective kick 228
age/phase analysis 28
Aksentijevic, A. 61, 115, *116*, 150, 175, 177
alapana – I 37
'all-or-none' response 154–155
amplification, sensory modification 68
applied musicology 1, 249, *256, 257*
arbitrary relationships, sound and place 80, *80*
arm movements 90–92; artistic awareness 90; 'continuity, fluidity and rhythm' of 92
Arnheim, R. 87–89, 92, 93, 95
art(s) **70**, 70–71, 84–105; 'abstract' elements of 89; children's, developmental stages in 85; 'conceptual' art 101, *101*; drawings and paintings 84, 85; language and

drama 105; Machón's pre-schematic stage 96; movement, gesture, mime and dance 101–104, **102–104**; perspective value in music 94; senses, relationship of 71–72, **72**
artistic accomplishment level 85
artistic awareness 90
artistic development: in children 84, 85; conceptual frameworks of 69; developmental model of 84–85; framework of **99–100**; Lowenfeld's sixth stage of 97; *Sounds of Intent* approach 90
artistic production 39, 71, 83, 90, 93, 96
asymptotic curve characteristic *125*
auditory domain 65, 75, 80; cross-domain mapping 251; extra-musical meanings 80; 'object of reference' 80; *Sounds of Intent* levels 11; working memory in 57
auditory processing system (APS) **180**, 251
auditory system, evolving capacity of 50
autism spectrum 36, 43, 67, 68, 77, 84, 97

babies, aware of sound 29
Bacharach, Burt 60
Baddeley, Alan 251
Bamberger, Jeanne 249–250, 252
'bar' notation 173
Beethoven: cuckoo 78; 'fate knocking on the door' 78; piano sonata *8*
Beethoven's 5th Symphony 7, 36
Berz, W. 251
'binary logic' 153
Boolean algebra 153, **154**

272 Index

'bottom-up' disintegration 59
British-English-speaking tradition 73
Burt, C. 85

Cheng, Evangeline 50, 51
child-led musical activity 23
children: art 84–105; artistic
development 84; 'coordinated
scribble' 92; drawing realism (9–11)
86; drawings and paintings 85; early
expressive movements 87–88; human
figure drawings of 84; Machón's
taxonomy 90; musical development
of 13; musical engagement 14, 22;
naturalistic stage 85; natural speeds
movement 39; period of decision
(adolescence) 86; 'pot pourri'
songs 96; preschematic (4–7) 86;
proxy longitudinal approach 28;
pseudorealism (11–13) 86; schematic
(7–9) 86; schematic stage 85; scribbling
(2–4) 85, 86; scribbling stage 85;
Sounds of Intent project 22, 31; surface
rhythm songs 21; 'uncontrolled
scribble' 90
chronic mental deterioration 58
'C in the 4th octave' 73
Clarke, Eric 248
cognitive abstraction 7, 75
cognitive decline model 58, *58*
cognitive processes model **186**, 198,
219, 251
cognitive restriction model 57, *57*
cognitive systems *233*
commercial imperative of
manufacturers 69
communal emotional reaction 37
complex metrical framework 37
'conceptual' art 101
Continuous Response Measurement
Apparatus (CReMA) 117, 146,
165, 174
contour maintenance **188, 204**, 213
'controlled' scribbling 93
conventional cognitive-psychological
view 166
Cook, Nicholas 248
Cooper, Jenny 105, 107
'coordinated scribble' 92
Cotgreave, S. 84
Cox, M. 84, 97
creative multisensory environments
68–70
cross-cultural analysis 115

cross-modal mapping 78, 80, *252*
cuckoo 78

data visual realisation *133*
'deceptive'/'interrupted' cadence 142
Deutsch, D. 176
diatonic melody 115, 174
digital recording 141
Duchamp's Fountain *101*
dynamic systems model 31

'early pictorialism' 87
'echolalia' 78
E flat 76
Eliot, T.S. 2, *2*
Ellington, Duke 67
'empirical musicology' 248
environments design 69
'episodic' and 'semantic' forms 113
episodic buffer 251
event-related electric brain 61
events: level of 14, 109, 127;
sound-making 21
'exceptional early cognitive environment'
('EECE') 57
expectation in music: expectations
collide 142–145; musical experience,
element in 141–142; Trower's doctoral
research 174–246; zygonic model
145–174
expressive non-verbal vocalisations 4
external relationships *91*
extra-musical behaviours 64
extra-musical imitation 80, *81*
Eye Level (Trombey) 109, *111, 112, 113*

facial expression 60
fantasy themes 69
'fate knocking on the door' 78
female vocalist 37
'flat line' expectation 174, 239
formal-graphic domain 90, **92**
frameworks, level of 109
free-flowing musical interactions 22
Frère Jacques (children's song) 144, *144*

van Geert, P. 31
Gestalt perception and information
theory 115
'goodbye' song 14
Greek cross 86
group projections **192**
groups: level of 109; proto-musical
structure appears 21; structures 14

Grundy, Ruth 108, 119, 121, 150
gustatory domain 65

haptic domain 65
Hargreaves, D. 85
Haydn piano sonata *143*, 144
hearing chord V7 155, *155*, 156, *156, 157*, 160, *160, 161*
Hearings 1 (H$_{H1}$) 169, 176–178, **211**, 214, **220**
Hearings 2 **211**, 212–218, 215
Hearings 3 218–223, **220**
Hearings 4 223–231
Hearings 5 231–236
Hearings 6 236–238
Hearings 7 238–241
Hearings 8 241–246
Henry's rhythm 251, *251, 252*
Hevner, Kate 249
higher-level music-cognitive functions 59
Howarth, C. 84
Hunter, P. 62
Huron, D. 115, 145

'ideograms' 95
'implication-realization' model 115, *116*
Indian (Carnatic) classical music 36
Indian listeners 37
Indian music 4
individuals, idiosyncratic nature of 69
infant song 21
'information' test 59
'interactive' ('I') 15
'interactive' domain 101
intermediate-term memory (ITM) 166, 168, *168*, **191**, 215, 234, 236, 246, 249
'internal' forces 214
internal relationships *91*
interperspective relationships 73, 74, *74*, 84
intra-personal and environmental factors 52, *52*
isolate correlations 69

Jessica's approach 251, 252, *252, 253, 254*
Joel, Billy 67
Jolley, R. 89, 90
Juvenile Tay-Sachs disease 59

Kellog, R. 86, 87, 95
Koelsch, S. 61
Kristensen, K. 59

language and general cognitive capacity 59
language-based art forms work 2
'learns' model 164, **164**
Lerdahl, F. 145
listeners' responses 254
logical relationship *5*, 109
Logic Pro 146
long-term memory (LTM) 7, 138, 142, 155, 156, 159, 160, *160*, 165, 166, 168, **191**, 236, 246
Lou, H. 59
loud dynamic levels 4
Lowenfeld, V. 85, 97

Machón, J. 90, 92; circular scribbles 93; controlled scribbling 93; coordinated scribble 92; developmental framework 97, **98**; ideograms 95; morphological 95; pre-schematic stage 96; stage of operations 95; stage of units 94–95; subjective realism 96; uncontrolled scribble 90
Malchiodi, C. 85
Malloch, Stephen 39
mandalas shape 86
Mang, E. 21
Margulis, Elizabeth 115, 142
'Marks of Intent' study 105, **106**, 107
mean predictability rating 117
melodic fragment 117, *119,* 149
melodic imitation 60
melodic narrative 176
melodic phrase 21
melodic stimuli *147–148*
melody's continuation **183**
mental processing 81, 84
Mervis, C. 49
Messiaen, Olivier 67
metacognitive activity 249
metaphorical (musical) narrative 6
Meyer, Leonard 4, 115, 142, 145
MIDI format 60, 117, 146, *255*
moment-to-moment regularities 77
Moog, H. 13, 85
mother's vocal sounds 34
'Movements of Intent' study 106
mridangam 37
musical ability 58
musical elements, unexpectedness of 228
musical events, model and proportion of **135**
'musical executive' 138
musical experience, element in 141–142

274   *Index*

musical narrative 37
musical structure: cognitive demands of 9; human cognition of 13; imitation of *79*; musical structure *8*; primary source 90; processing development 14; re-experience performances of 141; relationships underpinning logic 6; secondary source 90
music-cognitive growth model *47*
music curriculum 64
music-developmental literature 33, 85
music-developmental model 60, 62
music-developmental trajectory 58, 60
music-processing abilities 30
music-psychological work 4
music-specific qualities sound 4, 5
music-structural cognition: child's, leading edge of 30; child's potential 56; developmental features of 14; in girls and boys *61*; hypothetical model of 48; 'neurotypical' music development 21–22; phases of 39; postulated trajectory of 54, *54*; sequential model of *41*; *Sounds of Intent* project 13–20, 14, 50; standard logistic function *52*; by zygonic theory 33
music theory 1, 12, 139, 248

Narmour, E. 115, 142, 145
naturalistic stage, children art 85
natural sounds, imitation of *79*
negative correlation *217*
neural network model 159, 170
neurodegenerative conditions 58, 60
neuronal ceroid lipofuscinoses (NCLs) 58, 59
'neurotypical' children 50
neurotypical musicality 22
'neurotypical' music development 21
Ni (leading note) 37
non-domain-specific information 251–252
non-isomorphic transformations 35
non-musical sounds 78
non-sonic domains 80

objective correlative principal 2, 5
'Occam's Razor' 149
Ockelford, A. 36, 57, 59, 61, 63n2, 81, 94, 108, 115, *116*, 119, 121, 140, 141, 145, 149, 150, 175, 177, 251
olfactory domain 67
Optimusic® 60
OR function 159, 165, 170
'other-than-musical' approach 248, 253
oval 'diagram' 86

'overlapping' model *49*
overlapping waves theory 38

Papoušek, M. 34
Paravicini, Derek 97, 108, 119, 120, 124, 127, 132, 134, 139, 140
Parncutt, Richard 249
perceived probability of occurrence 149
'perspective value' 73, *74*, 93, 94
'phonological loop' 251
piano sonata 257
piece of music 77
pitch content 76
pitch framework 46
pitch proximity **181**
placement patterns 86
'pot pourri' songs 21, 35
'preference rules' 149
'pre-schematic stage' 95
'present moment' 108
pre-structural phase 15
preverbal communication 21
primary interperspective relationships 74, *75*
primary zygonic relationship 75, *76*
'proactive' ('P') 15
proactive zygonic relationships 109
probabilistic methods 177
proprioceptive domain 65
proto-musical structure appears 21, 34
proxy longitudinal approach 28

quasi-natural sounds 78

radials shape 86
radio play 71
'raga,' concept of 4
Raindrops Keep Falling on My Head (Bacharach) 60
'reactive' ('R') 15
reactive domain 71
Read, H. 90
recreational and artistic programmes 68
referent-guided improvisation 21
repeated hearings 174
representation manner principal 2
retrospective expectedness **193–195, 199**, 213, *213, 217*
retrospective verbal response strategy 247, 249
Rimsky-Korsakov, Nikolai 67
Robinson, B. 49
Roly Poly 43, 53
romantic rollercoaster study 119–127; eight bars of 120, *120*; musical

events probabilities *128, 129*, **132**; note in *121, 122*; onset and pitch domain *122, 123*; schedule of **127**; single structural relationship *129*; three zygonic relationships *123*; two structural relationships *130*; two zygonic relationships *122*; zygonic relationships 137
Romy adopts 78
Rosenzweig, M. 166

scale-degree transitions of +1 **181**
Schellenberg, G. 62
schematic and veridical processe 142
'schematic' memory 112
schematic stage, children art 85
'scribble,' definition of 93
scribbling stage, children art 85
secondary interperspective relationships 74, *75*
secondary zygonic relationship 75, *76*, 150, *150, 151*
sensory domains 81
sensory input 65–68; arts, relationship of 71–72, **72**; individual's levels of 69; psychological thinking 65–67; taxonomy of **66**
severe learning difficulties (SLD) 84
sheer complexity 69
Sherborne, V. 101
short musical patterns 21
Sibelius music notation software 146
Siegler, Robert 38
simplification, sensory modification 68
single musical activity model 48
Skoog 69
Sloboda, John 249
slow-moving melodic sequences 146
socio-cultural partiality 61
sound domain 71; categories of 80; loudness of 67; mental representation of 49; 'perspects' *(per*ceived a*spects)* of *73*; and place, arbitrary connection *80*
sound-making activity 15, 21
sound-making opportunities 14
sound qualities principal 2
Sounds of Intent in the Early Years: assessments **24–25**; basic logistic function 32, *32*; child age, range of *29*; distribution of *27*; 6-month age band **30**; musical development model 28; overlapping effect *48*; social contexts of *23*; zygonic hypothesis 22

Sounds of Intent ('SoI') model 10, 64; elements, Levels 1 and 2 *18*; elements, Levels 5 and 6 20; *equivalence* development 19; framework **16**; music-developmental framework 65; music-structural cognition 14; *sequence* development 19; visual representation of *17*
special-educational practice 68
spontaneous melodic production 35
spontaneous music making 23
Stalinski, S. 62
'Steinway concert grand' 73
Steinway grand piano 176
'Stickle Bricks' 55
stimulus melody 174–175, *175*
stylistic 'norm' 165
successive values 228
sung anticipatory responses *178*
suns shape 86
surface rhythm songs 21
A Survivor from Warsaw 110
Sweet Anticipation (Huron) 115
symbolic relationship 80
synaesthesia 67
'systematic musicology' 249
systematic theory 89

tactual domain 65
tertiary zygonic relationship 75, *76*
theoretical probabilities of anticipating *125*
Thorpe, M. 61, 78, 115, *116*, 150, 175, 177, **180, 185, 187, 192, 209**
tiniest movement 60
Tom's vocal sounds 14
tonal melody 39
'tonal pitch space' theory 145
tonal stability 21
touch-sensitive MIDI strip *255*
Trevarthen, Colwyn 39
Trombey, Jack 109
Trower, Hayley 117, *118*, 141, 145, 253; hearing 1, stimuli 165–166; hearing 2, stimuli 166–174; 'listening' and 'rating' conditions 146; long-term memory 155–165; melodic stimuli *147–148*; WM, function of 149–155
tugging 37
Tukey multiple comparisons test 241
two zygonic relationships: anticipatory effect of 151; combined effect of 153, *153*

'uncontrolled scribble' 90

276   *Index*

veridical expectations *144*, 144–145
'veridical' memory 112
vestibular domain 65
The Village School in London 84, 105, 106
visual domain 65
voluntary movement 69
von Hippel, P. 115
Voyajolu, Angela 62, 63n2
V–vi schema 144
Vygotskian 53

Welch, G. 61
Western Classical style 36
Western-encultured listener 142
Western music 155, 176
Western musical vernacular 14
Western music-developmental
    literature 35
Western tonal music 145
The Wheels on the Bus 43
Wiltshire, Stephen 97
'within-group' implication 115
working memory (WM) 142, 149, 155,
    156, 160, *160*, 165, 166, 176, **191**,
    234, 251

Xavier 14
'XOR' function 159, **159**

Yerik 15
young children: auditory environments
    of 28; musical development of 22;
    Sounds of Intent framework 22

Zeeshan's laughing and rocking 14
'zone of ambiguity' 41, 43, *44*
zone of proximal development ('ZPD')
    53, 54
'zygonic force' 153, **154**, *154*, 159
zygonic theory 1, 3, 6, 7, 13, 75; analysis
    of 36; conflicting expectations **189**;
    conjecture 70; Derek anticipating
    probability 124; general theory of
    81–84, **82–83**; hearing 1 framework
    165–166; hearing 2 framework
    166–174; implication and expectation
    in music 112, *114, 118*, 145, *168*;
    long-term memory 155–165; mental
    processing 81, 84; musical structure
    8; music, expectation in 108–119;
    nature and function of 94; of pitch
    7; presence of 124; principles of
    73; representation of 6; shape' and
    'position' thought 94, *94*; Trower's
    (2011) research 145–148; 'within-
    group' implication 115; working
    memory function 149–155

Printed in the United States
By Bookmasters